WORK–LIFE BALANCE

WORK–LIFE BALANCE

Janice Arenofsky

Health and Medical Issues Today

GREENWOOD™

An Imprint of ABC-CLIO, LLC
Santa Barbara, California • Denver, Colorado

Library of Congress Cataloging-in-Publication Data

Names: Arenofsky, Janice, author.
Title: Work-life balance / Janice Arenofsky.
Description: Santa Barbara, California : Greenwood, [2017] | Series: Health
    and medical issues today | Includes bibliographical references and index.
Identifiers: LCCN 2016040732 (print) | LCCN 2016054463 (ebook) |
    ISBN 9781440847134 (hard copy) | ISBN 9781440847141 (ebook)
Subjects: LCSH: Work and family. | Work-life balance.
Classification: LCC HD4904.25 .A74 2017 (print) | LCC HD4904.25 (ebook) |
    DDC 306.3/61—dc23
LC record available at https://lccn.loc.gov/2016040732

ISBN: 978-1-4408-4713-4
EISBN: 978-1-4408-4714-1

21 20 19 18 17   1 2 3 4 5

This book is also available as an eBook.

Greenwood
An Imprint of ABC-CLIO, LLC

ABC-CLIO, LLC
130 Cremona Drive, P.O. Box 1911
Santa Barbara, California 93116-1911
www.abc-clio.com

This book is printed on acid-free paper ∞

Manufactured in the United States of America

To my mother, Pearl Moster, one of the many thousands of spirited
women who launched careers for themselves in the 1960s
and enjoyed every moment of the freedom and independence that
paid employment conveys.

To my husband and pet family who boosted my spirits and never
complained while I struggled with my own work–life balance issues
in the research and writing of this book.

CONTENTS

SERIES FOREWORD

Every day, the public is bombarded with information on developments in medicine and health care. Whether it is on the latest techniques in treatment or research, or on concerns over public health threats, this information directly affects the lives of people more than almost any other issue. Although there are many sources for understanding these topics—from websites and blogs to newspapers and magazines—students and ordinary citizens often need one resource that makes sense of the complex health and medical issues affecting their daily lives.

The *Health and Medical Issues Today* series provides just such a one-stop resource for obtaining a solid overview of the most controversial areas of health care in the 21st century. Each volume addresses one topic and provides a balanced summary of what is known. These volumes provide an excellent first step for students and lay people interested in understanding how health care works in our society today.

Each volume is broken into several sections to provide readers and researchers with easy access to the information they need:

- Section I provides overview chapters on background information—including chapters on such areas as the historical, scientific, medical, social, and legal issues involved—that a citizen needs to intelligently understand the topic.
- Section II provides capsule examinations of the most heated contemporary issues and debates, and analyzes in a balanced manner the viewpoints held by various advocates in the debates.

- Section III provides a selection of reference material, such as anno-
  tated primary source documents, a timeline of important events, and
  a directory of organizations that serve as the best next step in learning about the topic at hand.

The *Health and Medical Issues Today* series strives to provide readers
with all the information needed to begin making sense of some of the most
important debates going on in the world today. The series includes volumes
on such topics as stem-cell research, obesity, gene therapy, alternative medicine, organ transplantation, mental health, and more.

ACKNOWLEDGMENTS

I wish to express thanks to all the scientific researchers and experts whose learned findings found their way into this book. Specifically, I'd like to thank Joan Williams, Distinguished Professor of Law and Hastings Foundation Chair at the University of California, Hastings College of the Law and the Founding Director of WorkLife Law Center, for sharing several of her papers.

INTRODUCTION

The phrase "work–life balance" or WLB has been tossed around by experts from different disciplines for decades, and still no one agrees on one definition. The multi-layered individuality of the term is the real reason because its meaning is shaped by the needs, goals, desires, and commitments of everyday working men and women from every ethnicity, profession, trade, country, and generation in the world. It is ludicrous to think that the WLB issues of a Baby Boomer contemplating retirement are exactly the same as a Millennial intent on advancing up the career ladder. Yes, both workers share the same WLB urge to establish boundaries between work and family and use technology and time management strategies to advance that goal, but both workers are not engaged by the same benefits or non-salaried perks. Human resource people know that child care benefits no longer attract talented Boomers in their 50s and 60s, and Millennials probably are more interested in tuition payoffs than onsite fitness clinics.

Where the commonality of diverse generations lies is in the desire for engagement, productivity, and managerial support in a culture that appreciates them and makes good use of their varied talents and skills. This is the domain and responsibility of all legitimate organizations interested in the bottom line as well as nurturing a culture responsive to the needs of their workers. All employees want to work in an environment where their ethnicity, gender, and religion is respected; where they can dress and wear their hair in a manner appropriate to their values and professional decorum; where they can communicate and contribute creatively with colleagues and supervisors; and where they can take advantage of flextime without fearing their co-workers and superiors will stigmatize them. All employees want to work in an environment that discourages incivility, harassment of any kind, and bullying and that disallows discrimination in any form. That kind of culture is conducive to a stress-free WLB for employees and management and is a hospitable environment that organizations and corporations can promote proudly as a community-minded, eco-friendly brand that attracts contented, highly motivated employees who reflect the demographics of the consumers they serve and espouses a commonsense credo of productivity and economic health.

But employers cannot do everything, and that is where local, state, and federal governments come in to help build an infrastructure of paid family leave, higher minimum wages, and affordable child care. According to Organisation for Economic Co-operation and Development (OECD), the United States needs to catch up in these areas and emulate other industrialized countries such as Sweden and Denmark.

This book, *Work–Life Balance*, is organized into three sections. Section I gives an overview of WLB. Chapter 1 traces the roots of work and the work ethic from early prehistoric times to the 21st century. Chapter 2 discusses the negative effects of poor WLB—the physical maladies, financial insecurities, relationship woes, and workplace aggression. Chapter 3 supplies the reader with a fight-back formula for minimizing workplace stress, focusing on value clarification, reaching out for family collegial support, and toughening up with resilience and emotional intelligence. Chapter 4 describes the flexibility options that employers offer and other benefits such as employee assistance programs (EAPs) and health and retirement plans. Chapter 5 chronologically lists the work-related legislation from the Fair Labor Standards Act of 1938 to current state and local laws mandating paid leaves and minimum wages. The comparison of United States legislation with that of other countries such as Japan and Sweden helps readers see the important omissions in our country that require national intervention for needed improvements.

Section II of the book focuses on controversies related to WLB. The following issues are examined objectively, and readers get to see the two sides of the equations. Chapter 6 explores why we are still underpaying, stereotyping, and disregarding women's desires for advancement. Chapter 7 highlights how demographics—marital status, parenting or non-parenting, ethnicity, white vs. blue-collar work—impact organizations as well as employees. Is there a way to level the playing field? Chapter 8 addresses the employer-employee relationship and how it can strengthen or weaken company culture. Chapter 9 discusses how organizations can provide attractive benefits and still afford the costs. Chapter 10 closes with a final look at how we might improve WLB.

Section III presents relevant primary sources, a timeline showing the evolution of the work and work–life balance concepts, and sources for further information. A glossary and index are also included.

Overview and Background Information

CHAPTER 1

Work–Life Balance: Its Meaning, Origins, and Modern Influences

Whether you are employed by a large organization, a medium-size company, or a small franchise, any worker must deal with work–life balance (WLB), which, depending on the person's stress tolerance, can be either fun or fatiguing.

WLB is not an abstract concept conjured up by erudite academics but rather a practical construct that affects relationships, finances, health, and happiness. Most WLB stakeholders—such as employees, employers, and human resource personnel—labor to improve WLB, but many struggle to define and delineate its parameters. That is because WLB lacks discrete borders because it interfaces with areas as diverse as feminism, parenting, multiculturalism, government, psychology, and geopolitics. Investigators explore multi-disciplinary issues encompassing everything from stress management, gender warfare, and digital technology to discrimination, family conflict, and political agendas.

This chapter endeavors to help readers understand WLB's lengthy and complex evolution from the centuries-old tradition of the Protestant work ethic through today's current trends, which have triggered physical and mental work stress in the United States and other places in the world and a below-average WLB rating. But first, let us see how "work" devolved into "work–life balance."

BIRTH OF WLB

If you google "work–life balance," thousands of hits appear, including a lengthy listing on Wikipedia. The term is even in the classiest English dictionary of all time: the OED, or the *Oxford English Dictionary*, where it is defined as "the division of one's time and focus between working and family or leisure activities."

According to the Society for Human Resource Management (SHRM), WLB may have been coined as late as 1986 or as early as the 1930s, when the W.K. Kellogg Company substituted four six-hour shifts for three eight-hour shifts and saw improvement in employee morale and efficiency. Use of the term WLB spread quickly following the publication of Rosabeth Moss Kanter's book *Work and Family in the United States: A Critical Review and Agenda for Research and Policy* (Russell Sage Foundation, 1977). By 1979, Working Families in London, England, popularized the term, and in the 1980s a number of American corporations began offering WLB benefits such as maternity leave, flexible scheduling, telecommuting, and employee assistance—women-oriented programs that ultimately accommodated both genders.

The Women's Liberation Movement of the 1960s accelerated the spread of WLB references, but it was endocrinologist Hans Selye's pioneering discoveries on human stress in the 1970s that brought it into prominence. Selye defined stress as the body's response to change. When applied to work, good stress, or eustress, can energize and excite, but too much or the wrong type of stress—distress—deadens the morale of employees and leads to burnout as well as to physical and mental illnesses such as depression, heart disease, obesity, and other diseases. Since Selye's seminal findings, WLB has become internationally recognized and respected as an important human issue.

Yet despite nearly total agreement from the media and experts that the U.S. workforce suffers from chronic work stress—and trails other countries in legislation and programs—there is no real consensus on the definition of WLB.

Definitions of WLB

According to Battalia Winston, a large woman-owned executive search firm, respondents to a survey agree that WLB is a "wax–wane" process in which workers constantly seek their own balance. However, a 2014 article in *Harvard Business Review* argues that WLB is an elusive ideal or a complete myth. Trinnie Houghton, an organizational coach with Sojourn Partners, also designates WLB as myth, but expands the harmony-is-at-the-core concept to nine areas including family, relationship, and wealth.

Harvard business professor Boris Groysberg says WLB invites people to choose which opportunities to pursue and which to reject while University of Pennsylvania Professor Stewart D. Friedman, author of *Leading the Life You Want: Skills for Integrating Work and Life* (Harvard Business Review Press, 2014), calls it "a misguided metaphor" where harmony is the focus and balance exists within work or school; home or family; community or society; and the individual's mind, body, and spirit.

The American Psychological Association (APA), borrowing from the field of economics, defines WLB as employee expectations and preferences blended with "finite" resources like time, energy, and money, and author Matthew J. Grawitch maintains WLB is the degree to which people's physical, mental, and emotional resources meet their expectations. Jim Bird, president of WorkLifeBalance.com, equates WLB with meaningful daily achievements and enjoyments in each of four areas—work, family, friends, and self.

Even everyday people continue to contribute their own personal meanings. In a *Fast Company* (October 6, 2014) article, interviewees introduced nine distinct definitions—for example, WLB means scheduling fun, merging individual obligations and challenges, and creating space and time. One interviewee—the co-founder of hair-color company Madison Reed—denied WLB's existence entirely. Yet despite the variance in opinions, the practical value of work—and now WLB—has existed since Biblical times.

THE EARLY HISTORY OF WLB

Work is an institution that rises to the level of a basic need. In fact, psychiatrist Sigmund Freud is reputed to have said, "Love and work . . . work and love, that's all there is."

Work has always existed, evolving over time in much the same way as humans have. In prehistoric eras, all Cro-Magnons worked to survive, except for the extremely young and old. Survival meant crafting stone tools for hunting, fishing, and foraging, but the Neanderthals took work to a new level by constructing permanent shelters with stone hearths. Once Homo sapiens appeared, however, they became more creative and devised hooks, needles, harpoons, spear throwers, and bows and arrows to kill prey and share the bounty with the community.

Life was not all work, however. As early as 15,000 BCE, storytelling and the production of decorative and narrative cave paintings like those in Altamira, Spain, and Sulawesi, Indonesia, emerged as recreational respites from the continual strain of survival. Prehistoric peoples illustrated and narrated their daily habits and tasks, which not only evolved into the tradition of oral storytelling but also provided aesthetic and artistic outlets. Around 12,000–10,000 BCE Neolithic humans started growing crops and raising livestock, building permanent cities, and delegating specialized workers for tool making, farming, herding, and soldiering. Surplus foods from farming gave rise to a small, select group of people who devoted time to thinking and innovation and underscored the distinction between work and leisure.

Then around 500–400 BC (the Classical Period), elitism began to emerge as a preferred lifestyle. While the majority of Greeks, Romans, and Hebrews worked at agriculture or another life-sustaining occupation, a minority (who privately and publicly disparaged menial labor) pursued intellectual aims. One of the best-known Greek intellectuals—the philosopher Aristotle— actually explored the concept of WLB in *Nicomachean Ethics and Politics* (HubSpot, 2015). He asserted that life combined business and leisure and that business denoted things "useful and necessary for the sake of things honorable." Aristotle and his erudite contemporaries generally regarded work as a waste of time for persons interested in art, culture, philosophy, leadership, and politics.

The Roman upper classes also viewed physical work with contempt except for agriculture and big business—the only two occupations deemed appropriate to accumulate wealth. The grand plan was for average laborers to amass monies from farming and mercantilism and not have to work for the rest of their lives.

By the Middle Ages (400–1400 CE), Christian values dominated, and people regarded work as God's punishment for man's original sin. At the same time they also recognized the charitable benefits of sharing with the poor. Gradually work for wealth became acceptable, and handicraft, farming, and small businesses gained greater approval. However, early Christianity equated social status with an individual's work, as noted in 1250 when the Catholic priest St. Thomas Aquinas compiled an encyclopedia citing the hierarchy of professions and trades. Agriculture was ranked first, followed by handicrafts and commerce, but the monastic life was at the apex. Work existed solely to meet a family's needs and avoid idleness, which was viewed as sinful.

During the Reformation (1517–1648), two Catholic dissidents— Frenchman John Calvin and German scholar Martin Luther—proclaimed that people might serve God best through an occupation. Luther viewed all vocations except commerce equally, but he regarded the monastic life as supreme, believing that incomes should meet basic needs and wealth was sinful.

This philosophy changed with John Calvin, whose credos in predestination and eternal life led to approval for worldly success. Citizens known as The Elect worked hard, earned money, reinvested their profits, and helped others. They were supposedly doing the will of God and might be rewarded with eternal life whereas idle people were doomed to damnation. Calvin's high esteem for the most profitable occupations demonstrated how the liturgical wheel was slowly turning toward materialism.

Much later, in 1904, Max Weber, a German economic sociologist, philosopher, and author of the *Protestant Ethic and the Spirit of Capitalism* (1905), popularized the phrase "the Protestant work ethic" and emphasized the values of diligence, punctuality, delayed gratification, and the importance of work. Some people believed these new values reflected Calvinist theology, but others thought they grew out of an economic restructuring. Weber's shift from utilitarianism, which rejected the intrinsic value of work, to a theological philosophy advocating work and riches marked the dawning of capitalism and the approval of regular systematic work.

Later WLB History: In the New World

These Calvinist precepts were adopted by the French Huguenots and the Swiss and Dutch Reformed Churches, and the attitude eventually permeated the American colonies in 1630 to 1640 with the arrival to the New World of the English Puritans, Quakers, and other Protestant groups. Researcher Roger B. Hill in "Historical Context of the Work Ethic," published in 1992 and republished by the University of Georgia in 1999, describes New World resettlement as one of hard work in which the colonists tried to prove their moral worth by imposing a European culture onto a primitive wilderness. Gradually the belief in hard work and monetary gains was assimilated into the values of the American colonies, especially around 1759 with the publication of *Poor Richard's Almanack*, when the popular adages of Benjamin Franklin (for example, "Early to bed, early to rise, makes a man healthy, wealthy and wise") seemed to validate the integrity and commonsense of the Protestant ethic.

Around then, many European-born colonists immigrated to the New World to amass riches and pursue a countryman's life of leisure, but the New England Puritans, the Pennsylvania Quakers, and other Protestant sects had no such grand illusions, regarding the colonies as a cruel hinterland where they could enjoy freedom but remain industrious. In fact, in the 1800s, visiting Europeans considered the northern colonists to be workaholics. As rural laborers, they were constantly improving their properties and homes, toiling on farmlands, and reinforcing the work ethic despite the seasonal nature of farming.

In 1764, the concept of work was turned upside down when James Hargreaves invented the spinning jenny, a machine that spun multiple spools of thread simultaneously. The Industrial Revolution had arrived to the Americas, and the next development on the 1770s American scene was James Watt's steam engine, an invention that radically altered transportation by powering trains, ships, and industrial machinery.

By this time, the work ethic had become secularized, and honoring God was replaced by public usefulness. Moralists stressed social duty, and social economists threatened poverty and decay if people abandoned their practical duties. Schools also reinforced the work ethic by preaching that idleness was a human failing and earnest work efforts could elevate peoples' social status.

This belief was partially justified, at least before 1850, when most manufacturing took place in homes and workshops where individuals hand crafted and assembled products, applied creativity, and enjoyed a fair amount of independence and enjoyment due partly to the lack of managerial supervision. All that changed in the early 1820s, when the Industrial Age relegated people to second-class workers. Craftspeople and farmers could still rise in the class system through hard work, but machines emerged as the stars of industry. The assembly-line-division-of-labor system slowly replaced manual labor and lowered employee profits. The first geographic center to feel this impact was the textile industry in Lowell, MA, where by 1830, 19 textile mills operated with 5,000 workers.

Competition increased when larger cotton mills were built, and the trend spread to other industries. Workers lost much of their independence and were forced to heed owner demands and regulations. By the end of the 19th century, large-scale factories usurped home production and piece work. By 1850 in Britain and the United States, the gulf between labor and management was wide; the average full-time worker clocked more than 3,000 hours per year and earned low wages. In the 1880s, output from factories exceeded demand, and salaries further plunged. The work ethic no longer guaranteed prosperity. Worse yet, automation reduced the need for skilled labor, fostering anonymity, intellectual boredom, and meaninglessness.

THE PSYCHOLOGICAL THEORIES OF WLB

Thus the "traditional model" was born and developed deep roots from a combination of technology and restructuring. Machines replaced raw human energy while bosses acted authoritarian, scoffing at the idea that workers adhered to a work ethic. They claimed that employees were lazy and motivated entirely by money. As a result, specialization and the division of labor increased, expanding into the early 1900s. Eventually, the authoritarian model failed to yield the hoped-for economic prosperity that management craved, and employees began reacting negatively to close supervision. Workers started to distrust their bosses, especially because some employees clearly demonstrated self-motivation.

By the end of World War II (late 1940s), the traditional dogma was permanently shelved. Psychological theories superseded it, with experts arguing that workers were not intrinsically lazy but became so if not sufficiently challenged. Finding ways to make jobs more meaningful, creative, and fulfilling became the focus, and human resource people began churning out company newspapers, employee awards, and company social events—tools they hoped might encourage people to feel useful and important.

In the 1950s, job enrichment theories spread the gospel of achievement, recognition, responsibility, advancement, and personal growth as the means to productivity. Experts introduced the Theory X and Theory Y models (the authoritarian vs. participatory approaches), advocating the cooperation and participation of management and workers toward a common goal. The rationale was that worker input in decision making provided valuable information and bolstered employee morale and self-esteem. Then along came a few radical changes that further restructured the concept of WLB.

Modern Trends Affecting WLB

Technology: The Computer Age

Psychological theories reigned supreme until the issuance of a 1977 U.S. Department of Commerce study by young Stanford University doctoral student Marc Porat. He investigated more than 400 occupations in 201 industries and determined that 46 percent of the gross national product (GNP) in 1967 came from jobs in the information sector and accounted for more than 53 percent of income. The decrease in goods-producing or manufacturing jobs was due to computers increasingly interfacing with machinery and requiring more human technical expertise.

In 1984, economists D. Yankelovich and J. Immerwahr wrote a book comparing Industrial Revolution jobs with Information Age positions and concluded that the latter required more thinking and decision-making skills. Coincidentally these jobs also correlated more closely with the basic work ethic, as workers who made independent judgments appeared to gain in self-fulfillment, challenge, autonomy, recognition, and work quality. These new decision makers tended to be better educated and comfortable with technology, so managers began to hire people with more problem-solving, supervisory, and application skills. These employees anticipated that their hard work would result in personal financial rewards and company productivity.

The Computer Age led to the eventual pervasiveness of technology—desktops, iPads, iPhones, and tablets—as Silicon Valley refined its products. No matter what the hour, workers could always be connected to their clients, patients, or bosses. As Maria Ferris, director of women's initiatives at IBM, pointed out to the U.S. House Subcommittee on Workforce Protections Education and Labor Committee in 2009, technology blurs the boundaries between home and work, and employees can opt for either constant conflict between their jobs and their life obligations or a reasonable compromise.

The digital revolution's challenges have been confirmed by more than 4,000 executives responding to a *Harvard Business Review* (March 2014) survey. The executives revealed mixed opinions regarding multitasking—using technology to be in two places at once. Some believed it caused more mistakes, and others thought 24-hour availability interfered with workers' abilities to exert initiative. A 2014 report from Project Time Off states that four in 10 Americans had 3.2 vacation days still available due to workers' inability to decrease use of digital devices.

Executives also said the new technology did not leave time for independent reflection, when creativity and good ideas often percolate, or for face-to-face meetings that build relationships. While some employees appreciated the flexibility, others disliked the intrusion into family time. Some companies such as Volkswagen and Atos enacted e-mail policies to reduce the technological umbilical cord, and Germany is considering legislation that would ban after-hours employer-employee communication. Furthermore, the French government is considering a bill to "disconnect" during off hours and vacations because the risk analysis firm Technologia found that 3.2 million French workers were emotionally exhausted from work and at risk of burnout, exhaustion, and chronic stress. Areva, a French nuclear power company, disconnected workers four years ago.

Employment of Women: Post WWII Uptick

With the advent of World War II and men enlisting in the Armed Forces, more and more women replaced men in vacant factory positions. In 1900, women comprised 18 percent of the nation's employed—in textile mills, office work, sales, and teaching—but the positions paid only about half that of men. By 1947, 28 percent of the workforce was women, a number that grew to 50 percent by 1990 (Hill, 1992). Women still comprise nearly half (46.8 percent) of the U.S. labor force (BLS, 2015), with six in 10 females ages 16 and older working outside the home.

Since 2002, women's employment has increased in 11 states and the District of Columbia, with Alaska having the highest employment rate at 68.3 percent, according to the Institute for Women's Policy Research in a 2014 paper titled "Status of Women in the States." Four in 10 women's jobs are in health care, non-governmental education, leisure, and other services. (Compare that to only one in four men's positions falling into these categories.) Construction, manufacturing, transportation, and communications employ only one in nine women, and the best-paying industry for women is government because private sector occupations in which women cluster tend to pay less than those in which men dominate the workforce.

Women also brought different attitudes to the work environment. They gravitated to more creative jobs that allowed them to interact with people rather than objects. While women wanted jobs with personal benefits like enjoyment, pride, fulfillment, and challenge, men were more concerned with salaries, supervision, leadership opportunities, and social prestige.

Working Mother Magazine: Guide to WLB

In 1979, when *Working Mother Magazine* debuted, 16 million working women with children turned to this pioneering periodical for advice. Women learned the hard facts, such as that they earned 60 cents on every dollar a man earned (Evans, 2009). This research caught the attention of Baby Boomers, who eagerly sought strategies to help women assimilate into the male workforce. They wanted mentors to guide, comfort, and inspire them, needed role models appropriate to the workplace, and appreciated the advice columns on maternity leave, child care, health, and sex.

Over the years, *Working Mother* has been extremely influential. Through its Research Institute, it helped participate in the reorganization of corporate and governmental policies and administrative options, and in 1985, when *Working Mothers 100 Best Companies* premiered, this annual became a cutting-edge publication highlighting companies that provided women-friendly benefits such as lactation rooms, paid maternity leave, protection from discrimination, multicultural support, and the special needs of single, adoptive, and normal care givers. Other WLB issues covered in the magazine include an increase in flexible schedules; extension of child-care centers to branches (not just headquarters); programs to shelter monies to cover child-care costs; paid leaves for fathers and adoptive parents; and programs for advancement to senior management.

Support from Executives and Educators

Media attention focused even more on WLB when researchers like Professor Lotte Bailyn of the Massachusetts Institute of Technology (MIT) wrote in 1995 about the state of women in science, and then reporters for *The Boston Globe* and *The New York Times* turned the information into headline news. Private companies urged their public relations departments to generate "family friendly" press, which Faith Wohl, the first director of work and family at DuPont, accomplished after two of her employee surveys were picked up by *The Wall Street Journal*.

Eventually more corporations got involved in gender causes; Exxon funded Catalyst, Inc., a national nonprofit for the advancement of women in business and professions, and then Fran Rodgers founded Work/Family Directions (now known as WFD Consulting) to provide child-care support services to IBM. By the late 1980s, the Boston College Center for Work & Family was established with corporate financial support. Soon local and regional networks of employers and foundations launched conferences, and more formal groups emerged with the support of corporate sponsors and universities. Cooperation and cohesion predominated and helped companies achieve common goals, says Ellen Galinsky, president of Families and Work Institute. Instrumental in the creation of the Conference Board's Work-Life Leadership Council in 1983, Galinsky says the formation of the Boston College Roundtable was a premier catalyst for changes in gender attitudes, and many other organizations have since held conferences to discuss trends, lobby for progress, share best practices, and stimulate leadership. Among them: the Institute of Family and Environmental Research, Center for Workplace Solutions at MIT, Work-Family Program (Alfred P. Sloan Foundation), Center on Families at Purdue University, Center for Work Life Law at University of California Hastings College of Law, Glassdoor, and the Great Place to Work Institute.

Empirical Research on Work Stress

After scientist Hans Selye introduced the concept of good and bad stress in the 1970s, the academic and professional world—psychologists, sociologists, and occupational health experts—began spewing out a plethora of evidence-based studies that documented Selye's findings and validated the negative impact of work stress on health. To this day, researchers are still exploring how work stress affects not only the physical and mental aspects, but parental relationships, work conflicts, and discrimination. For example, Fierce, Inc., a global leadership training company, interviewed 1,000 women in a 2014 WLB survey, and more than 34 percent of women said they experienced depression; 45 percent gained weight; and another 45 percent were plagued with insomnia.

Increasingly, the research links physical disorders to work stress. A recent Japanese study (*BMJ*, May 2016) on 1,764 men and women with chronic pain revealed that pain prevalence was higher among males reporting job dissatisfaction, and the same study noted that diminished stress resulted when social support was given by supervisors and co-workers. A Stanford University professor determined that job insecurity factored into poor health by 50 percent, and long work hours increased mortality by almost 20 percent. Another stress study (*Obesity, Fitness & Wellness Week*, March 14, 2015) examined ten workplace stressors, including job insecurity, low job control, overtime, exposure to shift work, and high job demands, and concluded that job insecurities ranked highest in causing poor health and increased mortality.

Over the past two to three decades, hundreds of research studies have confirmed the deleterious role of stress, especially in psychologically demanding jobs in which employees exert little control. Workers often develop chronic health problems—especially cardiovascular disease, musculoskeletal disorders (back and upper extremities), and psychological disorders. They also develop minor health problems such as headaches, upset stomachs, and insomnia. These ailments have increased from 2002 to 2008, with more than one in five employees receiving treatment for high blood pressure, which is linked to strokes or heart attacks. Furthermore, 15 percent of employees are treated for high cholesterol.

Not surprisingly, stress research has shown that lifestyle choices have gotten less healthy, too. Despite widespread efforts to reduce or ban smoking in American workplaces, 21 percent of employees still smoke, most workers do not exercise regularly, and nearly two of three are overweight or obese. Some studies even suggest a relationship between stressful work environments and suicide, cancer, ulcers, and impaired immune function, but more research is needed to confirm this. One thing is certain: Depression and burnout relate to stress, with one-third of the workforce showing signs of clinical depression. A 2015 Internet search on the National Institutes of Health (NIH) clinical trials website turned up 16 stress-related studies, including investigations into mindfulness, yoga, and meditation.

Note: Much of the stress-related information referred to here is based on research from The National Institute for Occupational Safety and Health (NIOSH), the American Psychological Association (APA), the Society for Occupational Health Psychology, and the Families and Work Institute.

Delayed Worker Retirement

Rising levels of stress and accompanying health problems may co-exist with another trend: older workers. Baby Boomers (born between 1946 and 1964), many in need of retirement funds, are now working alongside younger Gen Xers and Millennials. Since 2006, the percentage of people in the workforce 65 or older has risen to more than 80 percent, according to *Business Management Daily* (August 19, 2015). A recent Wells Fargo survey states that 34 percent of older workers plan to work until they die, and the Employee Benefit Research Institute's 2014 survey found that 36 percent of people plan to work past 65. Moreover nearly one in five 70–74-year-olds is already in the workforce. This older employee work phenomenon is not only a function of the U.S. economy but also extends to Western Europe and certain Asian countries such as Japan.

Why are so many older employees staying on the job? Some see themselves as younger and more energetic than their parents who retired, but others cite financial factors rather than enthusiasm. Some saw their IRAs implode in the 2008 recession; others never saved for retirement or had a benefits plan.

The result is that businesses must engage both younger and older workers. For example, the Society for Human Resources Management (SHRM) started a project to identify best practices for utilizing older workers. Mark Schmit, executive director of the SHRM Foundation, believes retaining older workers gives employers a competitive edge by allowing them to pass on knowledge and skills to younger workers. Called "phased retirement," this program has been implemented by 8 percent of private employers. The U.S. Congress passed phased retirement legislation in 2012, but federal employees can access it only at the discretion of the agency where they are employed.

There is a downside, however, to retaining older workers. They may require special programs related to care-giving responsibilities and health concerns, and their tenure can complicate career advancement for younger workers and contribute to intergenerational conflict. Employment attorney C.B. Burns says there are also legal risks, such as disability accommodations and severance packages.

Expansion of Human Resource Departments: Directors Coordinating Benefits

Human resource (HR) departments have taken on expanded roles due to WLB. According to the SHRM, the five areas projected as most critical to WLB are nurturing talent, leadership development, diversity of demographics, recruiting and staffing, change, and cultural transformation. More than six out of 10 HR professionals say their director is strongly involved in business decisions at the board level, so this enables HR to exert a stronger influence on WLB.

But not everyone extols HR departments for their participation in coordinating WLB. According to a 2015 Deloitte survey of 3,000 HR and business leaders in 106 countries, only 5 percent of interviewees believe their organization's talent and HR programs are top notch, and only 34 percent rate them as good. The rest—nearly two out of three—believe their HR solutions are below par. For example, according to the U.S. Department of Labor, officials estimate that more than 70 percent of employers are out of compliance with the Fair Labor Standards Act (FLSA) because HR departments have misclassified employees and failed to pay them proper overtime. This law is complicated and may become even more so in the next few years with government intervention. According to *USA Today*, the recalculations double the salary threshold, making white-collar workers (for example, restaurant managers) eligible for overtime if their salary falls slightly below $47,000 per year and increasing the number of overtime eligibles to about five million salaried workers. The Labor Department's new rule was released May 2016 (*USA Today*, May 18, 2016).

Employee retention and better WLB have become HR priorities, so companies offer more non-monied benefits packages or incentives (instead of increasing salaries). Job hunters in search of better WLB are looking for top-salary jobs, but many talented applicants are tempted by WLB perks like merit pay increases, challenging job responsibilities, and other benefits like flextime and telecommuting. On the other hand, a new survey by the nonpartisan Employee Benefit Research Institute states there is a long-term trend toward wanting more cash and fewer benefits.

Building a workplace where employees are engaged is another WLB challenge for HR. The trend has been to offer positive reinforcement and feedback to team members and mentor or coach them to become top performers, but morale boosting is not straightforward, especially with an expanding labor force of culturally and ethnically diverse workers as well as a politically controversial women's sector that demands equal pay, promotions, daycare, flexible hours, maternity leave, and child health care.

Cultural Globalism

While the term "global economy" implies organizations delighting in diversity, the Western cultural tradition still predominates, especially in North America, influencing employees' understanding and approach to work as well as expectations. It also conditions their views of an organization's practices and outcomes. Although organizations strive to balance international employees' values and behaviors with their need to achieve corporate goals, the effort requires commitment and training. The latter is often provided by consultants or in-house diversity programs, but the learning curve is difficult what with work schedules becoming increasingly erratic and more people toiling evenings, overnight, or on rotating shifts. Even those who work more traditional hours may extend the work day (via e-mail) to accommodate clients and colleagues working many time zones apart. Cultural globalism has impacted everyone's WLB, and not everyone appreciates the "time travel."

THE WORLDWIDE WLB TREND

According to Ernst & Young's 2015 The Global Generations Survey, many full-time employees in Germany (49 percent) and Japan (44 percent) believe WLB is getting harder to maintain. One in four U.S. workers reports this too, but China has the fewest complaints at 16 percent. Working parents in all countries find it more difficult to manage WLB than non-parents, but especially employees in Germany (54 percent parents, 47 percent non-parents); the United Kingdom (42 percent, 34 percent); India (39 percent, 26 percent); and the United States (29 percent, 22 percent). Also struggling are Japan, Brazil, and Mexico, which saw a 5 percent WLB difference between parents and non-parents. Furthermore, managers also must wrestle with WLB, and 35 percent to 56 percent of full-time working parent-managers say the number of work hours has increased in the last five years. Excessive overtime is a top reason Millennials quit jobs in the United States, the United Kingdom, Brazil, Germany, India, Japan, Mexico, and China, but so are minimal wage growth and lack of advancement.

The following sections give an in-depth look at WLB in selected countries. Data is based on information from the 2015 Organization for Economic Cooperation and Development (OECD)—its Better Life Index—as well as United Nations Statistics and the Gallup World Poll.

United States

Although the United States ranks high in housing, income, and wealth, it scores below average in WLB out of 36 countries. One reason is about 11 percent of American employees work long hours (defined as 50-plus hours a week). Gender equality lags too, with 16 percent of men (compared to 7 percent of women) putting in extra hours. Men and women, however, share equally in leisure and personal care time (which includes sleeping and eating). Both genders spend 14.3 hours at these activities—less than the OECD average of fifteen hours.

In other WLB-related areas, the United States compares favorably: Average income is $41,355 a year, and 67 percent of people (ages 15 to 64) have paid jobs. Americans also are moderately satisfied with their lives, and on a scale of zero to 10, give themselves a 7.2—higher than the OECD average of 6.6.

Japan

Japan ranks slightly lower than the United States in WLB; correspondingly, employees are less satisfied. The income gap plays a role here: The top 20 percent of Japanese earn more than six times as much as the bottom 20 percent. On the plus side, 72 percent of Japanese are employed, and the average salary is $35,405. Compared to the United States, however, twice as many Japanese workers (22 percent) work more than 50 hours per week. As a result of this excessive overtime, Japanese parents find it hard to balance long workdays with strenuous commutes and family commitments. Furthermore, the high cost of housing and child education encourages couples to delay parenthood and limit the number of offspring. Parental leave entitlements allow women to return to work, but as in the United States, mothers often end up in temporary positions with low pay or leave the workforce.

United Kingdom

The United Kingdom (U.K.) ranks above average in most areas, such as environment, health, jobs, and earnings. Compared to the United States' 5.3 WLB rank, the U.K. dwarfs its former colonies with a 6.1. Similar to the United States, 13 percent of U.K. employees work long hours, and 71 percent have a paid job with an average annual income of $27,029. The top 20 percent of earners make around $53,000 per year while the lowest 20 percent have to eke by on about $23,000. As in all OECD countries, men earn more than women with an average monetary gap of 15.5 percent.

Switzerland

The standard of living takes a leap forward in Switzerland with its 7.2 WLB index. Eighty percent of people are employed and take home an average income of $33,491; only 6.7 percent work more than 50 hours per week. In general, men and women are treated as equals with a child-care voucher system that allows families to choose care providers. As a result, 74 percent of women have jobs, significantly more than the OECD average of 58 percent. Although Switzerland's WLB sounds nearly ideal, the OECD recommends the Swiss government further improve its employment opportunities for women.

France

With a WLB index of 7.6, France fares better than many OECD countries such as Greece and Portugal but not as well as others like Ireland and Germany. Sixty-four percent of French adults are employed, with only

8 percent working more than 50 hours per week. The average salary is $40,242 per year, although some employees earn only an estimated average of $12,267. France is one of several European governments working on intergenerational partnerships to create jobs for both younger and older workers. The national government also has invested in family policies that benefit different children's age groups.

Sweden

Only a few countries—Denmark, Norway, the Netherlands, Belgium, and Spain—have a higher WLB index than Sweden. Around 74 percent of people are employed, and only 1 percent work more than 50 hours per week. The average employee earns $40, 818 per year. Probably the greatest contributor to Sweden's top WLB is the national government's online accessibility to benefits. The government recently launched a smart phone app so parents can apply for benefits (such as temporary leave) in a convenient, timely manner.

The Top Ten WLB Countries

Based on OECD data, the United States does not make it into the "Top Ten WLB Countries" list because unlike the majority of European nations, Americans have not passed a federal mandate for paid holidays, vacations, or maternity leaves. This contrasts with French employees (on the list) who receive a total of 40 paid vacation days, and Sweden (also on the list), which has earned the title of most generous parental leave benefits country in the world. Sweden offers as much as 16 months with 60 days reserved for fathers; an additional 36 paid vacation days each year is another perk as well as permission to use a total of 480 parental leave days until the child is eight.

The remaining eight countries with best WLB benefits are Bulgaria, Brazil, Finland, the Netherlands, Germany, Norway, Denmark, and Lithuania. Lithuania is celebrated for offering the most paid vacation days in the world—41—and one full year of maternity leave at 100 percent salary. If parents opt for two years of maternity leave, the first year is compensated at 70 percent of the salary; the second year is downsized to 40 percent.

Denmark, which the OECD ranks as number one in WLB, gives 52 weeks of paid maternity leave and 34 days of paid vacation while its Scandinavian sister, Norway, is a world leader in paid parental leave, doling out 47 weeks at 100 percent salary (nine weeks for mothers, 12 weeks for fathers, the remainder shared). Norwegians also receive 35 days of paid vacation.

Employees in the Netherlands fare almost as well. They receive 28 paid vacation days and 16 weeks of paid maternity leave at 100 percent of salary. The Dutch also get tax breaks on an additional 26 weeks of unpaid maternity leave if needed. Finland offers up to 40 paid vacation days a year, 30 of which are mandated and 10 taken as public holidays. Brazil takes a similar approach, but increases the ante to a paid total of 41 vacation days. As for Bulgaria, the government excels at maternity leave, giving a generous 410-day total at 90 percent of salary. Parents can also take a second year at minimum salary and substitute grandparents as caretakers. The last of the "top ten" is Germany, where employees work just 27.8 hours per week—one of the lowest measures in the OECD. Despite this, workers maintain a high standard of living, a strong economy, and a healthy WLB.

SUMMARY

Although WLB means different things to different people, physicians and scientists agree that physical and emotional stress are influenced by globalism, technology, and gender discrimination—not just in the United States but throughout the world. Stress is also influenced by other factors—for instance, what are the socio-economic, educational, and psychological factors that contribute to work stress? Chapter 2 takes a closer look at this as well as recounts the story of one employee who succeeded in overcoming her WLB obstacles.

CHAPTER 2

The Causes and Effects of Work–Life Imbalance

No one factor detracts from WLB. Its quality usually depends on a constellation of socio-economic, psychological, and physical stresses that impact workers and trigger medical, emotional, and legal repercussions. One environmental cause that can have a profound effect on workers can be a high-powered, demanding job.

Take teaching, for example. According to a 2015 analysis of teacher burnout at the University of Tennessee–Knoxville, teachers face many challenges like high accountability, curriculum aims, school safety issues, and legislative mandates. These responsibilities can lead to burnout, which can manifest itself as gastrointestinal disorders, headaches, and emotional exhaustion as well as decreased energy and increased absenteeism.

Although intense one-on-one work interactions such as teaching, police work, and health care can exacerbate tension, even quiet desk jobs can drain people if, for instance, you are a Wall Street investment counselor. One Goldman Sachs analyst literally worked himself to death to meet his company's expectations. In May 2015, he apparently committed suicide. Mental problems as extreme as this can develop when people experience high job strain and little social support at work, as seen in a study of 12,000 Swedish workers in the *Journal of Occupational and Environmental Medicine* (August 2015). Researchers determined that employees with high-stress jobs took more mental health sick leave than workers in less demanding fields.

IMBALANCES CAUSED BY GENDER ROLES

Although social pressure to procreate affects both genders, women also have to deal with the nerve-wracking ticking of their biological clocks. The

Population Reference Bureau defines social pressure as explicit and subtle influences from family, friends, and work colleagues. Additionally, years of intensive social learning and community expectations to reproduce are drummed into women's heads from the time they are born. It is the rare woman or couple who does not succumb to this pressure. Statistics support this, according to the Pew Research Center.

While the childless or childfree trend gained some momentum in the 1970s and 1980s, this demographic has peaked, and today's educated working women often delay childbearing for careers. If necessary they use high-tech reproductive procedures such as in vitro fertilization (IVF) and egg freezing or surrogacy to attain their family-minded goals.

Gender bias also continues its influence following the birth of children. According to the Council on Contemporary Families (2015), 182 couples reported equal divisions of labor (on the job and in the home) before the birth of their first child, but nine months after the babies' births, both genders reported increased workloads. However, only the women's responses approximated accuracy. Men overestimated the time spent in caretaking, and these time discrepancies generally reflect the inequitable environment in which working couples play out their lives. Data collected between 1965 and 2011 (2014 American Time Use Survey) corroborate this. In 1965, mothers and fathers worked an average of eight hours and 42 hours respectively per week; housework occupied 32 hours for women and four hours for men. Women put in 10 hours a week caring for children and men two and one-half hours. In 2011, however, the charts change, but still illustrate the unequal distribution. Fathers do more housework (10 hours a week) and more child care (seven hours) while working a little less (37 hours), but women are still responsible for the greater portion of home duties. Although men are edging toward greater gender fairness—research firm Yougov shows 33 percent of dads do the laundry once a week—women still bear the brunt of the child care and housekeeping tasks.

At the same time couples face significant public pressure to be fantastic parents, and that too is gender oriented, per the Pew Research Center (2013). The survey documented the ongoing social debate over working parents and the negative or positive effects they might or might not have on children. In general, six out of 10 adults say children are better off if one parent stays home, but the percentages change depending on gender. For example, 45 percent of women versus 57 percent of men say children are better off if their mother is at home, and 38 percent of women versus 29 percent of men say children fare as well if their mother works. Moreover, 76 percent of adults believe children are just as well off if their father works, according to the *National Review* (May 29, 2013). The varying percentages appear to be gender-related and may indicate the high cultural expectations society imposes on women to be both the perfect mother and the ideal worker.

The pendulum, however, is beginning to swing, with increasing social pressure on business men to become nurturing parents. For instance, the male founders of Silicon Valley software firm Quip leave work at 5:30 p.m., no later, and American Express holds an Occasional Fatherhood Breakfast Series where men trade WLB hints. The reframing of the male parenting role is in transition, according to the Center for American Progress. Earning money is no longer enough for men; new social trends are infiltrating the WLB, pressuring men to become true partners in parenting and domestic responsibilities.

Media bias also plays a part in keeping gender inequities alive. For instance, in a recent Reuters analysis of 400,000 reports, researchers found "he" pronouns used nine times more by reporters than "she" pronouns; the "he" contexts were also more positive, which reinforces gender stereotyping and inequities. Furthermore, gender stereotyping pervades film, television, and video, according to the *International Journal of Communication* (September 2015, 2370–90). Women are underrepresented, often sexualized, and portrayed as victims; men are overwhelmingly portrayed as violent perpetrators. In contrast, advertisers seem to be incorporating the new message more rapidly. Although *Vogue USA*, and *GQ USA* display images showing demure women with beguiling stances as well as rugged men in virile postures and leather jackets, these same publications also portray models in non-traditional gender roles such as independent career-oriented women and sensitive androgynous men. Still, the old macho-male vs. nurturing-female myth persists.

IMBALANCES CAUSED BY FINANCIAL PRESSURES

Gender inequity also carries over to salaries, exacerbating financial pressures for singles and couples alike. Women of all statuses receive less pay than men and that includes relatively high-paid women engineers, who sometimes quit their jobs due to unequal salaries. Lower salaries currently are affecting the entire workforce, putting pressure on everyday employee expenses such as groceries, mortgages, car payments, utilities, and caretaking costs for aging relatives. Wages have not kept up with employee productivity, according to the OECD's 2015 "The Future of Productivity," and this fuels financial stress.

Paradoxically, HR professionals describe the financial health of employees as fair, according to the 2014 Employee Financial Stress Survey from the SHRM. In reality, Millennials are on a financial precipice because although some own homes and cars and have investments and retirement accounts, others—especially singles—live at home with their parents and carry heavy debt in the form of high monthly credit card balances with hefty interest rates. Other factors affecting bank accounts are rising apartment rents and heavy debt on student loans. Not surprisingly, the 2015 Workplace Flexibility Study of 1,087 professionals shows a high percentage of employees ranked financial support such as tuition assistance high in importance.

Even more than weekly salaries, however, workers worry about future financial security—keeping their jobs and advancing through the ranks. This outweighs income pressures alone by a factor of three, says a Gallup survey. It is also another reason why some workers disregard the unpaid leave provision of the Family and Medical Leave Act (FMLA). Male earners with larger incomes cannot afford time off without reimbursement, although 80 percent of them said they would use leave if it were paid, according to a 2000 survey of eligible employers and employees for the U.S. Department of Labor. Furthermore, workers concerned about financial security fear "flexibility stigma" (which will be discussed in Chapter 4) because they dread the possibility of losing their job or not receiving promotions.

Some companies do offer educational programs to help employees manage their finances, but according to a Gallup poll, only 7 percent of employees think this assistance is effective. Research from the National Partnership for Women and Families (June 2014) reveals that workers do not understand financial basics. Nearly three-quarters of respondents face hardships when managing work, family, and personal responsibilities. Some low-wage, low-benefit workers (many of them women) face particularly difficult conflicts such as a choice between staying home with a new baby or going back to work to support a grown child. According to the 2015 Global Benefits Attitudes Survey, 28 percent of workers admit that these pressures prevent them from doing their best at work. Highly distracted in the job, they may also have higher rates of absenteeism (12.4 days per year compared to 8.6 days for those financially secure).

Also, approximately one-third of employees give elder care and they sometimes wrestle with the problem of whether or not they should reduce the number of work hours or quit to nurse the sick relative. Either option takes its financial and psychological toll as employees know that their decision impacts their long-term retirement payout. (According to AARP's Public Policy Institute, workers who terminate employment lose an average of $300,000-plus in wages and benefits over their lifetimes.)

IMBALANCES CAUSED BY FAMILY VALUES

From the time toddlers are in high chairs, children absorb values and attitudes about work through observations of and conversations with parents and other relatives. In a 2005 Los Angeles study, anthropologist Amy L. Paugh videotaped dinnertime conversations of 16 middle-class working families. By analyzing 900 messages, she found both males and females received clear signals that work should be enjoyable and enriching. Yet they interpreted the subtext in a manner most closely associated with gender. For instance, young girls and women internalized the message that their careers should dovetail with family obligations, so "stopping work" messages were inferred from phrases such as "full-time mothering is best for children" and "not regretting the missing out" of a child's early years. Some women find themselves in double binds that can easily limit their career options. Also in Paugh's study, men heard some blended family wisdom. Instead of the usual dad-must-provide-for-the-family theme, young boys also had to process conversational phrases such as "children always come first" and "you must save time for kids."

Irrespective of gender, children pick up work habits and attitudes of their parents, says Robert Nickell, a Los Angeles parenting expert. Nickell notes that if parents come home stressed out from work and say it is a grind, perhaps talking poorly of the boss and their co-workers, children may approach their work in a similar way. Also, if parents take too many mental health or recreational days off or show a lazy attitude toward career tasks, then parents may be instilling a poor work ethic in their children. The parent–child bond is a significant factor in determining a person's work ethic, says Wayne Baker, a University of Michigan business professor. Baker advises parents to be conscious about the messages they send—for instance, if parents communicate an overwhelming desire to retire, their children may equate work with drudgery (Fast Company, October 2015).

IMBALANCES CAUSED BY WORK–FAMILY CONFLICT

Generally, families run into work–life imbalances when work responsibilities (such as attending a late meeting) affect family obligations (such as watching a son's soccer match). The *Journal of Applied Psychology* (March 2015) surveyed 125 employees at five information technology companies for three weeks, and researchers observed that in the context of regularly-occurring conflicts, emotional exhaustion sets in and employees become verbally abusive to co-workers and loved ones. Furthermore, personal health behaviors start to slip. A 2014 study in *Sociological Focus*

Magazine explained how negative physical or emotional health correlates with declining workplace productivity and poor parenting.

Irregular shift times can be a formidable work–family conflict for the 65 percent of black women who must cope with this scheduling, which unfortunately is associated with lower job and life satisfaction, according to the Economic Policy Institute (EPI) in Washington, D.C. (The study also notes that women of all ethnicities—single or married—experience greater work–family conflict in shift work.) Even the 35 percent of single black women in non-shift, managerial, or professional positions struggle with work conflicts, so no one ethnic group is immune to work–family stress, especially singles. In fact, two large surveys of 18,000 U.S. and European women showed single women were more likely to smoke and have a higher risk of heart disease and stroke (*American Journal of Public Health*, June 2016).

IMBALANCES CAUSED BY PERSONAL GOALS

Personal goals can determine self image, and their achievement or non-achievement ultimately contributes to feelings of work–life balance or imbalance. For instance, definitions of success affect how people feel about themselves, their work, and their intimate relationships. People whose criteria are high can feel depressed if they fail to meet self-imposed standards.

Success goals in the workforce can run the gamut—from realistic to perfectionistic. American psychiatrist Carl Rogers perceived success as unconditional acceptance of oneself and others while U.K. Prime Minister Winston Churchill said success was proceeding from failure to failure and tolerating it all in good spirits. John Wooden, who coached UCLA's basketball team, considers success the peace of mind gained from people acknowledging they did their best. In contrast, perfectionists set extremely high goals and hardly ever feel they achieve them, which is why psychologist Leonard Felder proposes avoiding "normal" standards altogether. Instead he suggests daring to think, create, live, and solve problems differently from other individuals. His comprehensive success definition opens the door to a wide world of varied challenges.

Of course, definitions of success can evolve. For example, at the outset of her media career, Arianna Huffington, author of *Thrive: The Third Metric for Redefining Success and Creating a Life of Well-Being, Wisdom, and Wonder* (Harmony, 2015), pursued money and power, but after sustaining a serious fall from exhaustion and lack of sleep, Huffington rethought her definition of success and made healthier changes.

For most people, however, enthusiasm about their jobs and advancement are part of their definitions of success. That is why, according to Randstad's 2015 Employer Branding Survey, more U.S. employees leave jobs for career growth than money. While salaries are important to workers, employees need to maintain healthy self-esteem if they intend to stay in a position for the long haul.

IMBALANCES CAUSED BY HOME PROBLEMS

Parental anxiety over children does not end at the door of the daycare center or schoolyard, which is why the number of latch-key kids and after-school programs has multiplied since the 1970s. The APA reports that 52 percent of employees say job demands sometimes interfere with family or home responsibilities while 43 percent say just the opposite. In any case, family contentment is at least partly a function of the degree to which work affects the behavior of family members.

Research suggests that children's language and problem-solving skills may suffer due to their parents' irregular schedules and that children may be at greater risk of later smoking and drinking, according to the EPI. Also, the Families and Work Institute says 75 percent of working parents worry they do not spend enough time with their children, and a 2010 Penn State University study suggests their anxiety is well-founded. Findings indicate that parents who are physically and emotionally unavailable to their children (for example, worried about job problems) can impact children's sleep habits and affect family functioning, says Kelly Davis, a family studies expert at Penn State. Lack of parental presence also can reduce the quality of diet and exercise, according to Temple University's Center for Obesity Research and Education. Full-time employed mothers report fewer family meals, more fast food consumption, and less encouragement for eating healthy dishes.

Perhaps the most serious fallout from work that impinges on home life is found in a 2014 New York University study on children's exposure to parental verbal and physical aggression. Psychology professor C. Cybele Raver researched the backgrounds of 1,025 children and found that higher exposure to parental aggression was linked to children's difficulties in identifying emotions. For example, children exposed to parental squabbles faced greater problems regulating their reactions to classroom conflicts and remained at higher risk for anxiety and depression in later years.

The "sandwich" generations (those who care for children and elders) especially struggle with family problems, and the majority of the 66 million adults in the United States are family caregivers in some way. According to the University of North Carolina Business School, the care of loved ones can provoke anxious and threatened behavior. Employees who feel overwhelmed and isolated may compromise their moral principles and rationalize inappropriate work actions as acceptable—for example, they might insult a co-worker in front of others on the team or utter profanity. Jobs in inflexible environments are especially difficult for caregivers, and around 40 percent of elder caregivers say the imbalances often force them to reduce their work hours or quit. In a study of 823 information technology employees who took care of children, elders, or both groups (*Journal of Family Issues,* May 2015) researchers found that compared to non-care givers, the elder and child caregivers reported tremendous psychological distress and partner strain.

A real-life "sandwich stress" story from the *Washington Post* (November 16, 2014) involved Samira and Shaz Siddiqi, a dual-earning couple who struggled with four elderly parents and two daughters. Samira felt guilty that she was too exhausted from her job to read to her children at night, and her husband was plagued with a stress-induced eye disorder.

Family imbalance can be particularly hard on women because experts say they are primarily responsible for bolstering the emotional psyches of other family members, including their spouse or partner. According to psychologist Melissa E. Mitchell in the book *Gender and the Work-Family Experience* (Springer, 2015), this traditional empathetic role increases the female burden of responsibility. If you add this to the women's "second shift" of housework, child care, and other domestic duties, WLB can deteriorate fast. The result can be a lot of unhappy mothers and wives wanting to discuss problems with their partners but unable to because males characteristically withdraw.

Family-related imbalances also can lead to marital conflict, anger, and divorce. Researchers at Queen's University, Kingston, in Ontario, Canada, investigated 266 females who experienced sexual harassment at work. In a 2014 study in the *Journal of Organizational Behavior*, the researchers noted that women and their partners felt angry due to this harassment. The problem was so acute it caused turmoil in their romantic relationships. Other common negative marital reactions to work stress include conflict or withdrawal as observed in a 2009 Croatian study of 340 married couples. When one partner comes home feeling despondent about work (for example, weekend duties) and sulks about it (*Health Sociology Review*, 2014), this kind of depression can be contagious, especially to the female partner because women generally value domestic interactions more than men and are more vulnerable to discord.

On a more positive note, however, an American study of dual career couples found that among the 639 couples who worked in the same occupation or organization ("work-linked"), there were greater degrees of spousal support, WLB, and family and job satisfaction (*Journal of Occupational Health Psychology*, 2015). Researchers said the benefits doubled for work-linked couples compared with non-work-linked couples. In other words, partners employed at the same organization had fewer conflicts and better WLB.

IMBALANCES CAUSED BY CO-WORKERS

Pressure from bosses and colleagues can be obvious or subtle, vocal or tacit, but employees are all susceptible to the subtexts. Take, for example, vacations. Employees say they receive negative and mixed messages from their bosses regarding vacation days although a 2015 survey of 500 managers by the U.S. Travel Association concluded that 80 percent of managers believe vacation time increases team productivity and 69 percent say they encourage their employees to take off time. Do managers talk out of two sides of their mouths? Some employees doubt their bosses' sincerity. Only 67 percent of employees believed their supervisors value vacations, and others say they are afraid to take time off because the workload might worsen or they might appear less committed to the job. According to the 2015 Workplace Flexibility Study, one in five employees spends more than 20 hours per week working outside of the office just to demonstrate her loyalty. If managers also suffer from job insecurity, this further complicates the situation and adds to the pressure-cooker effect.

Another negative influence from co-workers is a shortage of personal recognition, which some managers nurture accidentally or intentionally. Managers sometimes forget or do not realize that praise, appreciation, and commendation energize employees. According to Quantum Workplace, the number-one reason employees get stressed and leave their jobs is lack of recognition.

Another area of miscommunication or misdirection is bosses who do not participate in wellness programs or who do not encourage personal development. It may be a case of "do as I say, not as I do," but managers sometimes discourage or antagonize workers by failing to transmit HR announcements of on-site health programs, networking, or mentoring opportunities. This may be because some Millennials look for career development opportunities, and older managers do not always perceive them as important. The result? The generational gap can inflict harm on workers hoping to advance to upper-level positions. In a 2015 study on managerial behavior in the *Journal of Applied Management and Entrepreneurship*, University of Texas Professor Ann Gilley suggests that same-generation managers can also exhibit different degrees of success in promoting WLB. So the cause is not always generational; sometimes it comes down to individual attitudes and habits.

Another cause of co-worker stress is colleagues who expect their co-workers to be reachable outside of the office on personal time—either by e-mail or phone. The Workplace Flexibility Study reported that 65 percent of employees say both their manager and HR representative exert pressure on them to be digitally available 24/7.

IMBALANCES CAUSED BY PERSONAL VALUES

Even personal values such as integrity and respect for the environment can detract from WLB if these life directions, personal qualities, and moral standards have relevance to the individual but not to the employer. (People can pinpoint their values by using the APA ACTraining exercise "Lifetime Achievement Award," a self-questionnaire focusing on career contributions.) This conflicting situation can create insurmountable pressure. In fact, the greater the distance between employees' beliefs and expectations and those of the corporate culture, the more the employees may experience stress in the form of burnout or emotional exhaustion. Psychologists call this "cognitive dissonance," and Senior Manager Goran Prvulovic writes about one example on LinkedIn.com, describing the case of a project health and safety advisor asked by his manager to downplay a safety investigation. Chronic ethical bouts of cognitive dissonance can lead to depression, aggression, or other negative behaviors.

IMBALANCES CAUSED BY LACK OF RESOURCES

Knowledge can be the key to easing your workload or exacerbating it, but the opportunity to learn, acquire, or develop skills (such as expertise in time management) often varies. Some workers never seem able to apply time management tips; others seem to have an intuitive grasp of basic techniques such as "to do" lists and prioritizing. Also, some employees are dissatisfied with their company's educational development programs and outdated processes and want greater career flexibility to gain additional skills, says Kate Bravery, with Mercer Consultants.[1]

Employee training programs provided by HR departments and managers also vary in the quality and depth of coverage. According to the 2015 Emerging Workforce Study, 31 percent of workers do not feel they have been trained sufficiently, and just 33 percent say the training and career development opportunities in their organization are good.

Some HR professionals are uninformed about company culture and do not communicate the range of flexibility programs available to employees. This can put pressure on employees to stick to the traditional 40-hour week instead of taking advantage of part-time, telecommuting or other flexible options. Some HR departments also may aid and abet employee job insecurity by failing to bolster employee optimism and morale with one-on-one interactions, career coaching, or transition services. Worse, only 34 percent of HR departments (surveyed by Workplace Trends) currently offer outplacement services, so employees are on their own if they lose their jobs.

Another HR omission that places pressure on employees is HR's ignorance of workers' views on WLB. Sixty-seven percent of HR professionals think employees lead a balanced work life, but 45 percent of those same employees say they lack enough personal time, according to the Workplace Trends survey of June 2015. This kind of informational disconnect hurts communication and places undue duress on workers to refrain from giving truthful feedback on employee surveys.

IMBALANCES CAUSED BY DISCRIMINATION AND AGGRESSION

The newest stress demon may be the pervasive, costly problem of workplace bullying and harassment, says lead researcher Jagdish Khubchandani, a health education instructor at Indiana's Ball State University, who analyzed 17,542 people in a national 2010 study in the *Journal of Community Health*. Khubchandani found that over a 12-month period, about 8 percent of all respondents said they were threatened, harassed, or bullied in the workplace. Higher rates of bullying occurred among hourly workers, state and local government employees, multiple jobholders, night-shift employees, and those working irregular schedules. In 2014 when CareerBuilder.com surveyed 3,372 employees in a variety of industries, 28 percent reported bullying incidents, and 19 percent reported leaving a job due to bullying.

Workplace bullying can contribute to job loss due to the lies, humiliation, shame, rejection, and other emotional tortures victims endure. Bullying also can induce loss of sleep, depression, and anxiety, according to the *Journal of Community Health* (November 16, 2014). The Workplace Bullying Institute, which reports that 35 percent of U.S. workers have been bullied on the job, also links bullying to many physical ills, including cardiovascular problems, gastrointestinal diseases like inflammatory bowel disease (IBD) and colitis, auto-immune disorders, diabetes, and skin problems.

Employers that allow bullying can experience high employee turnover, absenteeism, and lawsuits. According to the Bullying Institute, the most common employer reaction to bullying is to deny (25 percent) or downplay (16 percent) the issue, which further stresses victims. Although no employment laws regarding bullying are yet on the books, the Healthy Workplace Bill website reports that 30 states and two territories are currently considering bills.

Certain bullying cases with "malicious intent" have even yielded large recoveries. In October 2014, a Texas jury awarded $11 million to a Microsoft employee who proved that he was retaliated against and bullied after ending a romantic relationship with a female co-worker/boss. The abuse included false accusations of sexual harassment, expense account fraud, marginalization (being pushed aside as less important), and blocked promotions. The judge later reduced the award to $2 million, which included compensatory and punitive damages as well as legal fees.

Besides bullying, sometimes stressed-out employees get aggressive and argue. Often they cannot concentrate on their job tasks, which lead to accidents, impaired decision making, inattention, and inadequate performance. Employees spend at least three hours a week dealing with conflict, and this results in lower company profits, productivity, and WLB. Research shows that managers spend from 25–40 percent of their time managing conflict, HR coach Sue Jones told the SHRM.[2] That is a considerable portion of the day dedicated to playing mediator or assuaging the ruffled feathers of workers suffering from mental stress.

Far worse is when certain individuals reach a breaking point and turn to violence due to problematic jobs, demotions, or layoffs. Other triggers also can include irregular hours, depression, criticism, financial problems, marital difficulties, and inferior performance. About 50 percent of businesses with more than 1,000 employees experience workplace violence each year (BLS, 2006). A 2014 FBI report found that shootings in the United States now occur, on average, once every three weeks, with nearly half of them taking place at businesses. The FBI also reports that 16 percent of workplace violence is due to assaults or other violence such as stalking, rape, intimidation, or bullying. In the United States alone, 20 employees are estimated to be murdered and 18,000 assaulted each week, according to *Industry & Higher Education* (February 2012).

Unfortunately companies and other organizations have been slow in devising prevention strategies. A 2006 study by the SHRM found that 40 percent of organizations did not have any formal policies for responding to violence, according to *Industry & Higher Education*. This can lead to legal problems for employers and an immense work–life imbalance for employees. For instance, in a 2007 Houston, TX, case, a human resources assistant at a Veterans Assistance Medical Center sent threatening e-mails to his colleagues, later claiming his stressful job had made him develop aggressive behavioral problems.

No wonder employees are taking an increasing number of stress-related leaves under the Family and Medical Leave Act (FMLA), which allows up to 12 weeks of unpaid leave for a serious health condition (defined as requiring physician treatment and lasting three or more consecutive days).

The case of U.S. Marine Adam Brant eased the way for people with posttraumatic stress disorder (PTSD) who encounter workforce stress. After suffering several seizures as a maintenance technician for a Pennsylvania pipe fittings manufacturer, Brant filed a suit based on the Uniformed Services Employment and Reemployment Rights Act of 1994 and the FMLA. (Veterans like Brant must be rehired following FMLA leaves regardless of the time interval between diagnosis and work resumption.) The EEOC sued the company under the Americans with Disabilities Act (ADA), and the company later settled. Administrators recognized that six weeks of unpaid leave was a more honorable (and less expensive) outcome than prolonged litigation.

Although many non-veteran workers have legitimate stress claims, they end up losing psychiatric claims of "invisible" stress and disability (under the ADA) because stress is regarded as intrinsic to the workplace. But since the ADA Amendments Act of 2008, more psychological disorders have been added: major depressive disorder, bipolar disorder, PTSD, (post-traumatic stress disorder) obsessive–compulsive disorder (OCD), and schizophrenia.

Although courts usually dismiss psychological disabilities (except for the ADA diagnosed disorders) and generalized stress, the *Denver Post* says courts have awarded monetary compensation to employees when mental problems (such as panic attacks, high blood pressure, and headaches) were documented.[3] For example, in 2007, Khosrow Kamali, a civil engineer for Caltrans (California Department of Transportation), requested a transfer due to interpersonal stress and anxiety with his supervisor. Caltrans denied it, but the jury not only awarded Kamali the transfer but also extended his leave for 615 workdays.

The courts switched sides, however, in *Higgins-Williams v. Sutter Medical Foundation*—a California case that made national headlines. In 2010, Michaelin Higgins-Williams, a clinical assistant at Sutter, complained about hostile interactions with her manager and HR representative. She was diagnosed with adjustment disorder with anxiety and granted a stress-related leave under the FMLA. When Higgins-Williams returned to work, she insisted that a negative performance review had induced a panic attack. She left work and did not return for several months. Her employer fired her, and the court upheld it, citing the litigant's failure to provide convincing documentation of a mental disability.

Stressed employees have the burden of proof in compensation claims because the legal consensus is that normal stress is inherent in every job as in the case of *Knight v. Audubon Savings Bank* in New Jersey. Here the employee claimed that her supervisor's screaming and massive workload made her so stressed she had to seek out psychiatric care. The court denied her claim, maintaining that her stress (for example, her manager yelled at her while the employee spoke on the phone with a customer) was of normal quality and quantity.

One of the most stressful causes of work–life imbalance is sexual discrimination, what with the legal hoops employees must jump through if they are to get justice. In 2014, the Equal Employment Opportunity Commission (EEOC) filed around 26,000 charges of sex discrimination alleging firing, harassment, and sexual harassment. Those cases, which recovered $106.5 million, comprised nearly 30 percent of EEOC cases, many of them relating to gender discrimination (almost every major U.S. bank was sued). Thousands of women also filed charges alleging pregnancy discrimination in hiring, promotions, assignments, retaliation, and failure to accommodate pregnancy-related work restrictions. So far the EEOC has recovered $14 million under the ADA, the FMLA, and the Pregnancy Discrimination Act (PDA), which is an amendment to Title VII of the Civil Rights Act of 1964. (The Civil Rights Act of 1964 was landmark legislation that outlawed discrimination based on race, color, religion, sex, or national origin.)

According to employment attorney Lara de Leon of Ogletree Deakins, the EEOC announced a new Strategic Enforcement Plan targeting pregnancy discrimination, and a 2014 jury trial against AutoZone returned a record verdict of $188 million in damages following the demotion and then firing of an employee who had just given birth.

Things could get a lot more stressful for employees before they get better, says Marcia McCormick, co-director of the Wefel Center for Employment Law at Saint Louis University School of Law. Under U.S. employment law, any workplace rule that is not a "business necessity" cannot disproportionately affect one group (or gender), so any industry that prevents a group of employees such as women from taking advantage of flextime options—for example, working part-time or telecommuting—could be interpreted as acting illegally under U.S. employment law, says McCormick.

The ubiquity of computers and smart phones might make it difficult for employers to insist that traditional work structures are essential to the job.

PHYSICAL AND PSYCHOLOGICAL HEALTH CONSEQUENCES

As a result of the pressures discussed so far in this chapter, employees often suffer from emotional and physical illnesses. The American Institute of Stress estimates that job stress costs the United States more than $300 billion per year while the Global Wellness Institute puts the sum at $2.2 trillion if you include everything from absences to legal judgments to medical expenses. The World Health Organization (WHO) cites among a long list of symptoms such mental ones as irritability, poor concentration, inability to relax, difficulty in decision making, poor logic, fatigue, and anxiety; and such chronic physical conditions as heart disease, diabetes, obesity, digestive system disorders, high blood pressure, headaches, arthritis, cancer, and musculo-skeletal disorders like low back pain and upper limb disorders. In 2015, medical bills and lost productivity for diabetes and pre-diabetes cost Americans $322 billion, according to the ADA.

Only heart disease at $320 billion approaches that drain on the health care system. NIOSH says workers age 55 or less and employed in service and blue-collar occupations are more likely than those in white-collar occupations to report a history of coronary heart disease or stroke. A 2015 study in *Lancet*, which pooled data from 600,000 adults, underscores the damaging effect of long work hours (defined as more than 55 hours per week) on coronary heart disease. Researchers reported a 13 percent increase in coronary heart disease and a 33 percent increase in stroke risk. Work–family conflict, in particular, was linked to increased cardio-metabolic risk and poorer mental health (measured by job satisfaction, emotional exhaustion, perceived stress, and psychological distress), according to a 2015 Family and Health Network study. Moreover, in October 2015, an analysis of studies on work stress and stroke in *Neurology* found that people with high-stress jobs (big demand, little control) were 58 percent more likely to have an ischemic (obstruction of blood flow in an artery) stroke than those with low-stress jobs. Based on this data, neurologist Jennifer J. Majersik says strategies aimed at increasing job control, such as decentralizing decision making and encouraging job flexibility, should be tested.

Such positive interventions in the workplace are also warranted based on a NIOSH study on skyrocketing suicide rates after 2007. Even doctors—medical school students and practitioners—are at high risk for self injury. A *Journal of the American Medical Association* (JAMA) study published in December 2015 found that 29 percent of residents had significant signs of depression. According to a 2015 study by VITAL WorkLife and Cejka Search, 46 percent of physicians were severely stressed in 2015 compared to 38 percent in 2011. Burnout was so high that 89 percent of survey respondents desired some degree of job change, ranging from switching positions to leaving medicine entirely. Health practitioners worried about their own well-being and a decrease in patient safety. As with health care workers, lawyers also suffer from higher rates of depression than in most other occupations and, according to the Centers for Disease Control (CDC), 54 percent are more likely to commit suicide than non-lawyers.

Workaholism may lead to psychiatric disorders such as depression, anxiety, and OCD, say researchers at the University of Bergen in Norway. For example, Antea Group, an international environmental consulting firm based in Shoreview, MN, knew some of their 450 employees were struggling with mental health challenges so the company adopted the Learn to Live online program. Based on cognitive behavioral therapy (CBT), the Internet program might appeal particularly to Millennials who prefer technology to face-to-face therapy. Studies in Amsterdam and the United Kingdom have garnered mixed results thanks to support from the CEO, who kicked it off in his quarterly update, and HR people who participated in a two-hour online Webex to provide feedback to employees.

Also linked to mental health disorders such as suicidal thoughts is obesity, according to a 2015 Swedish study of 12,000 workers in which employees with demanding jobs, high strain, and little social support took more mental health sick leave and gained more weight. According to a 2015 CareerBuilder survey, 44 percent of workers say they gained weight in their present job, blaming it on sitting, not exercising, and a lot of performance and productivity pressures. In fact, workers say their busy workday prevents them from taking advantage of wellness benefits such as onsite workout facilities and gym passes. Although obesity directly impacts workers, it also hurts organizations as a whole. Obese workers cost employers thousands more a year than normal-weight workers, according to the *American Journal of Health Promotion*; Columbia University's Mailman School of Public Health puts the U.S. figure at $8.65 billion per year due to absenteeism.

Work stress often triggers insomnia as well. Nearly one-third of Americans and 40 percent of night-shift workers say they get less than six hours of sleep on workdays, said Charles Czeisler, MD, chairman of the board of the National Sleep Foundation. Czeisler also says 70 percent of working Americans call themselves sleep-deprived.

SUMMARY

Stress in workplace and home zones can cause work–life imbalances that lead to physical and mental disorders. Imbalances also can kill by means of heart disease, suicide, or chronic illnesses. Stress can force workers to quit or sue their employers for bullying, discrimination, and more. Individuals can, however, minimize these imbalances by taking decisive and positive actions to avoid or dissipate stress. In Chapter 3 we learn about the gamut of coping responses, perks, and programs that employees can use to help restore WLB.

CHAPTER 3

Self-Help Strategies to Ease Employee Stress

A volatile economy and a multi-generational workforce have motivated organizations to start modifying their corporate cultures to better meet the needs and demands of employees. Organizations also are reacting to a national study by Harvard and Stanford universities that estimates that U.S. workplace stress contributes to at least 120,000 deaths each year and accounts for as much as $190 billion in health care costs (*Employment Benefit News*, February 2016).

Efforts to decrease stress have led to flexible scheduling and employee assistance programs (EAPs) in some organizations, and these provisions have benefited hundreds of families. For example, Patagonia—a California sports clothing manufacturer—now allows employees to set their own hours, use on-site daycare, and take regular exercise breaks. Not all workers are as fortunate, but most have access to other tools to lessen stress if they choose to be proactive. Here are some time-honored and innovative techniques for helping to improve WLB.

STRATEGY 1: CHANGE JOBS

This may sound defeatist, but it should be reassuring to know that workers always have the option to change jobs—or careers—if the WLB proves untenable or contrary to important goals. A job or career reorientation may be the best choice depending on such variables as an individual's age, experience, family status (for instance, a husband in graduate school or an ailing parent), or a decreasing (or increasing) passion for another field or industry.

What are the reasons most people switch jobs? According to a Swedish 2015 University of Gothenburg paper: Improved psychological environment, social support, and work task satisfaction are common reasons. So are WLB issues such as low pay growth, inadequate salary, or dislike of a manager or supervisor. According to HRM Recruit, a Dublin, Ireland, talent acquisition company, lack of job enjoyment is a legitimate reason to switch jobs. For example, when Audrey Gauss graduated from college, education was her chosen career path,[1] but health problems and conflicts with a large urban school system led her to abandon those goals. Today she teaches yoga, uniting her passion for health with the need for a steady income.

Discontent with location, compensation, security, or managerial support can also play a part in job change, but many workers list dissatisfaction with WLB as the number one reason for change (59 percent of 1,000 professionals, according to FlexJobs). The desire for more meaningful work ranks second at 47 percent; 40 percent cite current career stress; and 37 percent attribute it to financial pressures. Respondents also said they anticipated that a career change would improve their personal relationships and permit them to enjoy a healthier lifestyle. In a similar survey by Ernst & Young Global Limited (EY), a U.K. knowledge management company, people complained of poor wage growth, lack of advancement, overtime, a non-teamwork environment, and a manager who discouraged flextime.

Job-hopping and career change have become the rule instead of the exception. In January 2014, 21 percent of American workers said they planned to change jobs within the next 12 months, according to a Career-Builder survey. A 2014 Penn State study of 74 male biologists and physicists revealed that one-third of male scientists were willing to sacrifice advancement for better WLB. In a 2015 report by the American Institute of Physics, which focused on 503 physicists in the private sector (they used a variety of skills and not just physics), 85 percent worked in STEM (science, technology, engineering, and mathematics) fields, but others preferred positions in law or finance, admitting that these jobs were more intellectually stimulating, challenging, and rewarding. A recent survey of 432 STEM professionals reported that a third of Australian workers expect to leave that occupational sector within the next five years.

Some physicians also change careers, says Elizabeth Steiner, MD, in *Annals of Family Medicine* (January/February 2014). Some family doctors trade clinic or private practices for jobs in government programs, insurance corporations, politics, information technology, business, and law. Speaking of law, many lawyers are also defecting from larger firms to smaller ones to upgrade their WLB. A study from the Center for WorkLife Law reports that more than 50 entrepreneurial law businesses lured attorneys away from more prestigious and bigger firms.

Strategy 2: Be Your Own Boss

It is both easier and harder to be your own boss, says Matthew Salzberg, chief executive officer (CEO) and founder of Blue Apron, a food-and-recipe start-up. Salzburg transitioned to entrepreneur from prior positions as a private equity investor and venture capitalist. According to the National Association for the Self-Employed, 77.6 percent of small U.S. businesses are self-employed (U.S. Census 2006). One reason for the attraction is self-employment allows people to retain full control of hours and workload. The downside, though, saddles the owner with full responsibility for delivering a product or service efficiently and effectively. For example, Monica Galetti, the former sous chef at the French restaurant Le Gavroche in London, England, gave up her full-time position there to freelance, gaining the flexibility to write cookbooks, appear on television, and parent her daughter (*Huffington Post UK*, August 26, 2014).

By 2020, according to a 2010 Intuit Report, more than 40 percent of the U.S. workforce will choose contingent, freelance, or contract work. MBO Partners also projects a future flood of independent workers, affirming that by 2020 one in two American workers will either switch to independent work or spend at least part of their day self-employed. The top reasons: control over the type of work assignments, earnings potential, and flexible scheduling.

Freelancers, as opposed to entrepreneurs, are more likely to be older. More than half are Boomers (currently aged 51–66), with a third categorized as Gen Xers (aged 35–50); younger contractors are more likely to be women, which may indicate a generational move by both genders to embrace more contract work. These independent workers depend on technology even more than corporate workers, a 2015 U.K. survey says. Eighty-eight percent of all freelancers, contractors, and zero-hour workers (on call at the employers' discretion) use smart technology to search for work assignments to schedule around family commitments, according to a 2015 London PR Newswire.

In 2006, the U.S. Government Accountability Office found that 42.6 million people were "untethered," contingent, or independent workers, and that figure is probably higher now.[2] Although these work arrangements can potentially disturb family relationships, collective work spaces in cities like Austin, TX, Atlanta, GA, and Berkeley, CA, have arrived at a solution: day-care facilities in work spaces. Self-employed parents like Jennifer and

Steve Garcia, who run a web-development business out of their Texas home, can maximize their work time by bringing their sons to Plug & Play Daycare for four hours twice a week and hosting client meetings in the collective's conference room.

STRATEGY 3: CLARIFY YOUR VALUES

Spotlighting pressures that negatively affect WLB is important, especially when they are self-imposed. If workers pinpoint their values—what is important to them ethically and morally—it can help them discriminate between the "musts" or priorities and eliminate some of the "maybes" or possibilities. The APA defines values as "chosen life directions" and says people are more motivated to accomplish goals that synchronize with these life directions. Values energize people in the workplace, says Dan McCarthy, a management and leadership expert.[3] Employees are fueled by personal standards or guiding principles such as integrity, privacy, family, honesty, harmony, and loyalty.

Clarifying values, however, entails serious introspection. People do not usually work solely for money. By discerning what non-materialistic goals they strive for, they can make better decisions about careers, marriages, and other important life experiences. Engaging in values clarification can help employees sort the vital from the trivial, shorten their "to do" list, and take pride in their accomplishments. Employees can take advantage of the many online values clarification exercises that corporate consultants and behavioral health organizations post on the Internet, such as the following self-examination recommended by psychologist Harry Mills and his colleagues at www.mentalhelp.net:

- What are the five most important things in your life?
- How would you spend a week if you only had six months to live?
- What are the most important relationships in your life? Why?
- What are your long-range goals regarding family, career, and money?
- If you died tomorrow, what would you like others to say about you?

Author Stewart D. Friedman advocates that employees compare and contrast their personal values with their work decisions. He suggests employees notice if their daily activities are congruent with their core values and consider such questions as:

- Does the work task better serve the clients?
- Does a specific home chore help my family function better?

One exercise Friedman especially recommends is to identify a simple action aimed at a value-based goal. For example, a worker's core commitment might be to become a good parental role model; ongoing actions for accomplishing this might be complimenting the child for positive behaviors. At work, an employee's value-based goal might be conscientious attention to accuracy. Watch whether this person follows through on this goal by rechecking numbers, names, and other important data. Does the employer also take pride in this effort, or is this a value unshared by the organization?

Strategy 4: Build Support Networks

Emotional, intellectual, social, and physical support at home and in the workplace is wholeheartedly endorsed by most WLB experts. Finances permitting, dual-income parents who wish to participate in important moments in their children's lives might consider hiring support staff such as home assistants to manage physical chores like washing laundry, dressing children, cooking, and housecleaning. Nannies and au pairs can make the difference between balance and bedlam.

Besides drawing from financial resources, workers also need the emotional support of families and friends. Networking can ease conflicted feelings and help to share common problems such as finding competent caretakers to watch the children after school. According to *Harvard Business Review* (April 9, 2015), workers need opportunities to confide, vent, and receive advice from trusted sources.

In *Leading the Life You Want* (2014), author Stewart D. Friedman recommends ways employees can extend their support networks. For example, brainstorm the names of three to five important individuals in your career, family, and community; then find a way to support these people such as by means of an introduction to a significant contact or a volunteer activity at a police fundraiser. Employees also should identify areas in their life in which they need help—for example, requiring extra computer tutoring or rehearsing a product presentation—and then contact someone to assist them with that task. Rewarding the person with a personal note, gift, or some sort of sincere acknowledgement can bring a new helpmate into the support network.

Support also can come from receptive supervisors or managers, especially if employees confront problems related to specific job assignments or feel overwhelmed by certain projects. Strong bonds between co-workers and bosses, says *Harvard Business Review*, can determine whether careers crash and burn or grow and prosper. Sympathetic superiors can often help employees overcome difficult moments and unexpected crises. Even bonding with an employee in a similar situation on social media such as LinkedIn or Facebook can provide the impetus to make needed changes.

Research also indicates that health-geared social supports can lower levels of work–family conflict through peer consultation groups, personal psychotherapy, and mentors. The availability of mental health supports such as workshops or counseling sessions are more important than how many participants actually attend, and every industry or profession can organize them. Take advantage of them—for instance, in one study, women cardiologists with marital conflicts due to long hours and at-risk patients assembled regularly to discuss their fears in nonjudgmental ways. Some participants became stronger health providers and human beings through the sharing.

Most important, every worker needs a supportive partner or spouse who pitches in with domestic responsibilities. If this is not possible, employees should seek out corporate mentors, sympathetic department chairpersons, or a network of senior faculty or executives to help nurture confidence and balance. Especially in male-dominated professions like STEM, women lack confidence in their abilities and need supportive mentors, says Sandra Kentish, head of engineering at the University of Melbourne, Australia.[4]

STRATEGY 5: AVOID RUDENESS

Workplace incivility or rudeness is on the upswing and can produce stress, reducing an individual's resources, according to a 2015 Austrian study of 371 participants in *Psychology*. Increased incivility (doubling between 1998 and 2011) continues to take its toll on employees' physical and mental health, Persistent unpleasant interactions between employees and supervisors or other co-workers can lead to emotional exhaustion, the precursor to burnout. Christine Porath, a Georgetown business professor, says her father encountered protracted incivility from two bosses and ended up hospitalized.[5] While managers and bosses need to keep their behaviors in check, the same also applies to employees. Engaging in incivility adds negativity to the workplace and galvanizes an employee's "fight or flight" reaction, releasing the stress hormone cortisol and perhaps contributing to cardiac problems. How can staff cultivate a civil atmosphere? Porath suggests several techniques:

- Do not interrupt employees or be judgmental.
- Try to express interest in others' opinions.
- Say "please" and "thank you."
- Do not patronize or put others down.

- Do not swear or make obscene gestures.
- Do not pat yourself on the back too much.

STRATEGY 6: VOLUNTEER IN THE COMMUNITY

According to a 2013 study co-sponsored by United Health Group and the Optum Institute, 75 percent of 3,351 employees who volunteer say it makes them feel physically healthier and lowers their stress. About 25 percent say volunteering helps them manage a chronic illness. Similar results emerged from a Swiss online study of 746 workers in the *Journal of Occupational and Environmental Medicine* (February 2015). The authors concluded that volunteering was associated with less work–life conflict, burnout, and stress and that it nurtured mental health. Helping others gave people a greater sense of balance.

For instance, automotive retailer AutoNation, with more than 26,000 employees, partners with many cancer charities throughout the United States, such as Atlanta's CURE Childhood Cancer. Employees volunteer by serving meals to hospitalized children and parents, providing holiday gifts, and participating in special events such as Lauren's Run and the annual picnic to raise research funds.

STRATEGY 7: PRACTICE MINDFULNESS

Positive psychology deals with mindfulness techniques, which are currently being implemented by companies and corporations given their success in education, dieting, and other areas. Mindfulness teaches people to keep their thoughts in the present, and studies show that people who apply this technique in a nonjudgmental way can help relieve stress and improve their concentration. In 2014, the American Management Association conducted a major survey with the Business Research Consortium, and researchers learned from 991 respondents that 49 percent of organizations provide mindfulness-related training to some degree. Among workers receiving this training, 85 percent reported it was somewhat beneficial, and researchers saw improvements in leadership abilities, emotional intelligence, and decision making—all skills associated with the practice of mindfulness and cognitive behavioral therapy (CBT). According to *Employment Benefit News* (March 2016), mindfulness studies also show that restaurant servers, physicians, managers, hospital admissions teams, and psychotherapists perform better after training because mindfulness does not just improve productivity; it helps regulate emotions, making everyday activities feel important and enjoyable by emphasizing intrinsic instead of extrinsic motivators. One resource available for practicing mindfulness-based cognitive therapy is the book *Mindfulness-Based Cognitive Therapy for Depression* by Zindel Segal et al. (Guilford Press, 2013).

STRATEGY 8: AVOID TRANSFERS AND TRAVEL

Travel or relocation is one of the top perpetrators of stress and poor WLB. Even managers on extended business trips admit to needing assistance from their employers. The combination of late-night phone calls from headquarters in distant time zones together with distress from unhappy partners or spouses can lead to a chaotic lifestyle. Culture shock can discombobulate and frustrate even the most experienced employees traveling internationally.

Foreign relocation can be particularly troublesome when the whole family makes the trek. Family members relocating overseas rely on each other for support, says Mila Lazarova, a business professor at Simon Fraser University in Vancouver, Canada.[6] Despondent spouses or depressed children affect work duties, and family tensions can quickly escalate. In a 2013 study, Harvard business professor Boris Groysberg surveyed nearly 4,000 executives. Twenty-eight percent said they turned down international assignments in order to protect their marriages, and 32 percent said they had done the same in the past to save their family the stress of relocation.

According to a 2002 Global Expatriate Study, 75 percent of expatriate workers agreed that international assignments were difficult, especially on dual-career families. Steve Poelmans, assistant professor at the International Center of Work and Family at IESE Business School in Barcelona, Spain, says expatriates have to cope with intense levels of work–family conflict, facing challenging new demands while being separated from vital resources such as family support, childcare arrangements, and school facilities. The challenges are so extreme (such as leaving friends and family) that more than seven out of 10 adults say they are unlikely to relocate to a new position, according to a June 2015 American Staffing Association report by Workforce Monitor.

Employees who perceive that the advantages of transfer outweigh the disadvantages still need special assistance such as access to certain employer resources like counseling help, preparation assistance to build family support and communication, and an employee assistance program (EAP) specifically tailored to meet the needs of international or long-distance assignments.

STRATEGY 9: MAKE SMART USE OF TECHNOLOGY

Whether employees like it or not, smart phones, tablets, instant messaging, and texting—not to mention e-mails—are here to stay and do create a non-stop 24/7 work world. Rather than regarding it as punishment, however, employees need to figure out how to take advantage of the benefits.

In a 2012 survey of 483 employees, researchers at the Center for Creative Leadership found that 78 percent of workers used smart phones to accompany flextime, and 60 percent were connected 13.5 hours or more a day five days a week. They also spent about five hours on weekends scanning e-mails. Despite the long hours, 60 percent said they appreciated the flexibility and liked the option to leave work to attend to a child or the ability to lunch with a colleague while still being connected to work. They also appreciated that they could peruse e-mail before and after work.

A 2011 U.K.-wide survey in *Industrial Relations* also described freelancers' enthusiasm about technology because it gave them greater freedom, expanded choices, and saved filing time on paperwork. The British Psychology Society says that control of e-mail—not volume—determines the stress factors for workers, so Richard Mackinnon of the Future Work Centre in Nottingham recommends skipping early-morning and late-afternoon e-mail checks. He says first plan your day and prioritize work tasks before acknowledging your e-mails and turn off "push notices" and any e-mail app for those portions of the day when you want better control.

What really stresses workers, according to the same survey, are managers who constantly revise decisions and thus produce a lot of e-mails. Furthermore 73 percent of employees disliked outdated computer infrastructures and, according to *MIT Sloan Management Review* (Winter 2015), were disheartened by the all-too frequent downtimes required for new software training. Researchers advise employees anxious about technology to engage in "mindful technology use" (approach it objectively and non-judgmentally) and establish an e-mail-free weekday afternoon. Also, experiment with various software applications to improve comfort levels. Furthermore, employees can arrange brown-bag meetings to share "tech woe" stories. According to the *MIT Sloan Management Review* (Winter 2015), employees who shared their tech stories had 20 percent lower stress levels than those who did not participate in these sessions.

STRATEGY 10: RESPECT BOUNDARIES

Boundaries refer to the divide between work and real life, and experts say it is sometimes possible to combine them through multi-tasking but only in safe environments (for example, texting at home but not while driving). For example, First Lady Michelle Obama juggles tasks but also knows how to create boundaries such as ensuring her family dines together as often as possible. At the White House Forum on Workplace Flexibility in 2010, work–life author Stewart D. Friedman noticed that the First Lady, despite her innate reserve, interacted with the public in a relaxed manner, matching boundary-appropriate behaviors with specific venues.

Physician leadership strategist Francine Gaillour also emphasizes the necessity to maintain and protect work–life boundaries and for employees to weigh options carefully regarding responsibilities, schedules, and interactions. She especially encourages practicing good communication skills such as the transitional phrase "Do you realize?" to broach a question of possible negative boundary crossover. For instance, an employee might say, do you realize that scheduling that meeting at 4:30 p.m. means we will have to abbreviate it so I can be out of here by 5:30 p.m.? This question signals to other colleagues that some things in life are not negotiable and work commitments cannot encroach on personal life.

STRATEGY 11: MAXIMIZE RESILIENCE

Work expert Stewart D. Friedman says resilience can de-stress workers. Workers can increase their integrity (and thus their resilience) by clarifying expectations, becoming active listeners, raising uncomfortable topics, and being open to constructive feedback. Integrity also can be honed by searching for opportunities to help colleagues and creatively drawing from one's personal resources to help co-workers meet their goals.

Claiming autonomy also helps employees build resilience, so they can more easily embrace change and challenge the status quo. Autonomy energizes people, says Professor Ivona Hideg of Wilfrid Laurier University's School of Business in Canada.[7] She cites a study of 103 administrative workers given the discretion to use their lunch time or other times to schedule job tasks. Employees developed a more meaningful investment in the outcome, and that made them more motivated, industrious, and productive.

An article on the website Inpower Women gives specific information on how employees can build autonomy by querying their managers on the latter's project goals and what constitutes a successful project. After employees understand their supervisors' vision, they can ask permission to implement an idea they think might expedite or ameliorate the project. The double payoff may be that employees become more empowered and earn increased trust from the boss.

Other ways to strengthen resilience include teaching people to examine the other person's point of view as well as how to express gratitude or thankfulness. Some organizations have adapted this training in innovative ways. For example, some employees list "appreciations" at the beginning of staff meetings and nominate someone or something for which they are grateful. Some examples:

- "My appreciation is for Sarah. Last week she showed me how to complete my spreadsheets and since then I've been finishing on time."
- "My appreciation is for Frank. He knows my father passed away last month, and his support and understanding have made a real difference. Coming into work has actually been helpful for me."

STRATEGY 12: SYNCHRONIZE GOALS WITH YOUR PARTNER

When both partners in a marriage or long-term relationship value each other's work and life goals, WLB is enhanced. Partners learn to compromise to retain certain priorities, and this helps them better cope with marital hurdles and pressures. In a 2013 study, Harvard Business Professor Boris Groysberg surveyed nearly 4,000 executives from around the globe and found that ambitious types determined to achieve success chose partners with similar goals and outlooks. What do you do, however, if your spouse is not on the same page? Groysberg suggests that partners with conflicting goals should resolve their differences through better communication and move toward greater acceptance of shared views.

For instance, common goals are usually at the heart of entrepreneurial ventures, said Dawn Casale, who co-owns One Girl Cookies with her partner David Crofton. Shared goals are how and why partners can work diligently together except when occasional discord rears its ugly head, says Jeremy Robinson, an entrepreneur and editor of Indie Brand Builder (www.indiebrandbuilder.com). If that happens, sometimes couples therapy or individual therapy can put a couple's shared goals back on track. Either the couple themselves or with a therapist can help review and reprioritize their shared goals whether they may be career advancement, living in a certain geographic area, or starting a business (*Harvard Business Review*, April 2013). By using a flexible "team orientation," couples can adjust and realign their approach to help maintain WLB, says the International Federation for Family Development.[8]

STRATEGY 13: PRIORITIZE TASKS

One of the most useful coping tools is prioritizing—discriminating between activities necessary to fulfill work goals and activities vital to happiness. When *This Morning* TV anchor Gayle King interviewed Michelle Obama, the First Lady did not mince words in laying out her priorities. She said her career gives her life meaning, but motherhood is also her priority.

The inability to re-evaluate goals regularly and prioritize tasks is one of the biggest causes of burnout, says Kelsey D. Howard, a researcher at Parkland College in Champaign, IL.[9] Morgan Norman, founder of Work-Simple, acknowledges that prioritizing, though it sounds easy, is not so simple because people must guarantee that the priorities are realistic and do-able in a designated time frame. Once priorities are established, workers can more easily resist the disruption of interruptions, said Cyrus Foroughi, co-author of the paper "Do Interruptions Affect Quality of Work?" at George Mason University in Virginia. Foroughi says optimum prioritization occurs when employees clearly know their managers' goals and work level units so they can rank-order tasks efficiently.

Prioritizing is also effective in dealing with multiple roles, not just work issues, says the Canadian Policy Research Networks.[10] One strategy is for employees to rank-order work tasks and delegate family-role responsibilities to others. Another strategy is to put family first and modify work schedules. Those who use such strategies suffer less from work–life imbalance, says Italian sociologist Vilfredo Pareto, who applies the 80/20 optimality rule to prioritization (*International Journal of Administration and Governance*, July 2015). Pareto attributes 80 percent of success to 20 percent of a person's actions, so by using this formula, employees should direct 20 percent of their activities toward achieving their priorities.

Priorities of course not only vary from person to person, but according to generations. Experts say Gen Xers put a high value on compensation, career advancement, and perks such as offices (as opposed to partitioned areas) while other employees are more concerned about job security because their finances are reduced and they cannot afford to risk unemployment. On the other hand, Baby Boomers (those between 52 and 70 years old in 2016) have an autonomous work style—a leave-me-alone-and-let-me-do-the-job attitude—and are focused more keenly than other generations on benefits such as retirement plans and health care. (Caution: Generalizing about any one group is dangerous and sometimes totally inaccurate.)

Millennials prioritize paid time off, work flexibility, and the opportunity to accomplish things quickly as well as receive professional development. According to Fidelity Investments' March 2016 online job survey of 1,500 respondents ages 25 to 70, Millennials will quickly relocate to another job if discontented. For example, Chris Loos, 25, quit a job as a sales representative in Oakbrook, IL, because his new job at a tech company in Santa Monica, CA, offers more opportunities for career growth, a younger office staff, and a pleasant start-up culture—even though his salary was $7,000 less.

STRATEGY 14: TAKE CONTROL

Although absolute control of work–life situations is impossible, employees still can get the upper hand by taking advantage of flexibility options and employment assistance programs (EAPs) available to them and by not being intimidated by rumors or fear mongering that flextime and vacation time will relegate them to lesser career positions.

Also, employees who take control of their finances as well as their health probably will enjoy better WLB, says Pam Sartell, president of an information technology firm in Minneapolis, MN. Chris Novak, CEO of the National Pork Board in Clive, ID, agrees and says that a comprehensive approach to benefits motivates exceptional employee service because workers can more easily take control of what matters to them.[11] In a 2011 study in *Industrial Relations,* workers controlled the start and finish times of their workdays; set their breaks, vacation days, and days off; and distributed their workdays over the work week.[12] The result was they exhibited more productivity, organizational commitment, and job satisfaction as well as significantly less stress and exhaustion.

Another means by which employees can exert control is by ensuring their performance goals are realistic and coincide with those of managers and supervisors. Employees should participate as much as possible in SMART goal making (Specific, Measurable, Attainable, Relevant, and Time-bound objectives), and employees who are confused or unsure about any changes should talk them over with a trusted friend, colleague, or senior leader, says CEO Teressa Moore Griffin, founder of a leadership company.[13]

STRATEGY 15: GET SPIRITUAL

Spirituality can lead to clearer life purpose, better stress management skills, and an improved WLB, says Lisa Miller, director of the Spirituality Mind Body Institute at Columbia University in New York City.[14] Miller also believes spirituality protects against illness. She may be right as 10 years ago *Nightline* and *Good Morning America* co-anchor Dan Harris had an on-air panic attack that made him realize he needed a remedy for his mental stress. Harris explored religions, meditation, and mindfulness and found that Buddhism helped him cope better with depression and stress. His explorations peaked when he wrote the meditation book *10% Happier* (It Books, 2014).

Spirituality works for non-celebrities too, according to *The Journal of Business Ethics* (2010), which reviewed the literature on spirituality and work. Spirituality enhances employees' well-being and quality of life and provides them with a sense of purpose and interconnectedness. In fact, many organizations, including Intel, Coca-Cola, Boeing, and Sears, incorporate spirituality in their workplaces, strategies, or cultures. Spiritual practices include holding Bible, Quran, or Torah study groups; forming voluntary prayer groups; hosting "higher power lunches"; forming interfaith dialogue groups; organizing reflection 6 sessions (awareness of God); offering meditation exercises; and organizing servant leadership development programs (to cultivate positive working relationships).

Experts say acceptance of the whole individual, including his spiritual focus, is a genuinely practical and holistic approach to stress relief. In a 2014 study of 600 Christian employees from various U.S. and South Korean industries, researchers found that those who revealed their religion at work showed higher job satisfaction and perceived well being. Kansas State University psychologist Sooyeol Kim believes that masking your identity, pretending, or lying can be stressful and negatively impact relationships with co-workers.[15]

STRATEGY 16: USE EAPS

EAPs are the corporate perks that help employees cope with physical and mental stress as well as promote social connectedness, job satisfaction, and financial security—all the ingredients for WLB. Onsite health programs such as fairs, screenings, flu shots, and risk assessments have high participation rates of 80 to 90 percent, according to a survey by the National Business Group on Health (NBGH) and Fidelity in early 2015. Published research (in *The Journal of Occupational and Environmental Medicine*, 2015) shows 68 percent of employees participating in hypertension workplace screenings were unaware they had this serious condition.

In contrast, a recent study from the University of Pennsylvania reported that financial incentives do not necessarily motivate participation in workplace wellness programs. In a study of 197 obese participants, even a $550 incentive for completing the program did not spur weight loss. Perhaps more creative weight-loss programs to combat diabetes are needed, say *Health Affairs* (January 2016) and *Benefit News* (April 2016). One suggestion is biometric screening, which uses smart phones and wearable tech devices to transmit information such as body mass index (BMI), blood pressure, cholesterol, and glucose. Employees can choose the most convenient screening method such as home kits, retail pharmacies, labs, or doctors' offices, and employees can be directed to educational modules to complete the screening at their own pace. Another successful in-house program is the subsidization of health foods at workplace canteens and cafeterias.

Another health perk that appears to be gaining ground (and has already been mentioned) is resiliency training. According to the ComPsych 2015 StressPulse report, 56 percent of employees say they feel extremely stressed, especially on financial issues. Research shows that 30 million American workers report feeling seriously distressed about their finances, but Dr. Richard A. Chaifetz, founder of ComPsych, says other popular topics in resiliency training include change, conflict, and relaxation techniques.

Financial wellness and literacy programs also can lower employees' stress levels says Bruce Elliott, manager of human resources at the SHRM. JumpStart coalition for Personal Financial Literacy (hectorqkmc.soup.io/) suggests tailoring programs to the worker's degrees of financial wellness. For instance, financial education for an employee in high financial distress should include budgeting, credit education, and coaching on how to prepare for retirement.

One popular financial perk is tuition payments. For example, PwC, an audit and tax services company announced in 2015 that it will pay associates and senior associates (one to six years of work experience) $1,200 a year to help reduce their student loans. Starbucks did something similar in September 2015 when the company announced that employees working at least 20 hours per week and enrolled in Arizona State University's online bachelor's degree program would receive a $6,500 (about half their tuition) reimbursement for the first two years plus full tuition for the final two.

STRATEGY 17: USE COGNITIVE BEHAVIORAL THERAPY (CBT) AND OTHER POSITIVE TOOLS

CBT helps people examine their negative thoughts and minimize them. Some companies, such as Antea Group—an international engineering and environmental consulting firm—and Facebook include CBT on their list of online resources for employees. Along with CBT, workers can consult books and articles on positive psychology, which suggest honing such character traits as honesty, compassion, objectivity, and a sense of humor.

Also, common sense recommends such rejuvenating strategies as meditation, mindfulness, or deep breathing; a healthy diet; regular exercise such as yoga, gardening, or hiking; and seven to nine hours of sleep each night. These behaviors promote good work attitudes, and as Southwest Airlines founder Herb Kelleher says, bosses do not want employees with bad attitudes, no matter how skilled they are.[16]

Summary

Employees can modify their thoughts, actions, and behaviors to lower their stress levels and successfully navigate an increasingly global and technologically advanced economy. As proactive workers, they also can take advantage of support networks, spiritual avenues, and EAPs. In Chapter 4 readers will discover how employers can also help employees. Organizations can ease everyone's stress by modifying their culture, extending benefits packages, and offering flexible work options.

CHAPTER 4

Employer Techniques for Minimizing Stress and Maximizing Return on Investment

Most organizations use benefits packages and other perks as techniques to minimize employee work stress and maximize their bottom lines, but since 2010 most organizations have neither increased nor decreased their employee benefits in areas like leave, flexible work, and career development, according to the SHRM 2015 Employee Benefits report. Unfortunately these are three areas employees prioritize, so let us look more closely at their current status.

TECHNIQUE 1: OFFER FLEXIBLE SCHEDULING

Telecommuting is a technique offered by three out of five organizations, 56 percent on a case-by-case basis, 36 percent part-time, and 22 percent full-time. Employees value this flexibility, with 55 percent citing its importance in overall job satisfaction, according to the 2015 SHRM Employee Job Satisfaction and Engagement report. The 2015 SHRM Employee Benefits study shows a steady trend toward more telecommuting (all types)—53 percent in 2011 and 60 percent in 2015. Telecommuting on a full-time basis increased from 20 percent in 2011 to 22 percent in 2015. Since 1996 the percentage of organizations offering telecommuting has tripled—from 20 percent to 60 percent.

Telecommuting is not appropriate for everyone, but some professions such as librarianship minimize face time anyway. For instance, technical librarians, such as systems and digital service librarians, often complete their tasks behind the scenes. "How to Hack it as a Working Parent" (*Code 4 Lib Journal*, April 2015) describes how librarian–caregivers telecommute several times a week so they can parent young children or take care of ill parents.

Among the top companies offering telecommuting, according to *Forbes Magazine*, are Amazon, Kaplan, First Data, Convergys, Nationwide Insurance, CIGNA, ADP, and CVS Caremark.[1] One smaller online marketing company, Blue Global Media in Scottsdale, AZ, established a three-days-a-week work-from-home program.

Job sharing is a benefit offered by 10 percent of organizational survey respondents—a decrease of three percentage points since 2011. Two employees share the responsibilities, accountability, and compensation of one full-time job. For example, Julie L. and her work colleague Julie R. have successfully shared a management position at Ford for more than five years. Julie L. now has the time to volunteer at her children's school as well as exercise and participate in other activities. Her job arrangement also allows her to show her children that her career is as important as her spouse's.

Compressed work weeks, where full-time employees work longer days for part of a week or pay period in exchange for shorter days or a day off during that same week or pay period, are offered by one-third of organizations. This option, like shared jobs, has decreased over the past five years, going from 35 percent of organizations in 2011 to only 31 percent in 2015. People opting for this choice like having a full day off during a work week while earning a normal income, according to www.workoptions.com. They also like missing rush-hour commutes and saving on gasoline and automobile wear and tear.

Some **part-timers** (those who work less than 35 hours per week) do not opt for part-time work but are forced into it due to a "stale, machine-dominated economy," says Derek Thompson in *The Atlantic* (July/August 2015). Known as involuntary part-time workers, according to the Bureau of Labor Statistics (BLS), six and a half million people were in this group as of August 2015. They work part-time because their hours have been cut back or they were unable to find a full-time job due to child care problems, family or personal obligations, school or training, retirement, Social Security limits on earnings, or other reasons. Almost 20,000 in this group worked in nonagricultural industries, with some of the more popular part-time jobs, according to NBC News, being a translator, tutor, freelance writer, dog walker, yoga instructor, analyst or consultant, adjunct professor, computer programmer, and Uber driver.

Many people cobble together livelihoods from two or more part-time jobs, scheduling around life commitments. This is one reason why the number of temporary help service workers has grown by 50 percent since 2010 (according to the BLS) as exemplified by companies like Uber (for drivers), Seamless (meal deliverers), Homejoy (home cleaners), and TaskRabbit (catch-all).

Alternating locations is another flextime arrangement, according to the SHRM 2015 report. Although only 5 percent of employers offered it in 2011, that number increased in 2015 to 8 percent. Employees work part of the year in one location and the rest of the year in another. For example, "snowbird" employees who move from colder climates to warmer ones in the winter fall into this category. Canadian employees are adopting this work structure more quickly than workers in the United States—47 percent of Canadians work in alternative locations at least once a week compared with 22 percent of Americans. One reason for the discrepancy is the Canadian government offers location moves to help seniors coordinate care giving. Employees can be transferred to different locales across the country or internationally (depending on the organization) and choose their work location or work off-site (for instance, from home). For example, the city of Calgary, Alberta, promotes "hub" spaces so staff members can work at alternate locations.

In a survey by Intelligent Office, a virtual office staffing agency, 70 percent of employees chose alternate work spaces rather than one standard workplace location, reported *Business Daily* in 2012. More than half of those worked in three or more places; 29 percent used libraries, hotels, and restaurants while 28 percent preferred local coffee shops, using these alternate locales for working independently, traveling, or holding meetings.

Shift work is fairly common, according to the 2015 SHRM report, which announced that 21 percent of organizations currently offer it, but this is a 3 percent decrease from 2011. This option requires employees to coordinate with co-workers and adjust their schedules by trading, dropping, or picking up shifts. Whether shift work is acceptable or unhealthy is unclear. According to a study in Finland, shift work may lead to a poor diet and too little exercise, and other research shows workers have an increased risk for cardiovascular diseases, metabolic syndrome, and Type 2 diabetes (*Occupational and Environmental Medicine*, April 2015). Recent researchers think they also may have found a "shift" connection to breast cancer.

Our bodies repair problems when we sleep, said Dr. Christina Lawson, an epidemiologist with the National Institute for Occupational Safety and Health (NIOSH), and night-shift work confuses sleep–wake patterns, possibly harming health. Research from Texas A&M (published in *Endocrinology*, June 2016) indicates that some 15 million American shift workers are potentially susceptible to more severe ischemic strokes (greater brain damage, sensation loss, and limb movement) due to body-clock changes in the timing of waking, sleeping, and eating. Males are at higher risk than females.

Flextime options offer employees the opportunity to arrive later or leave earlier, according to their needs and commitments. This schedule choice saw an increase of just one percentage point to 54 percent in 2015. Customizing schedules within a certain range of hours and days can allow employees to attend to child or elder care, a second job, schooling, or doctor's appointments. Employees with long commutes can schedule around rush hour traffic. Examples of flextime schedules include Tuesday to Friday, 7 a.m. to 5 p.m., and Wednesday to Sunday, 9 a.m. to 5 p.m. According to *Employee Benefits*, flextime works best if the industries are not customer- or client-driven, meaning employees mainly complete their duties independently of direct contact with customers.

The crown jewel of flextime is a results-only work environment (ROWE), which is offered by 5 percent of organizations and allows employees to work wherever and whenever they want as long as projects are completed on time. ROWE implementation has shown a steady increase since 2011, when just 2 percent of organizations used it.

Breaks are another option but offer far less latitude. Thirty-seven percent of employer-respondents said they provide break arrangements that give employees more scheduling flexibility. Forty-two percent offer mealtime flex, which allows employees to take longer meal breaks or to leave work earlier if they choose to take a shorter meal break. Overall, break arrangements decreased as an employer option; they went from 45 percent in 2011 to 37 percent in 2015.

TECHNIQUE 2: PAID MATERNITY AND FAMILY CARE LEAVES

Overall leave benefits, according to the 2015 SHRM Benefits report, increased between 2014 and 2015, with a total of 27 percent of organizations extending paid family leave (up from 19 percent). Only 21 percent and 17 percent of organizations, respectively, offer paid maternity and paternity leave, but this too represents an upward trend. The same can be said for paid sick leave, parental leave above federal FMLA leave, and parental leave above state FMLA leave.

Several months after publication of the 2015 SHRM survey, Netflix raised the bar on paid maternity leave. The company offers a year of paid leave to employees following the birth or adoption of a child. Kaiser Foundation said Netflix did this to forestall wholesale resignations from

Millennials.[2] Another Silicon Valley company copied this approach in August 2015 by increasing total paid leave for mothers from 12 weeks to 20 weeks; new fathers gained eight weeks for a total of 12 paid weeks. Furthermore, 17 percent of organizations offer paid adoption leave, and 5 percent give paid surrogacy leave. Bank of America recently extended its paid leave by four weeks, and one Arizonan Glenda Frantz is pleased that she can use her leave time all at once (16 weeks) for her kindergarten-age son and a newborn.[3] As for elder care, 13 percent of organizations offer elder care leave above federal FMLA requirements and 12 percent offer elder care above state FMLA, but these figures tend to fluctuate from year to year.

TECHNIQUE 3: CAREER DEVELOPMENT

Coaching and mentorship programs have dipped since 2011, although career counseling has been offered more frequently, probably due to layoffs. Another hopeful sign is that 42 percent of organizations offer cross-training to develop skills not directly related to employees' current jobs. Cross-training can increase understanding and communication between departments. Also, the percentage of organizations offering certification fee benefits has increased compared with 2011. So did college selection referrals, which provide employees with information and help them link to colleges. Generally, however, off- and on-site professional development opportunities have lagged since 2011, which accounts for some of the Millennial stress.

Both coaching (short-term with results- and task-orientation) and mentoring (a long-term commitment with a broader focus) involve a one-on-one partnership, but workplace mentors, who can be other employees or outside professionals, provide guidance to less-experienced employees. Acting as role models, they share knowledge and advice and support the mentee's professional development. Some organizations provide this benefit via contracted corporate training firms; other organizations offer a less expensive, in-house version in which coaches or mentors may be part of the HR department. Consultant Elizabeth P. Cipolla says mentoring programs can be cost-effective, worthwhile alternatives to expensive traditional training programs.[4] For example, many organizations in the nonprofit, private, and governmental sectors use mentoring. The State Correctional Institution in Huntingdon, PA, offers mentoring to promote professionalism as well as diversity, and so does Anadarko Petroleum Corporation in Woodlands, TX. Anadarko Vice President Kurt McCaslin says he values the program because it helps to retain younger workers, especially during slower times.[5]

Another effective mentoring program is at SWBC, a San Antonio-based financial services company. Mandy Smith, vice president of training, says the program has an excellent effect on company culture and efficiency.[6] Developed by eLogic Learning, the turnkey program helps participants form goals at regular meetings where they also informally share success stories.

TECHNIQUE 4: EMPLOYEE PARTICIPATORY DECISION MAKING

Employee participatory decision making produces a positive effect on job engagement (*Consulting Psychology Journal*, March 2015). Volkswagen, for example, relies on their participatory councils to promote efficiency and high-quality work conditions. The Gallup Organization, which studied 7,939 business units in 36 companies, found participation was positively associated with increased customer satisfaction, profitability, productivity, and reduced employee turnover. By giving employees of all levels some decision-making authority (including determining which products would be designed and sold, creating work schedules, hiring, and firing), employees were motivated to excel. Not every employee became more engaged, but most saw the intrinsic value in their work and outdid expectations, according to a 2015 Rutgers report ("A New Framework of Employee Engagement"). The Center for Effective Organizations endorses employee participatory decision making, especially in team-based organizations.

Other countries also praise participatory decision making. Aluminerie Alouette, a Canadian metal producer based in Quebec, endorses the sharing of ideas and employee decision making, and Bill Harley, management professor at the University of Melbourne, Australia, and leader at the Centre for Workplace Leadership, predicts a future increase in participatory decision making. He says organizations that use sophisticated recruitment, performance, and training techniques also give employees opportunities for input.[7] Harley may be referring to HR analytics in the form of regular pulse surveys that measure and track employee engagement. By careful analysis of this information, HR departments can get better insight into the causes of turnover, develop a feedback culture, and attract great talent.

TECHNIQUE 5: EMPLOYEE ASSISTANCE PROGRAMS (EAPs)

Financial literacy programs are popping up in organizations due to their ability to maximize employee productivity and the business's bottom line. Workers worrying about the $73 billion credit card debt they racked up are stressed and not clear-headed enough to do their jobs well. The website www.wallethub.com says around a million people miss work every single day due to stress. Financial literacy programs aim to reduce anxiety and give people control of their finances. How do they do that? By shaping financial behaviors, such as establishing measurable financial goals and realistic plans to achieve them; by using a budget to control spending; by maintaining adequate insurance; by paying credit charges in full every month; and by maintaining an emergency fund equal to three months of take-home pay.

Financial plans also should help people save for retirement with an employer's tax-sheltered plan or a Roth 401(k). Similar plans have grown in popularity among organizations; more than 50 percent of large employers offer them in 2016 compared to 2011, according to The SHRM Employee Benefits survey. Still, only 10 percent of employees use them, says Kevin Wagner, senior consultant for Willis Towers Watson.[8] Wagner recommends motivating strategies such as dividing employees by needs based on age and other characteristics and communicating facts and benefits clearly and concisely with actionable goals.

Some employees ignore retirement plans because they can cause stress, says *Benefit News,* which based its conclusion on a 2015 Harvard School of Public Health survey that said 53 percent of respondents agonized over finances. Because common wisdom informs couples that they need $250,000 or more to cover retirement's medical expenses, employees can easily become overwhelmed. Experts suggest addressing money concerns through an approach linked to health care planning. For instance, the HR department could recruit a few employees to promote financial literacy services through education and integrating 401(k) contributions with health savings accounts.

Health and wellness have always been crucial parts of an employee benefits package to attract talented employees. In fact, about 175 million people nationwide get their health coverage through an employer. According to the 2015 SHRM Employee Benefits report, over the past five years an increased percentage of organizations offered mental health assistance (91 percent), contraception coverage, vision and short-term disability insurance, health savings accounts (HSAs), critical illness insurance, employer contributions to HSAs, and laser-based vision surgery coverage. In 2015, fifty percent of organizations offered HSAs—an increase from the previous year's 43 percent; 30 percent offer employer contributions to HSAs, a 10-point climb over the past five years.

In 2015, 96 percent of organizations offer a prescription drug program, although organizations have seen Affordable Care Act (ACA)-related increases in their health insurance programs (HMOs, PPOs, and exclusive provider organizations [EPOs]); 96 percent of organizations offer dental insurance; 87 percent, vision insurance; 69 percent, medical flexible spending accounts (to help employees manage co-payments, deductibles, and vision and dental expenses); and 80 percent, long-term and short-term disability. Some employers also include nontraditional healing methods such as acupuncture and experimental drug treatments, and 29 percent of organizations cover infertility treatments other than in vitro fertilization (IVF).

Preventive health programs also have expanded due to spiraling health costs, especially those targeting chronic health issues. Strategies include health and lifestyle coaching, weight-loss programs, on-site fitness centers, and nutritional counseling. Forty percent of organizations offer bonuses for the completion of certain healthy activities, but fewer organizations offer stress reduction programs such as massage therapy and nap rooms. Other emerging benefits reported by the *Wall Street Journal* include genetic testing; fitness trackers; and diagnoses, treatments, or prescriptions available by phone or video.[9]

The return on investment (ROI) varies from organization to organization, but a 2013 Rand Wellness study of 600,000 workers showed the financial savings from these health programs was not that dramatic—the average annual difference was about $157, not a statistically significant amount. One Fortune 100 company lost about 50 cents for every dollar spent. Other studies have found more positive results.

To save money participation must be high, but at least one survey (by Brodeur Partners) revealed employees' distaste for health prevention programs. Half of workers surveyed cited privacy concerns for their nonparticipation, and other reasons included misgivings about the programs' helpfulness (31 percent) and lack of confidence in the programs' management (19 percent). Moreover, resistance to health programs increases with age. About one-quarter of workers under age 35 said they do not or would not participate, and a third of 35–54-year-olds and 45 percent of those over age 54 also opted out. According to *Employee Benefits News* (December 4, 2015), one reason is the excessive number of health care plan choices and confusing information avenues. For instance, some Millennials prefer to receive health information through websites, texting, and social media, but other generational groups like to speak one-to-one or use traditional hardcopy correspondence.

Social service programs provide help and therapy for a broader, more holistic range of emotional, physical, familial, and organizational issues. Some employers refer employees to special programs for treatment of alcohol or drug abuse, eating disorders, stress or depression, and financial or legal problems. The city of Seattle, for instance, offers the mentioned programs as well as ones for critical incidents or catastrophes; family, relationship, or emotional concerns; job-related problems; co-worker conflicts; elder care; gambling or other addictive behaviors; and grief.

According to the 2015 report "Demonstrating the Impact of EAP Services on Workplace Outcomes" (EAP Association), these services significantly improve depression and anxiety symptoms. An unexpected finding was the diminished effect on hazardous alcohol use. Generally, though, findings support the communications value of mental health-related EAPs for employee productivity and healthy functioning.

Some EAP addiction programs in the United States have been adapted for international use. For example, in 2015, U.S. experts counseled Shanghai workers on smoking cessation. Counselors completed three days of face-to-face therapy and skill-building workshops, then added on web-based meetings for reinforcement. The result was a reduction in the number of Chinese smokers.[10]

TECHNIQUE 6: PERKS TO ENGAGE WORKERS

Child care benefits rank high for recruitment and retention, which explains why 22 percent of organizations allow employees to bring their children to work in a child care emergency. Nine percent of organizations offer a child care referral service, and 2 percent allow parents to bring infants to work on a regular basis. Organizations are less generous, however, with more costly benefits. For example, only 4 percent provide access to backup child care or subsidized payments, and 2 percent offer non-subsidized child care programs. Less than 1 percent provides consortium child care centers, and though rare, onsite childcare is offered—one example is Baptist Health South in Florida, where there are a high number of parent-employees. According to smartcare.com, which provides software for daycare centers, employer-paid child care (especially on-site) is virtually unheard of in the United States.

Business Week says the pros and cons of onsite versus off site care are about equal. The most cost-effective child care benefit, which most companies adopt, is to help pay by providing employees with flexible spending accounts. Further complicating the child care debate is feedback from a 2010 study by the National Association of Child Care Resource and Referral Agencies, which found that users of on-site child care programs were neither more engaged nor more satisfied with their jobs. The study recommended that more research should be done on how on-site versus off-site child care affects employee absenteeism, productivity, and turnover.

Egg freezing is a relatively new perk, and according to NBC News, tech companies Apple and Facebook provide up to $20,000 for this. Employees may also use the sum for infertility treatments and sperm donors. Apple helps with adoption costs, too. Critics, such as writers for *Contra Costa Lawyer*, favor more realistic and practical benefits like on-site daycare, increased daycare benefits, and more telecommuting. On the other hand, sociology professor Shelley Correll at Stanford University says the peak time for establishing a woman's career often coincides with her narrow biological window for fertility, and high-tech benefits like egg freezing prolong women's fertility. The SHRM 2015 Benefits report shows that egg freezing for non-medical reasons is funded by 2 percent of organizations, and paid surrogacy leave is provided by 5 percent. The most commonly offered women's health benefit, contraceptive coverage, is compensated by 83 percent of employers.

Vacations are automatic perks to fulltime employees whether it is the more flexible PTO (paid time off), the cash-out option (getting paid for non-use of vacation time), or the donation program (employees donate unused time to a general pool of workers), but less than 1 percent of organizations provide their employees with unlimited paid vacation time like Netflix did in 2004. Social Strata joined the elite pack in early 2010, while in 2015 Richard Branson of Virgin Group offered it along with Sparksight and Thumbtack. According to the 2015 Employee Benefits, SHRM notes that compared to 2011, fewer organizations offer paid vacation leave donation programs and paid vacation cash-out options.

The U.S. Travel Association and SHRM conducted a survey of HR opinions regarding vacations, which showed that the majority believed vacations led to positive outcomes such as better performance, morale, wellness, productivity, and retention, yet some employees hesitate to take vacations due to job insecurity, work culture, and other reasons. According to a 2015 Oxford Economics Assessment of paid time off, more than 42 percent of American employees store an average of eight days of unused vacation time. According to the U.S. Travel Association, employers lose $52.4 billion annually in revenue (in the form of employee resignation, rehiring, and training) when employees fail to use their paid time off.[11]

Sabbaticals are unpaid perks that 13 percent of companies grant, but according to SHRM, another 5 percent have paid sabbatical programs. Some diverse examples are Adobe, Boston Consulting Group, General Mills, Quik Trip convenience stores, and the Cheesecake Factory. Catherine Allen, co-author of the book *Reboot Your Life* (Beaufort Books, 2011), says sabbaticals rejuvenate employees, and not one person she interviewed was demoted or penalized for taking time off.

Concierge services such as banking, travel, and dry cleaning are only some of the personal services that some companies provide for their employees, says Cathy Leibow of Leverage Life and a pioneer in the field of work–life and concierge services. In an October 2007 article in the World at Work publication *workspan,* Leibow said that company feedback informed her that these programs help employees become more productive and less stressed by saving them time. She says employer-sponsored concierge programs generally return 150 percent to 200 percent in savings through improved retention, recruitment, and productivity. The 2015 SHRM Employee Benefits survey reports that 3 percent of organizations offer concierge services, but since this survey, the number may have increased due to add-ons in boutique services such as on-site haircuts, take-home meals, dry cleaning services, and travel planning.

Ken McCollum, vice president of human resources for North Bay Health-Care in California's Solano County, says his company's onsite car wash increased employee engagement, with scores rising from 74 percent to 87 percent and the company earning a listing on the Great Place to Work website.

Pets on work premises is a growing phenomenon although statistics vary on its prevalence. A survey of Americans and Canadians in the late 1990s found that 24 percent brought their pets to work (*HR Magazine,* June 1998) while the most recent SHRM survey reported only 8 percent of companies provide this benefit with 9 percent offering pet health insurance. Pro-worksite pet companies include well-known ones like Purina, Google, Ben & Jerry's, Domino's, Procter & Gamble, Amazon, Replacements, Marcus Thomas, and the Humane Society of the United States (HSUS); Trupanion in Seattle offers one paid pet bereavement day while Kimpton Hotels offers up to three days bereavement leave for both salaried and hourly employees.

Discrepancies on the exact number of dog-friendly companies depend on the source. For instance, www.dogfriendly.com lists more than 370 pet-friendly employers in the United States, Canada, and England, and a 2010 telephone survey of 90 Swedish employers found that 40 percent allowed dogs in the workplace. The *Bark Magazine* website lists a substantial number of 2015 pet-friendly workplaces, including pet insurance company Etsy in Brooklyn, advertising agency Archer>Malmo in Memphis, and American Stonecraft in Lowell, MA.

Why so much attention to pets in the workplace? According to a 2015 dissertation at Southern Illinois University, stress levels decrease when businesses offer dog-friendly policies. The researcher interviewed 188 full-time employees from 23 industries and found that 43 percent of dog owners already do or would choose to bring their dogs to work if allowed. The results also indicated that 78 percent of dog-owning respondents at pet-friendly companies bring their dogs to work once a week or more.

Another study from Central Michigan University revealed that dogs in the workplace lead to more collaboration and friendliness among team members. In fact, according to a survey from www.3MillionDogs.com, 66 percent of American workers said they would consent to a pay cut if allowed to bring their dogs to work. Ninety-five percent said they would be less stressed, happier, and more productive. When Virginia Commonwealth University professors Randolph and Sandra Barker spent a week at Replacements, a china and crystal retailer, they measured cortisol (stress) levels in employees' saliva and not only did they find dogs made people happier and less stressed, but also more productive.

"Comps" or **direct compensation** for job-related expenses are still legitimate benefits, but more organizations offer spot bonuses, non-executive sign-on bonuses, and donations for charitable causes. Fewer provide credit unions; flexible benefits plans; payroll advances; and automobile subsidies for business use of personal vehicles.

Also, travel compensation has increased for daily meals and first-class or business airfare, according to SHRM, but is down for personal telephone travel calls. The good news is 84 percent of organizations pay membership, certification, and license application fees under the umbrella of professional development.

Another fast-spreading compensation category is student debt repayment. For example, Boston-based Natixis Global Asset Management announced it will pay up to $10,000 of an employee's student loan debt provided the employee has been at the company at least five years and has taken a federal Stafford or Perkins loan. The company will also contribute $1,000 a year for the next five years.

Housing and relocation benefits for new hires or transfers are usually in the form of a one-time, lump-sum benefit. According to SHRM, this benefit is offered by 32 percent of organizations; 17 percent also provide assistance for house hunting, and because temporary relocatees often have to maintain two households, 23 percent of organizations provide help for this. As for new home purchases, few organizations offer assistance there.

Miscellaneous benefits were also cited in the 2015 SHRM report. Two-thirds of organizations offer annual company outings; almost one-third offer discount ticket services; and 23 percent offer company-purchased tickets to cultural and sporting events as well as theme parks.

Almost half of all organizations offer time off for volunteer programs; 5 percent offer ESL classes; and 14 percent sponsor sports teams. Other benefits include on-site ATM or debit cards (8 percent); personal shopping discounts (13 percent); self-defense training (9 percent); legal assistance (23 percent); and postal services (13 percent). Some of the newest benefits are foster child leave and company-paid wedding expenses as well as corporate mindfulness programs. A 2016 study by the National Business Group on Health and Fidelity Investments reveals that 22 percent of survey participants currently have mindfulness programs and 21 percent plan on introducing one in 2017. Programs are designed to help improve focus, memory, relationships, and self-control as well as issues like stress, anxiety, depression, chronic back pain, tobacco cessation, weight, and diabetes.

TECHNIQUE 7: COMPANY CULTURE CAN ATTRACT TALENT

Culture is that intangible something that keeps employees engaged and proud of their accomplishments and the overall reputation of their organization. Various components contribute to a satisfactory culture, and diverse hiring is one. Diversity encourages staff productivity and creativity, and consumers of different ethnicities want to patronize an organization employing people like them. However some businesses face difficulties in hiring a varied workforce, says Tom Borgerding, president of Campus Media Group. Fortunately new recruitment tools, such as Mytasca database, connect companies to universities and can target LGBT, disabled people, and veterans as well as ethnic groups such as Hispanics and African Americans.

Although company culture needs to be diverse, it also needs to involve the local community through volunteer efforts. For example, the Cincinnati-based software firm Paycor was chosen as a top workplace for 2015 because it demonstrates a solid social conscience with employees volunteering at Cincinnati's annual Flying Pig Marathon. Monsanto received the Work-Life Seal of Distinction for offering substantial benefits, among which was community support. Another example is Robert W. Baird & Co., a Milwaukee, WI, financial services firm that gives associates two paid days off every year to volunteer for a nonprofit. Also, the Baird Gives Back Associate Resource Group coordinates a week of group events at charities in more than 60 cities.

Employee **recognition** also helps create a stronger culture and healthier profits, according to the 2015 Employee Recognition Report by SHRM and Globoforce. The SHRM survey found that recognition is the driving force behind employee engagement, happiness, retention, safety, wellness, employer brand, and even cost control. Known as values-based recognition, these programs reward the traits and moral characteristics employers would like to see in their workers. For instance, at content marketing agency Influence & Co., managers reward creative employee achievements with "The Belt," a professional wrestling-style championship belt. At Zappos, an online retailer, managers created a $50 coworker bonus program to award influential team participants. Illinois custom graphics company Silkworm believes rewards are so important that the business regularly gives on-the-spot personalized appreciation gifts for extraordinary performance, including customized brand name jackets, coats, pens, cups, bar glasses, stemware, watches, briefcases, and Bluetooth speakers and other tech gadgets.

Self-managed teams also contribute to a healthy culture. Many large, highly successful companies like W. L. Gore, Semco, and Barry Wehmiller have used this strategy for nearly 50 years. Kraft Foods Inc. operates 62 plants in the United States, Canada, and Mexico, with many employees working within self-directed teams.

Self-managed teams allow freedom and flexibility for innovation and creativity, but only if team goals are consistent with those of the company and the team's decision makers have consistent access to accurate information. Accountability is necessary as well as clear context. In short, self-management works when employees know the goals of the organization and how they fit into those goals, said Sharlyn Lauby, an HR consultant.[12]

The principle behind self-management is simple: Psychological ownership and power stems from decision making. When people become "owners," they become more motivated and invested in outcomes. *Inc. Magazine* (November 25, 2014) calls self-management "giving people back their brains" and says companies functioning this way grow faster and end up more productive with less turnover. Researchers found that workers within self-managed teams have greater self-government, discretion, and flexibility. They also have more opportunities to hone their skills, which leads to increased job satisfaction, intrinsic rewards, and enhanced performance.

Getting people to contribute is not only important, says Maxine Attong, a corporate coach, but necessary for work culture.[13] It ultimately engenders trust if input is welcomed nonjudgmentally and the team leader refrains from knee-jerk reactions to unorthodox or poorly articulated suggestions from team members.

THE FOUR COMPONENTS OF RETURN ON INVESTMENT (ROI)

When employees are less stressed, employers get a higher return on investment (ROI) in the form of improved staff morale and attendance, reduced health costs, and enhanced company image.

Healthier Employees

Some positive studies say employers receive an average of $3.48 back in reduced health care expenses for every dollar spent on employee wellness. Studies also show that healthier employees increase morale. In a 2014 study of 380 depressed employees, those who received telephone counseling improved their productivity by 44 percent. In another of health-compromised workers published in 2016 in *Population Health Management*, results suggested poorer productivity was related to poorer emotional health and obesity-related health risks (for instance, higher BMI and less exercise).[14]

Unfortunately, most studies also show less than 40 percent of employees actively participate in employer sponsored wellness programs, but all this could change with the Millennials because more than half of those interviewed say such programs help increase their satisfaction with their employers, according to the National Business Group on Health and The Futures Company in the 2016 "Consumer Health Mindset Study." Millennials will dominate the workforce in the next few decades, and though they admit to high levels of stress, they rate "overall well-being" as a priority. Millennials even advocate imposing negative consequences on co-workers who indulge in less healthy behaviors.

Eighty-four percent of large-company CEOs view incentives as the key to healthier employees and larger profits, according to a study by Price Waterhouse Coopers. IBM has paid out about $160 million in wellness incentives—for example, encouraging employee participation in team walks or basketball games during lunch breaks. Other companies offer free smoking cessation classes, cholesterol tests, or regular use of the treadmill, and some employees can accumulate points toward company-funded shopping sprees or even trips. A strong incentive strategy—whether it offers cash, non-cash, or a combination of the two—is critical to the success of any health management program, said Michael Dermer, president and CEO of an incentive solutions provider.[15]

Good Attendance Record

Reductions in presenteeism (going to work sick) and absenteeism are two other benefits employers hope to gain from less stressed workers. These two problems cost American businesses $180 billion a year and $6 billion in Canada, says David Gallson, associate national executive director of the Mood Disorders Society of Canada.

Organizations are fighting back with on-site flu immunizations, EAPs for mental health and wellness, and job engagement methods, all of which supposedly lower stress-related illnesses. A 2015 study of employees with rheumatoid arthritis showed that programs that reduced functional limitation and pain (due to biologic products) improved workplace absenteeism and contributed to less presenteeism. A 2008 Michigan study of a utility company showed that chronic health conditions, stress, and their interaction directly affected absenteeism.

High Employee Retention

According to 40 percent of respondents to the 2015 SHRM/Globoforce Employee Recognition Survey, reducing turnover is the number-one benefit employers gain from relieving stress. As Josh Bersin of Deloitte explains, the costs of employee turnover are increasing to as much as 1.5 to 2 times an employee's salary.[16] Other, softer costs, such as lowered productivity and a decrease in employee morale, also increase turnover costs.

According to tech information website www.CIO.com, minimizing turnover means offering the right type of benefits package. Change.org, an online social change platform, recently announced its plans to offer employees up to 18 weeks of paid parental leave as a carrot to forestall turnover. Employers also reap rewards offering flexible scheduling because employees on flextime are less distracted and resentful, thus less liable to quit. According to the 2015 National Healthcare Retention & RN Staffing Report, the average cost of turnover for a bedside registered nurse ranges from $36,900 to $57,300, resulting in the average hospital losing $4.9 million to $7.6 million a year. The report concludes that enhancing culture and creating the right benefits programs, such as on-site child care, flex scheduling, and tuition assistance, are critical to retention.

Because Millennials, the largest demographic in the current workforce, are more mobile than their elders, many will leave their jobs and relocate if the benefits are not there, according to a 2015 survey by *Crain's Detroit Business*. Finances are uppermost in their mind as nearly two-thirds are still paying off college loans, and nearly three-quarters find the payments burdensome. Employers who respond to these needs improve their chances of employee retention.

Enhanced Company Brand

An enhanced company brand or culture encourages employees to criticize their managers less and interact with their colleagues more. They use their initiative and become more creative because they know their efforts are appreciated. That all adds up to higher morale, which is usually infectious, increasing productivity and attracting talented job seekers. When Robert Levering and Milton Moskowitz assembled the first 100 Best Companies list in the early 1980s, the two researchers said the secret to a great workplace was not just a prescriptive set of employee benefits, programs, and practices, but the nurturance of high-quality relationships, which today reflects the company's image or brand.

Quality relationships nurtured by caring managers support team building, collaboration, and cultural sensitivity, according to global forecasting firm Oxford Economics, and trusting, respectful relationships are the foundation for great company culture. Deloitte's 2016 annual survey of 3,300 executives in 106 countries confirms this, suggesting that through relationships built on integrity and worth, emotionally intelligent managers can project a healthy company image that differentiates the organization, adding value to the service or product it sells. Most people want to work hard for a brand they admire.

Summary

Employers seeking a fair ROI need to encourage WLB in employees through flexible scheduling, appropriate benefits, and a healthy company culture. That being said, let us look at what national and state governments have also done to encourage better WLB. In Chapter 5 readers get a short review of the history of U.S. work legislation and get to compare current American policies with legislation from the United Kingdom, Asia, and Scandinavia.

CHAPTER 5

Past and Present Government Support for WLB

Many countries have pioneered programs and legislation to manage WLB. Federal, state, and local laws have improved things in the United States; however, compared to European and Scandinavian nations, U.S. public agencies and private businesses have passed fewer bills and regulations to encourage healthier work patterns. Read on for a summary of past and present governmental interventions.

FAIR LABOR STANDARDS ACT OF 1938

The history page at the U.S. Department of Labor website recounts an anecdote that helped to change the course of labor legislation. When President Franklin Roosevelt was campaigning in Bedford, MA, in the late 1930s, a young girl tried to pass him an envelope, but a policeman refused permission. Roosevelt told an aide, "Get the note from the girl." The note read:

> I wish you could do something to help us girls. . . . We have been working in a sewing factory . . . and up to a few months ago we were getting our minimum pay of $11 a week . . . Today the 200 of us girls have been cut down to $4 and $5 and $6 a week.

As a result of this and other federal unfairness, President Roosevelt's administration vowed to prevent abusive child labor practices as well as long hours and punitive wages. In its final form, his ground-breaking legislation, known as the Fair Labor Standards Act of 1938 (FLSA), applied to industries whose combined employment represented only about one-fifth of the labor force. In these industries, the law banned oppressive child labor and set the minimum hourly wage at 25 cents and the maximum workweek at 44 hours.

Prior to the FLSA and as part of the New Deal legislation, President Roosevelt and his advisors developed the 1933 National Recovery Act (NRA), a fair-trade bill to encourage less competition and higher wages. One section, known as the President's Reemployment Agreement, was to raise wages, create jobs, and bolster businesses. In 1935, however, the Supreme Court ruled against the NRA and similar state and federal labor laws; so by 1936, wage hour legislation became a big campaign issue. The President pursued a federal wage minimum law with the Public Contracts Act of 1936 (Walsh-Healey). Most government contractors had to adopt an eight-hour day and a 40-hour week, employ only those over age 16 if they were boys or age 18 if they were girls, and pay a "prevailing minimum wage" to be determined by the Secretary of Labor (at this time it was Frances Perkins). The bill had been hotly debated and watered down before it passed Congress on June 30, 1936. Though limited to government supply contracts and weakened by amendments and court interpretations, the Walsh-Healey Public Contracts Act was hailed as a federal milestone intending to lead the way to better pay and working conditions.

Then in 1937 the Supreme Court unexpectedly heard the case of *West Coast Hotel Company v. Parrish*, the civil suit of a former Wenatchee, WA, chambermaid who sued her employer for $216.19 in back wages. Elsie Parrish said the hotel paid her less than the state minimum wage, and the Supreme Court agreed. This decision as well as Congress' willingness to pass child labor laws (initiated by a Labor Department survey of the Children's Bureau that revealed nearly 25 percent of 449 children in several states worked 60 hours or longer a week) helped expedite the passage of the FLSA. Finally, after several proposals, Roosevelt agreed to a compromise bill, and the FLSA was signed into law on June 25, 1938.

EQUAL PAY ACT OF 1963

Still, it was not until the Equal Pay Act of 1963 (EPA) that the federal government amended the Fair Labor Standards Act to abolish wage disparity based on sex. According to the SHRM, the Equal Pay Act requires that men and women be given equal pay for equal work. The jobs need not be identical but must be substantially equal in skills, responsibilities, effort, and environmental conditions.

Some businesspeople opposed the Equal Pay Act, including the U.S. Chamber of Commerce and the National Retail Merchants Association (NRMA), arguing that women cost more to employ than men due to women's higher rates of absenteeism and turnover and certain state requirements for benefits such as rest periods, longer meal times, and separate toilets. To allay the business community's fears, President John F. Kennedy added the Equal Pay Act as an amendment to the FLSA.

1964 CIVIL RIGHTS ACT AND TITLE VII

A year later came the 20th century's greatest contribution to anti-discrimination legislation: the Civil Rights Act of 1964. It outlawed bias based on race, color, religion, sex, or national origin; and ended unequal application of voter registration requirements and racial segregation in schools, the workplace, and facilities that served the general public. Title VII of the Civil Rights Act of 1964 specifically impacted the workforce because it prohibits employers from discriminating against employees on the basis of sex, race, color, national origin, and religion. It applies to employers with 15 or more employees and to federal, state, and local governments.

Title VII's coverage is much broader than the EPA of 1963, which prohibits wage discrimination based on sex. Title VII bars employment discrimination (including hiring, firing, promotion, and wages) based on race, color, and national origin as well as gender. Title VII not only protects workers from biased recruiting, hiring, and advancement, but also from harassment, retaliation, and segregation. As a result of Title VII, the Equal Employment Opportunity Commission (EEOC) was formed to implement and enforce this law.

The most often-cited racial discrimination case resulting from Title VII is *McDonnell Douglas Corporation v. Percy Green*. During a reduction in force (RIF) at the aerospace company, Percy Green, an African-American mechanic and lab technician, was laid off. He said this was racially motivated due to a "stall-in" (car blocking) protest in which he and other activists participated. Though qualified, he was not rehired for another advertised mechanic position. The EEOC sued, and the Supreme Court ruled in Green's favor.

More recently the drug company Novartis was hit with a $110 million gender discrimination lawsuit by two female plaintiffs, Elyse Dickerson and Susan Orr. Alleging the company fostered a "boys' club" attitude that was hostile to women, they maintained the company violated Title VII of the Civil Rights Act of 1964 and the U.S. Equal Pay Act. That lawsuit was settled earlier in 2016 for $8.2 million.

AGE DISCRIMINATION IN EMPLOYMENT ACT, 1967

According to the Department of Labor, the Age Discrimination in Employment Act of 1967 (ADEA) protects applicants and employees 40 years of age and older from discrimination on the basis of age. It covers hiring, promotion, discharge, and compensation and applies to employers with 20 or more employees in federal, state, and local governments. It also applies to employment agencies, labor organizations, apprenticeship programs, and job notices or newspaper ads. Workers cannot be exempted from company benefit plans because of age, and employers cannot reduce benefits based on age unless the cost of providing the benefit increases with age. Since 1986 it has prohibited mandatory retirement in most areas, with phased elimination of mandatory retirement for tenured workers, such as college professors, in 1993. Mandatory retirement based on age is permitted for executives over age 65 in high policy-making positions who are entitled to a pension over a minimum yearly amount.

A 2010 ADEA case, still in litigation, is that of Theresa Seibert, who worked 26 years for Quest Diagnostics, a large medical lab. At age 52, Seibert had her sales territory changed, making it difficult for her to earn money or reach new quotas. In 2010 she was fired for poor performance and denied severance. Seibert sued Quest, alleging that her termination was a managerial pretext to drive out older sales representatives and replace them with younger people. The court stated that company management had coerced some employees into "voluntarily" leaving the company and denied Quest's motion for summary judgment. One of Seibert's lawyers said Quest violated laws by deliberately firing Seibert and about 100 older workers on trumped-up claims of poor performance in order to avoid paying them severance. He also said that litigants must prove these cases circumstantially because other employees at the company would be afraid for their jobs if they wrote or stated the actual reasons for dismissal. As of this book's publication, the suit is pending. Meanwhile Seibert returned to school to study organizational leadership, and in the process, drained half her 401(k) account to pay her bills including college tuition. She has been without permanent work for more than three years and asserts that retirement is not part of her future plans.

PREGNANCY DISCRIMINATION ACT, 1978

According to the EEOC, the Pregnancy Discrimination Act (PDA) of 1978 is an amendment to Title VII of the Civil Rights Act of 1964. The PDA makes it illegal to discriminate on the basis of pregnancy, childbirth, or related medical conditions as this would constitute unlawful sex discrimination. Pregnant women must be treated in the same manner as other applicants or employees similar in their ability or inability to work. Pregnant employees also must be permitted to work as long as they are able. If an employee is absent as a result of a pregnancy-related condition and returns to work, her employer may not require her to remain on leave until the baby's birth. Also, an employer cannot prevent an employee from returning to work at any point following childbirth.

One high-profile case—*EEOC v. High Speed Enterprise, Inc. d/b/a/ Subway*—gained attention in June 2011. The EEOC Commission sued a Phoenix, AZ, Subway franchise under Title VII because the general manager admitted pregnancy was the reason for not hiring Ms. Belinda Murillo. The district court found for the plaintiff, maintaining that a reasonable jury would conclude she had been discriminated against. The jury also awarded punitive damages.

FAMILY AND MEDICAL LEAVE ACT (FMLA), 1993

According to the SHRM, the FMLA (the Family and Medical Leave Act) of 1993 entitles eligible employees to take up to 12 weeks of unpaid, job-protected leave in a 12-month period for specific family and medical reasons. In 2008, the FMLA was amended by the National Defense Authorization Act (NDAA), which allows eligible military employees to take up to 12 weeks of job-protected leave in a 12-month period for any "qualifying exigency." This latter provision applies to military members on active duty or those notified of an upcoming call to duty. The NDAA amendment also allows eligible employees to take up to 26 weeks of job-protected leave in a 12-month period to care for a service member with a serious injury or illness.

The FMLA has certain restrictions, however. Eligibility as defined means not just holding down a job; eligible employees are those who worked for their employer at least 12 months prior to the request and put in at least 1,250 hours (about 156 days). A crucial requirement is the organization must employ at least 50 workers who perform their duties within 75 miles of the employer's location.

The fight for the 1993 FMLA lasted a decade, however, and was initiated and preceded by a track record of state family leave legislation. Prior to its national passage, if a worker had a heart attack or needed time off to take his or her spouse to chemotherapy, nothing guaranteed that the worker could not be fired. For example, in *Saroli v. Automation and Modular Components, Inc.*, the District court ruled on the discharge of comptroller Maria Saroli who had recently returned from maternity leave. The Appeals court instructed Saroli to produce evidence that her employer created an intolerable working environment that forced her to resign. Saroli replied that when she requested maternity leave, the employer informed her that his son had been hired as manager and that she would no longer report to her original boss. The employer did not tell Saroli until the day she resumed work that she would need a doctor's note, and when Saroli returned to work, she found her computer account inactivated and her work cleared from her desk. In 2005, Saroli won her case since the FMLA says an employer may not interfere with an employee's right to apply for and take leave.

Another more recent case involved a payroll administrator and an HR representative at the Culinary Institute of America in Hyde Park, NY. When the employee's teenage son was diagnosed with Type I Diabetes, she filed FMLA forms and returned to work after 12 days. A week later her 12-year-old son fractured his leg, and the employee applied for a 10-day FMLA leave. However, the HR director stalled, asked her to send in a doctor's note, and then informed her that the paperwork was inadequate. Then the employee was terminated. During the ensuing EEOC case for FMLA violations, the court agreed with the employee's claim that the HR director (representing the employer) had ignored the employee's communications and had ultimately made the recommendation to terminate her.

LABOR-RELATED LEGISLATION FROM 2009 TO 2014

On January 29, 2009, President Obama signed the Lilly Ledbetter Fair Pay Act to help restore protection against pay discrimination. Ledbetter, an Alabama woman who worked at a Goodyear plant for 20 years, filed an EEOC suit after learning about her huge salary inequity. The jury awarded her back-pay and approximately $3.3 million in compensatory and punitive damages, but the Appeals Court reversed the decision, basically negating Title VII. The Appeals Court argued Ledbetter did not file a claim within the set time frame. President Obama thought this decision was unfair and signed the Lilly Ledbetter Act, which restored pay equity by extending the time period in which women can recover wages lost to discrimination.

On December 9, 2010, President Obama signed the Telework Enhancement Act, which requires all federal executive agencies to incorporate telework for better WLB. One provision was a written agreement between the employee and manager and a requirement for both parties to complete interactive telework training.

Also in 2010, the ACA, or Affordable Care Act (also known as Obamacare) was launched, requiring individuals to have or purchase health care coverage or pay a tax. Employer health care plans must meet certain minimum standards, and as of 2015, employers of 50 or more full-time workers (putting in more than 30 hours per week) who did not offer health insurance (or offer unapproved health insurance) paid a penalty. Experts at the Congressional Budget Office are not certain what the long-term effects of Obamacare will be, but Dean Baker of The Center for Economic and Policy Research (CEPR) reported in 2015 that the number of part-time workers has increased because people no longer need to work fulltime for health care insurance. According to *USA Today* (Dec. 29, 2015), some low-income part-timers find themselves in a predicament. Their employers are not legally responsible for their health care insurance and workers cannot afford to purchase it for themselves (especially if the state does not offer Medicaid for employees to buy subsidized insurance on the exchanges). According to a recent SHRM article, 20 percent of about 750 HR managers said they have reduced workers' hours below the 30-hour insurance mandate or plan to due to rising health care costs.

Some of these workers have joined ShiftPixy, Inc, which some restaurants and hotels in California now turn to for employees. These employers wish to avoid paying for health insurance so they reduce workers' hours. Then ShiftPixy acts as a third party and lends them out to restaurants and hotels in need of additional workers.

STATE LAWS REGARDING LEAVE

State pregnancy disability leave laws, such as in Montana and New Hampshire, require employers to offer disability when a woman is temporarily unable to work due to pregnancy and childbirth. These laws usually do not provide a specific time frame but require employers to provide a "reasonable" amount of time or mandate a maximum time limit.

Adoption leave laws, as in Maryland, require employers to offer the same leave to adoptive parents as biological parents, and Small Necessities laws, as in Massachusetts, require employers to permit time off for family needs such as school events, dental or medical appointments, or eldercare. In Vermont, private-sector employees can take leave for any reason.

Another category of leave is domestic violence. Some states have laws enabling employees to take leaves for seeking a restraining order, getting medical care or counseling, or relocating to a safe environment.

In the past decade, some cities and states including California, Iowa, Massachusetts, Oklahoma, Oregon, Rhode Island, and South Carolina have enacted laws to grant greater flexibility to state employees, according to the National Conference of State Legislatures. Some states and cities have even applied them to the private sector. So far, only five states—California, New Jersey, New York, Rhode Island, and Washington—have passed paid family leave laws. California pioneered the first one in 2004, providing up to six weeks of paid family leave at up to 55 percent of weekly earnings (the maximum is $1,104 per week). All private sector employers are also covered. During the first year of the program, 135,000 Californians used it to spend time with their children and about 25,000 of them were men. Last year, about 190,000 Californians used the program after birth, and roughly 60,000 of them were men, according to State Employment Development Department figures. Younger men are increasingly more interested in WLB, said Ruth Milkman, a sociology professor at City University New York speaking to the *Sacramento Bee*.[1]

New Jersey granted paid leave insurance in 2009, offering six weeks for family care and 26 weeks for employee disability. The weekly benefit rate is 66 percent of a worker's average weekly wage with a cap of $604. In 2014, Rhode Island enacted a state leave law for pregnancy, adoption, sick relatives, and personal disability: four weeks for family care and 30 weeks for employee disability with a maximum weekly benefit of $770. In 2007, Washington State signed a law (five weeks of family care at $250 per week), but due to lack of funding has not implemented it yet. In 2016, New York State signed an employee-funded program in which workers can take as many as 12 weeks of employee-funded paid family leave. Washington, DC, is considering a 16-week proposal.

Some employees are entitled to both the family leave rights outlined by state legislation and the federal FMLA. They can opt for the law that offers the most liberal benefits. For example, certain state leave laws apply to small businesses and are similar to the FMLA in that they require employers to provide medical, caretaking, and/or parental leave, but some laws overlap with the FMLA and offer additional benefits such as inclusions of more family members or longer periods of leave.

Paid sick leave is offered in 34 places in the United States, including five states, 28 cities, and one county, including San Diego, Chicago, Vermont, Massachusetts, Oregon, and Connecticut. The National Partnership for Women and Families supports this benefit.

STATE LAWS REGARDING MINIMUM WAGE

The Obama Administration wanted to raise the minimum wage for all public and private employees from the current $7.25 per hour to at least $10. Some experts say the public endorses this, but Congress, businesses, and some public advocacy groups disagree. Some states are blazing a trail. California dominates a group of nearly 30 states with 60 percent of the U.S. workforce receiving minimum wages higher than the federal government's $7.25 an hour.

According to the National Conference of State Legislatures, nine states and the District of Columbia currently have minimum wages above the current federal $7.25 per hour minimum. The Rhode Island Legislature increased its state minimum wage to $9.60 effective January 1, 2016, and as of July 1, 2016, the District of Columbia's $11.50 an hour makes it the first jurisdiction to go beyond the $10 state level. Maryland's minimum is $8.75. According to *USA Today* (July 5, 2016), about 13 cities and counties have raised their minimums, including Seattle, Chicago, and Louisville (KY). At the same time, New York State voted for a phased $15 an hour minimum wage. The incremental increases in Oregon will eventually bring the minimum wage to $14.75 an hour (inside the Portland city limits) by the year 2022.[2]

In March 2016, California began a graduated program to raise its minimum wage to $15 by 2022, making it the nation's largest state to raise the incomes of low-wage workers. As of July 1, 2016, wages were bumped up in Los Angeles, San Francisco, El Cerrito, Emeryville, Los Angeles County, Malibu, Pasadena, Santa Monica, and Sunnyvale; the new amounts ranged from a low of $10.50 to $14.82, according to the Employment Policies Institute and National Employment Law Project.

San Francisco's progressive trend even extends beyond $13 hourly minimums. Employees can request flexibility to care for a child, a parent age 65 or older, or any chronically-ill family member, and private employers must consider employees' requests for flextime without reprisal. In 2014, San Francisco's Retail Workers Bill of Rights legislated predictable schedules for hourly workers with monetary consequences if employers renege.

Proposed Federal Legislation

In June 2013, the Flexibility for Working Families Act was introduced in Congress. It proposed to authorize employees to request a temporary or permanent change in the number of hours required to work; the times when the employee is required to work or be on call; where the employee is required to work; and the amount of advance notification the employee must receive for work assignments. On December 2015, the bill was referred to the House Subcommittee on the Constitution and Civil Justice, and no further action has taken place as of publication.

Other proposed legislation, such as the 2014 Schedules That Work Act, also might help working parents achieve flexibility and stability at work. According to CLASP (Center for Law and Social Policy), an agency benefiting low-income people, the act would give low-wage workers, who historically work shifts, the ability to request changes to their work schedules without fear of reprisal. Workers in retail, food preparation and service, and building cleanup would have more stability. In July 2015, the bill was read twice and referred to the congressional Committee on Health, Education, Labor, and Pensions, where it is still under review as of publication.

EXECUTIVE ORDERS ISSUED

On February 12, 2014, President Obama issued Executive Order 13658, "Establishing a Minimum Wage for Contractors," which raised the minimum wage to $10.10 for all workers on federal construction and service contracts. Later, in June 2014, Obama issued a Presidential Memorandum directing federal agencies to expand access to flexible work schedules and give employees the "right to request" flextime.

In April 2015, President Obama also enacted an Executive Order on LGBT (lesbian-gay-bisexual-transgender) Workplace Discrimination. It prohibits federal contractors and subcontractors from discrimination for gender or sexual orientation. Another 2015 executive order requires all federal contractors to offer their employees at least one hour of paid sick leave for every 30 hours worked. This gives about 300,000 workers access to paid sick leave for loved ones. The leave also applies to absences related to domestic violence, sexual assault, and stalking.

While many citizens, interest groups, and politicians object to these orders, Ellen Bravo at Family Values at Work wrote that government should model preferred standards for the country.[3] According to *USA Today*, the most controversial executive order Obama has so far issued is the 2014 Fair Pay and Safe Workplaces Order, which requires contractors to disclose any labor violations of city, state, or federal labor laws—or executive orders—against themselves or subcontractors.

In 2015, President Obama introduced an update to the FLSA to extend overtime protection to nearly five million full-time, white-collar workers. As proposed, it would set the new salary threshold in 2016 at the 40th percentile, approximately $46,000 a year (double its current level) and would apply to workers earning as little as $23,660 a year, a sum that would affect convenience store managers and other workers.

WLB LAWS IN COUNTRIES AROUND THE WORLD

United Kingdom

In 2014, the U.K.'s Children and Families Bill guaranteed rights for leave and pay for parents, adopters, and expectant fathers, who get time off work for ante-natal care (two appointments). All employees can request flexible working options, not just parents and other care givers. Employees can thus return to school for training, volunteer in a local community project, or merely avoid rush hour. Employers can turn down requests, but these must be appraised in a "reasonable manner." In April 2015, U.K. parents received 18 weeks of unpaid parental leave for each child under age 18 and shared parental leave up to 50 weeks (with 37 weeks paid at 90 percent of the employee's weekly salary).

Japan

Japan's 2008 Work–Life Balance Charter heavily revised features to limit overtime and prohibit employers from discriminating against leave taking (up to 18 months at 50 percent of salary). Employers cannot refuse a worker's request for childcare leave, which is guaranteed until the child is one year old. The 2009 Labor Standards Law revises Japan's overtime culture; government employees receive overtime payments of 50 percent when overtime exceeds 60 hours per month. Companies accept a weekly "No Overtime Day," and other related WLB laws legislate shorter working hours, gender equity, and part-time work.

According to the Japanese Ministry of Health, Labour and Welfare, 90 percent of eligible parents taking childcare leave were women in 2008, and only 1 percent were men (likely due to fear of stigmatized treatment, according to the Equal Employment Offices). Japan desires greater use of its paternity leave and is planning to raise salary compensation from 50 percent to 67 percent as a carrot to men, according to the *Japan Labor Review* (Winter 2014). Childcare also needs greater government sponsorship to lower costs and to benefit working women. As of April 2013, more than 22,000 children were still on childcare waiting lists.

Korea

The Saeromaji Plan 2010 promotes family size growth and improves the quality of life for the elderly. It requires on-site childcare facilities and monetary incentives toward child birth and childcare. Saeromaji Plan II (2011–2015) targets policies and programs aimed at raising the total fertility rate to 1.6 per couple by 2020 and promoting a higher socio-economic quality of life. The plan also supports economic incentives for childbearing, improving reproductive health services, fostering family friendly social conditions, and promoting gender equity. Dynamic Women Korea 2010–2015, a government plan, expands job opportunities and consists of 46 measures to build career paths for female youths and support for WLB, according to "Institutional Support for Women's Economic Activities" (United Nations Economic and Social Council).

Also, the 2015 Labor Standard Act extended paid maternity leave from 60 to 90 days and shortened the work week from 44 to 40 hours. The Equal Employment Opportunity and Support for Work-Family Reconciliation Act increased paternity leave to five days, three of them paid. Provisions also include parental leave for children under age eight and family care leave (up to 90 days and not just for children). Other proposals include increasing the number of public childcare facilities and after-school programs; providing career development support; and counseling women returnees to the workforce as well as certifying family-friendly organizations.

Sweden

In Sweden, workplace rights and regulations are determined by government labor law (such as the Annual Leave Act, the Work Environment Act, and the Working Hours Act) and collective bargaining between employees, employers, and unions. (About 90 percent of workers are protected by collective agreements.) Among the country's social benefits, parental leave provides a total of 480 paid days per child; leave is allowed from 60 days before the child's delivery date up until the child's eighth birthday; and sick days are reimbursed at 80 percent of the employee's daily salary. Also, flexible hours, while not in every organization, are as widespread as telecommuting. Long hours are extremely rare with only 1 percent of employees working overtime. Overtime is set by statute: Total working time cannot exceed 48 hours over seven days with a maximum of 48 hours every four weeks.

REASONS FOR SLOW ENACTMENT OF U.S. WLB LAWS

The slow progression of U.S. WLB legislation is at least partially due to the "ideal worker" model (the super worker), say experts. Also, Congress has roadblocked most legislative attempts to pass more progressive national bills providing affordable childcare, equitable wages, and paid leaves.

A shrinking workforce is another reason, according to CNN Money and a recent OECD report that studied 38 developed countries. The labor participation rate of the United States (which measures employees and those actively looking for work) has fallen 4.5 percentage points to a rate of 72.7 percent for those ages 15 to 64. The United States' retirement-age Baby Boomer workforce is starting to leave the workforce, and another factor is that some women are leaving the workforce to care for children and elderly relatives. Furthermore, the White House's Council of Economic Advisers says the problem may relate to the decreased demand for low-skilled workers earning low wages. Also, a large number of workers are on disability with chronic health conditions.

Furthermore, job insecurity (23 percent of Americans told Gallup they worried their working hours would dwindle, and 24 percent worried over wage reductions) is transforming traditional 9-to-5 employment into an "uber" society of freelancing, contracting, and part-time positions. Then, too, the outsourcing of some entry-level jobs may also be decreasing employment rates for less experienced candidates. Furthermore, the more than half of Baby Boomers who have delayed retirement are making it more competitive for new workers.

Currently in 2016, the economy is experiencing the lowest unemployment rate since 2007, with nearly 60 percent of callers to a job search hotline already employed. According to the June 2016 monthly Job Openings and Labor Turnover Survey (JOLTS), firms may be having difficulty finding qualified employees in a tightening job market.

EFFECTS OF LEGISLATIVE LAG ON FAMILIES

One result is Millennials often give up trying to land the perfect job, taking positions that are an inadequate match and that offer lower-than-average wages. Research suggests that even after recovery from a recession (such as in 2008), college graduates who enter the workforce during a weak economy experience a relative wage loss for at least 15 more years. Some Millennials are also trying to pay off college loans while building a family, career, and retirement fund.

Low-income workers are paying a harsher price. Paying for child care or elder care eats up about one-third of the average family's budget, according to the www.Halfinten.org annual report. Low-wage workers (many of them single women and minorities) must manage unpredictable work schedules that often interfere with child care arrangements, transportation, and the balancing of several part-time jobs. The stress often affects health, which in turn can lead to missed shifts, loss of wages, and increased medical costs.

Even for middle-class families, the financial pressures can be tough. Gender bias can relegate women to lower-salaried positions, and job insecurities can push them to put in longer hours and forego flextime. When a crisis arises, for example, in the form of a dyslexic child or a hospitalized parent, one spouse may have to take unpaid leave to tend to the sick relative while the other partner must pay the mortgage and other monthly bills and come up with emergency cash. Dual salaries are necessary, and according to the U.S. Census Bureau, nearly 1.4 million married couples with children relied exclusively on women's earnings at some time in 2013, and more than 14.8 million married couples with children relied on both parents' earnings.

WOMEN IN THE LABOR FORCE AND THE NEED FOR PAID LEAVE

The gross domestic product (GDP) would have been roughly 11 percent lower in 2012 if women had not increased their working hours, say WLB experts at the Washington Center for Equitable Growth. In today's terms, this translates to more than $1.7 trillion less in output. Stanford University experts agree; their results conclude that 16–20 percent of U.S. economic growth between 1960 and 2008 was due to women and people of color entering professional occupations.

This is profoundly important, say economists at the Center for Economic and Policy Research and CUNY's Murphy Labor Institute, who have researched paid family leaves and found zero evidence that family leaves negatively affect business operations; in fact, they increase labor-force participation and employee retention. A 2011 evaluation of California's family leave insurance program ("Employer and Worker Experiences with Paid Family Leave in California") found that nine out of 10 employers reported the program had either no effect or positive effects on business.

Naturally these economic effects have spurred political debate. A survey commissioned in 2012 by a pro-paid leave group found that respondents supported the idea by 63 percent to 29 percent; Democrats were strongly in favor (85-10), Independents favored it (54-34), and Republicans were evenly split at (47-48).

Kristin Rowe-Finkbeiner, CEO of www.momsrising.org, an advocacy group for family economic security, believes a federal paid family leave insurance policy is needed to pump up the national economy and support families. Detractors and proponents alike agree that the issue of paid leave will be a major 2016 campaign issue—a conclusion articulated by President Obama's Council of Economic Advisers (CEA). The report re-stated what most Americans already know and the previously mentioned data show: that the United States is the only developed country in the world not guaranteeing paid maternity leave of at least 14 weeks with costs covered by employers or special taxes. In a column in *The Washington Post*, Robert J. Samuelson concisely stated the two sides of the debate: Will more governmental mandates and money promote better WLB for families, or will they simply impose costly regulations on firms and discourage hiring? Only time and further legislative movement will determine the outcome.

SUMMARY

The United States is making headway in legislating WLB through federal, state, and local laws, but future progress is not guaranteed given the current divisive political climate and volatile economy. If, however, the United States wants to regain its premier standing among industrialized nations, experts agree that Congress will need to address vital WLB issues such as minimum wages, paid leaves, and childcare so employers can hire and retain a talented, engaged, productive, and physically healthy workforce.

In the next chapter, we deal with important issues surrounding the implementation of WLB, starting off with the problem of gender inequities.

SECTION II

Controversies and Issues

CHAPTER 6

Do Men and Women Compete on a Level Playing Field?

The issue of gender inequality has been hotly debated ever since significant numbers of women entered the workforce in the 1970s. Do women always get the short end of the employment stick, or do men also face disadvantages in their attempts to become providers and parents? Although much has been written and voiced about women suffering greater inequities in wages, scheduling, and advancement, this chapter presents both sides of the story and lets readers draw their own conclusions.

WOMEN: FLEXIBILITY STIGMA

The so-called flexibility stigma for venturing from the traditional 9-to-5 schedule has been associated with both women and men in the workforce, but women, especially those with children, more often opt for flextime than men. Coined in 2013 by law professor Joan Williams, director of the Center for Work Life at the University of California Hastings College of Law, the term "flexibility stigma" signals the bias workers face when taking advantage of flextime programs. Although 79 percent of U.S. firms allow at least some employees to change starting or quitting times, only 11 percent of full-time workers actually use this benefit.

The reason is fear of negative career blowback such as wage penalties, lower performance evaluations, and fewer promotions. Flexibility stigma has its origins in the "work devotion schema" or the "ideal worker" beliefs that work should be the central focus of life and that a strong work ethic establishes self-worth. In short, non-allegiance to an obsessive workaholic attitude denotes a lack of morality. Intimidated by this extreme characterization of employment, male workers usually default to this ideal worker status and make sure they are available anytime and anywhere.

Women, however, more often opt for flextime, but the flexibility stigma they must bear often disrupts their careers. Why is this so? Simply put, the work devotion or ideal worker schema clashes with the cultural expectations of being a good mother. While many flextime women workers are considered good mothers, they sometimes face the guilt of being less-than-ideal workers. In one study of women professionals, the switch to part-time work triggered the deterioration of work assignments. Flextime alone can doom a woman's career, writes expert Joan Williams. It can deprive women of professional training, mentorship, sponsors, and networking.

High penalties often come with career breaks, Williams says. These penalties are extremely disproportionate to the waste of human talent especially in the professions of law and science. In one example, a female Harvard law graduate was told that no headhunter would want her as a client because she had taken off one year to raise a child. In 2014, an Atlanta immigration attorney pleaded with a judge to postpone a court hearing scheduled during her maternity leave. Only when she appeared before the judge with her four-week-old child in her arms did the judge relent, all the while scolding her for having the audacity to bring the child to court even though she lacked an alternate child care arrangement. Joan Williams concedes that while the extent of flexibility stigma differs by professions (medicine is more receptive to flexibility and part-time employment), one in five mothers in a professional or managerial position will generally abandon the labor force due to flexibility stigma; others will work part-time. For example, according to the American Psychological Association (APA), 40 percent of women with engineering degrees exit the profession or never enter the field. Poor "workplace climates" (think flexibility stigma) and "managerial mistreatment" are the biggest reasons. In 2014, only 9 percent of electronic and environmental engineers and 11 percent of all practicing engineers were women. Compare that to the nearly 20 percent of females who graduate from engineering schools. A third of engineer dropouts stay home with children because the cultural perception of flextime withheld opportunities for advancement and handed out boring assignments. The employed women engineers stay in their jobs because they have supportive bosses and advanced training. Current women engineers are "flight risks," says Nadya A. Fouad, PhD, a University of Wisconsin-Milwaukee researcher.[1] Fouad explains that this is because corporate cultures stress taking work home or working on weekends with no support for managing multiple life roles.

Even in education, where administrators supposedly regard children, parents, and teachers with even-handed respect, three-fourths of the teaching staff (usually women) face flexibility stigma. Breast pumping stigma complicates that, and many teachers end up quitting to raise their children.

WOMEN: SALARY INEQUITY

It seems to be a given—at least in the minds of women—that females will not receive the same pay as men. The data supports this: A 2015 national survey from CareerBuilder reported that only 35 percent of female respondents believed there was equal pay in the workforce. Glassdoor reported in March 2016 that out of 25 industries, gender salary gaps range from 14 percent to 28 percent (in health care and computer science). Women generally get five cents less on the dollar than men in the same position. According to the American Association of University Women (AAUW), full-time female workers in the United States were paid 79 percent of what men received. A recent Australian STEM survey reported that full-time women workers earned 24 percent less than men.

Employers may not be completely responsible for this apparent inequity; it may be that women undervalue their own educational achievements, and this impedes salary negotiations. According to the *Arizona Republic* (May 2016), Small Business Association CEO Rick Murray said the salary gap still exists because of women's general reluctance to ask for a raise. He may be right, as a 2013 survey by LinkedIn showed that only 26 percent of surveyed women asked for a raise but of those who did ask for a raise, 75 percent received one.[2] According to a social psychologist at the University of Oulu in Finland, social anxiety disorder (SAD) in some women has helped widen the wage gap because women get anxious and worried in situations where they might be criticized such as negotiation and performance evaluations (*Women's eNews*, April 2016). Evidence from the National Institute of Health (NIH) also indicates that social anxiety correlates with lower incomes and employment rates.

On the other hand, a Stanford University sociology professor documented that salary inequity may also be due to the "motherhood penalty." This may force women with children to go head to head with childless women because employers appear to hire fewer mothers than childless women and pay mothers lower salaries. In a study of 600 published newspaper ads that were responded to with two different résumés (altered with subtle references to parenting or non-parenting), childless female candidates were twice as likely to get interviews as mothers. And the pay gap between mothers and childless women was even higher than the pay gap between women and men.

A Columbia University study also found that women with lower incomes than men (with similar levels of education and experience) were about 2.5 times more likely to have major depression than men. This suggests that women may be more likely to place blame for their lower incomes on themselves and not on gender discrimination.

Pay inequity among women can also be complicated by ethnic bias. Compared with white male workers, Asian-American women's salaries show the smallest gender pay gap, equaling 90 percent of white men's earnings. The gap was largest at 54 percent for Hispanic women.

Other factors like age and gender of the manager also affect women's salaries. Women typically are paid about 90 percent of men's earnings until age 31; then the wage percentage lessens until by retirement age (50+), women are paid 75 to 80 percent of what men earn. Contrary to common belief in women's empowerment, wage inequity for women does not decrease given female managers, according to a study at University of California, Berkeley (*American Journal of Sociology,* May 2015). Between 2005 and 2009, the authors analyzed 1,701 full time U.S. employees working for an information services firm and found that women employees with female managers do not necessarily earn higher salaries. A high-performing woman manager might, for example, worry about her own possible devaluation if she is perceived as associating with a low-performing female subordinate, says assistant professor Sameer B. Srivastava.

In July 2016, the New Jersey-based drug company Merck came under fire for unequal pay in a $250 million class action suit filed by more than 400 current and former female employees. The original plaintiff, Kelli Smith, was a sales representative who had worked for the company since 2004. Smith said she was demoted, received lower performance evaluations than her male counterparts, and was subject to a hostile work environment following her return to work from maternity leave in 2010. According to the litigants, Merck "systematically discriminates against female sales representatives and pregnant women in particular in promotion and other terms and conditions of employment" (BioSpace.com, July 22, 2016). These allegations are in addition to the complaint of unequal pay.

WOMEN: OCCUPATIONAL INEQUITY

As stated earlier, gender discrimination varies within professions or work areas, but nearly 40 percent of women are employed in occupations that historically offer lower wages, such as social work, nursing, and teaching. Fewer than 5 percent of men work in those fields.

Do these professions pay less because the occupations are valued less by society, or are wages lower due to gender discrimination? Perhaps history can answer this. In the early 2000s, when women began entering STEM (science, technology, engineering, and math) fields at a lower rate, men's WLB declined. Why did this occur? According to an online paper in September 2015, traditionally male occupations need to be gender balanced in numbers if both genders stand to gain better benefits. Yet a 2014 report indicated that if STEM women really want a pay advantage, they ought to work for the federal government where women are paid 87 percent of men's salaries compared with 78 percent in the workforce as a whole.

Medicine does not escape gender inequity. *JAMA* (May 2016) recently reported that 30 percent of female doctors face sexual harassment on the job, and close to 75 percent perceive gender bias. Compare that to only 22 percent of male doctors who perceive gender bias and 10 percent who experience it.

At least one state, however, is doing something about inequities. A landmark state law passed in October 2015—the California Fair Pay Act—ensures women equal pay for doing "substantially similar work" (not just "equal work") as their male counterparts. This extends to jobs at different employer worksites or positions with different titles but with approximately the same duties. For instance, female housekeepers cleaning hotel rooms would be paid the same as male janitors cleaning lobbies.

WOMEN: DISCRIMINATION IN PROMOTIONS

Although some women start out with ambitious career goals, they often wind up scaling back or seeking more flexible jobs to maintain a tolerable WLB. Compared to Baby Boomers and Gen Xers, Millennials are lowering their expectations for having it all. For instance, a survey of Harvard Business School alumni found that 37 percent of all Millennial women and 42 percent of those married plan on interrupting their careers for family. A Pew Research Center study found that 58 percent of working Millennial mothers said being an employed mother stood in the way of further advancement.

According to research at Pepperdine University, women worldwide face similar advancement challenges. Half of women age 30 and younger in the Harvard Business Survey said they thought being female was a work disadvantage so their decision was to choose a job with more flexibility;

26 percent slowed the pace of their career; and 9 percent declined promotions. These compromises may ease WLB for Millennials and other workers in the short run, but in the long term, the decision detracts from legitimate career goals and deprives the economy of talented workers.

In a 2014 report by Catalyst ("First Step: Women in the World "regarding the G7 countries (Canada, France, Germany, Italy, Japan, United Kingdom, and United States), women make up only 21 percent of senior positions."[3] Women run into hiring problems despite different leadership preferences in China, Saudi Arabia, and the United States because socially acceptable behaviors tend to be gender discriminatory. For example, aggressive, outspoken, and ambitious behaviors among men are admired, but women are sometimes criticized for the same attitudes.

Another barrier to promotional advancement is negative perceptions such as a loss of faith when younger women see fewer women in senior "glass ceiling" roles. For instance, U.S. women are underrepresented in top leadership positions in Fortune 500 companies (there are only 23 women CEOs). Although consulting firm Mercer says U.S. and Canadian organizations promoted and hired an increasing number of women to the executive ranks ("When Women Thrive 2016"), these organizations are mainly intent on quick solutions to gender diversity and actually hire women at lower rates for many mid-level jobs.[4] According to Anne-Marie Slaughter, formerly with the U.S. State Department and the author of a much quoted 2012 *Atlantic Monthly* article on gender advancement called "Why Women Still Can't Have It All," until corporate cultures value elder and child care duties and make structural changes in the workplace, women will be on the losing end regarding advancement.[5] In agreement is the 2003 publication *Bit by Bit: Catalyst's Guide to Advancing Women in High Tech Companies*, which points out that women also face barriers due to an "exclusionary" corporate culture in which women lack mentors and role models, feel isolated, and do not receive social support.

Business Management Daily says managers have to accept some of the blame for promotional bias.[6] When Bain & Company followed the career goals of 1,000 men and women, researchers learned that 43 percent of college-age women wanted to achieve executive-level positions, but a few years later, that number dropped to 16 percent. Bain partner Julie Coffman thinks the discrepancy corresponds with managers' failures to understand women's goals (less than 35 percent of American workers have female managers, according to Gallup in 2015).[7] Some managers (male and female) would rather spend one-on-one time conversing about humdrum tasks instead of helping women develop the skills and confidence for executive positions such as introducing them to role models, honing leadership skills, and hosting networking events.

In contrast, a 2015 report titled "Women in Leadership in the Real Estate and Land Use Industry" suggests that some women in certain fields do achieve leadership goals.[8] American women dominate in special fields such as construction, agriculture, forestry, and fishing. In fact, women actually outdistance men in transportation and warehousing. Furthermore, Australian mining, oil, gas, and engineering companies use female talent more extensively (despite their American values) because they extend flextime privileges to women.

Male entrepreneurs, however, still far out-earn women, according to *Inc. Magazine* (January 2016). Men are about 3.5 times more likely to reach $1 million in revenues than women. Over the past five years, although women entrepreneurs have generally seen a $9,835 decrease in average revenues, men gained $27,768. One reason might be that Small Business Association (SBA) loans are more likely to be parceled out to male-owned businesses.

WOMEN: SUBTLE STEREOTYPING

Second-generation gender bias is subtle but damages women, who may sometimes feel less connected to male colleagues. For example, women may be "advised" to take a staff (rather than a leadership) role to accommodate family. Or sometimes women find themselves excluded from key positions and are confused as to what they failed to do or not do.

The irony is, according to *Harvard Business Review* (September 2013), women often do not recognize that second-generation gender bias actually exists and is another form of stereotyping. Take, for instance, international assignments. In the 1950s and early 1960s, prestigious international posts automatically went to (male) employees who relocated with their wives (who of course had no careers to leave behind). Today, the reverse situation has not materialized: Men normally do not relocate for ambitious wives.

Another example of subtle gender bias is performance reviews. When a woman's name comes up in conversations, the decision makers sometimes "compliment" women as "nice," but attach a nuanced pejorative to her role. The same negative is usually never attributed to men. Women also are often excluded from power circles. In some instances, men take credit for women's ideas and are seldom challenged. Women sometimes inadvertently become "office moms," assuming support roles for men by allowing themselves to be relegated to note taking or staying late to meet deadlines.

WOMEN: PARENT, EMPLOYEE, PARTNER

In the past, Boomer women deceived themselves into thinking they could have it all: happy family, healthy marriage, fulfilling career. Some of the more high-profile types—for instance, Jill Abramson, former editor of the *New York Times*, and Anne-Marie Slaughter, former U.S. State Department employee—are revising their life philosophies and ranking care over work. Slaughter describes her conflicted choice to return home to her husband and sons in her *Atlantic Monthly* article.[9] She rants about a workaholic culture that ignores talented women. Abramson, who now teaches at Harvard, is also reappraising things. She says in a *Washington Post* article that there is something fundamentally wrong with a society that values managing money (and supporting the workaholic credo) more than parenting children well.[10]

According to Connie J. G. Gersick, PhD., in "Having It All, Having Too Much, Having Too Little," no one WLB strategy works best because success depends on the match between a woman's needs and her resources.[11] Gersick questioned 40 Boomers now in their 40s and 50s who answered "yes" to the question, "Can you have it all?" These Boomers claimed victory because they prioritized, limited, or excluded activities or events, experiencing events sequentially or delegating. Success came not immediately but as a journey through adulthood.

Today, feedback from CareerBuilder indicates that 78 percent of working mothers and 83 percent of working fathers say they too can have it all. Judging by that comparison, having it all may again translate to gender inequity. Although Millennial women say they want it all, they are not sure it is achievable because despite spending more quality time with their children, working mothers are nearly twice as likely as working fathers to say their job has negatively affected their relationships with their children (25 percent of working mothers versus 13 percent of working fathers). Millennial women are also likelier than Millennial men to say parenting has caused their professional work to suffer (17 percent of working mothers versus 9 percent of working fathers).

So, are Millennials really so different from their elders? Yes, says Katherine Y. Lin in her dissertation "Life's a Balancing Act" (University of Michigan, 2015). Younger workers no longer choose to be obsessed with work. Recent research verifies that young workers express a higher preference for leisure time. Moreover, Millennials worship the "super dad"—defined as the man who prioritizes family and respects female breadwinners. A Harvard Business School alumni survey found that 37 percent of Millennial unmarried women and 42 percent of those married planned to interrupt their career for family. Only 17 percent of Baby Boomers admitted to doing this.

So far Millennials are transitioning to the *Lean In* (2013) philosophy of CEO Sheryl Sandberg, who upon her husband's death in 2015 revised her picture of the perfect mom and perfect leader. Millennials might opt to lean in and work hard to get to a career status where they hope parenting will not hurt them. Once they reach that stage, however, they may not "lean" into future promotions or more responsibility but instead may seek careers with more flexible hours and better WLB.

Men: Flexibility Stigma

Men also face flexibility stigma if they request family leave or flextime. Fifty years ago, successful men and good fathers devoted themselves nonstop to work, but in some organizations today, the newer nurturing father wages war with the breadwinner and ideal worker models. The result is increasing flexibility stigma for men. In an online 2015 My Family Care survey of fathers, 50 percent of respondents said they worry that flexible working will affect their career progression.[12] These men are afraid to ask for flexibility due to the perceived stigma and impact on their careers, says Ben Black, director of My Family Care (*Employee Benefits Online*, 2015).

High-powered types—especially those in government—such as Speaker of the House Paul Ryan and Vice President Joe Biden—may receive less punishment for decisions to spend more time with family because, for one thing, they refrain from discussing it. They steal time from the office, walking out unnoticed, conference calling from cars, or responding to e-mails at home.

Some men in high corporate positions perform the same low-keyed behaviors, but when Daniel Murphy of the New York Mets openly took paternity leave in 2014, his public act came under fire. Ellen Galinsky, president of the Families and Work Institute, says few employers help working fathers arrange reduced schedules, and a 2014 paper from the University of Toronto's management school found that colleagues regard active fathers as distracted and less dedicated to their work. Law professor Joan Williams calls these men "caring in secret."

As with women, engaging in child care is seen as more legitimate as a reason to request flextime than other non-child-care-related reasons, says Christin Munsch, a sociology professor.[13] For instance, training for an endurance event as a reason for flextime might not hold weight for men or women. Also, as with women, at least one study in 1999 in the *Journal of Applied Social Psychology* found that men who took paternity leave got fewer organizational rewards such as promotions. Of course, that was nearly two decades ago, and some organizational attitudes have matured since then, but bias still exists.

For instance, a 2015 dissertation on flexibility stigma at the University of Minnesota found that fathers are heavily penalized for using flexibility benefits but in a different way than women. While women's gender-conforming prioritization of children over work is socially approved (unlike men's), and women can be upfront about their need for family commitments, men attempting to dodge the flexibility stigma sometimes lie or act sneaky about their domestic reasons for using flextime. These tactical differences also extend to male supervisors, who tend to permit or disallow flextime in gender-biased ways.

Of course, men sometimes cannot avoid advertising their allegiances. Take, for example, the San Francisco lawyer and father who worked at a large firm and was offered four weeks of paid leave. While he made himself available to clients by e-mail, a partner criticized his colleague's commitment and ability to service his clients and the father's bonus shrank. He eventually left the firm. In another example of gender bias, a male employee left his pharmaceutical job in 2012 to join another company that offered paid paternity leave and flexible scheduling.[14]

MEN: SALARY DISCRIMINATION

Women and men face salary disparities even in female dominated fields, according to two Adelphi University researchers who did a retrospective on salaries from the 1960s. The U.K. shows the same similarity. Male managers earn 22 percent more than female counterparts, which equates to women doing nearly two hours of unpaid work a day, according to a 2015 survey of more than 72,000 U.K. managers. Universum reports that men in business expect $3,263 more in wages than females in the same field; male engineers expect $3,179 more than women engineers.[15] Dana White, leadership expert and author of *Leader Designed* (Lulu, 2016), says women need to stop handicapping themselves with lower salary expectations.

A University of California, San Francisco, researcher studied nursing and found that male nurses (10 percent of the total in 2013) get $5,000 more per year on average than female nurses—a pay gap that has remained stable for the past 20 years. The reason? The researcher hypothesized that women nurses may leave the workforce to have children and then return at a lower pay scale than male colleagues. Another possibility is male nurses may be better at negotiating pay raises as has been suggested by other research. Of course gender discrimination also could be the underlying problem.

Salary inequity also pervades collegiate and professional sports. Although the World Major Marathon series, World Surf League, and Wimbledon tennis tournaments award equal-gender purses, not every event results in such even-handed treatment. For example, in 2016, the U.S. Women's Soccer team filed a complaint with the Equal Employment Opportunity Commission (EEOC) against the U.S. Soccer Federation for wage discrimination. The women's soccer team cited such actions as the men being paid four times more than the women's team despite the women's team attracting nearly $20 million more in revenue, according to the *Feminist Newswire* (March 31, 2016).

On the other hand, some men face the same wage penalties as women do if they exit the workforce for family obligations, say researchers in the *Journal of Social Issues* (2013). Scott Coltrane and his co-authors find few statistically significant differences between the flexibility stigma for men and for women. In short, men who exit work for family reasons suffer significant salary and promotional penalties.

Men: Advancement

In a 2013 Pew Research Study, fewer men than women reported negative impacts on their career due to career interruptions such as caring for a family member. Theories differ as to why men and not women advance more easily. In a 2015 series of nine studies of 4,000 participants at Harvard Business School, researchers found that men view professional advancement differently than women. Many men tend to assume a more career-focused perspective while some women embrace relationships, marriage, and family and indicate a fewer number of life goals associated with career power.

Another possibility is ethnicity, according to a Catalyst Study.[16] For instance, many Asian women feel overlooked by their companies' diversity programs and believe they lack HR support. They have difficulty finding mentors and forming positive managerial relationships. Co-workers feel uncomfortable around them, perhaps because some Asian women have difficulties with self-promotion and networking but sense the Western pressure to behave this way. The Ascend Foundation (a nonprofit Pan-Asian organization) found that Asian women are the least represented executives in the workforce. While Asians make up about 27 percent of employees at five large companies (such as Intel and Hewlett Packard), they account for

only about 14 percent of top executives. Their cultural profile may discourage advancement due to a perceived lack of appreciation for leadership skills, emotional intelligence, avoidance of risks, and desire to maintain
a low profile.

Generally speaking, some men are more confident or positive than
women and are likely to take advantage of professional advancement opportunities while women sometimes experience greater conflict, reasoning
that the tradeoffs and sacrifices might not be worth the power. Another theory advanced in *Atlantic Magazine* attributes men's greater advancement
to women's shortage of confidence.[17] While this may be true for some
women, according to an article in *Frontiers in Psychology* (June 2015), this
"confidence" theory ignores the organizational context and affixes the blame
to women's personalities instead. Perhaps, say experts, a subtle "second-
generation" gender bias—instead of overt discrimination—still exists in
some workplaces. A vicious managerial cycle may favor men at the expense
of women because managers sometimes incorrectly assume that men are
more motivated and offer them more career development opportunities.
Also, because some men regularly exhibit overconfidence, some managers attribute this behavior to actual leadership abilities. In short, some men
may score promotions more easily because the structure or culture of the
workplace may favor their gender.

The male model of social interaction also favors male advancement, says
Marilyn Nagel, co-founder of NQuotient, a technology company.[18] Men's
style of networking emphasizes informal, "cocktail" relationships regardless of conflicting values. In contrast, some women would rather network
in non-social settings such as at work. Not surprisingly, a major study of
nearly 30,000 employees in 118 companies found that women's odds of
advancement are 15 percent lower than men's, according to www.leanin
.org and McKinsey & Company.[19]

Men's networking efforts can also lead to more mentor sponsorship and
endorsements, according to "Men Still Get More Promotions than Women"
in the *Harvard Business Review*.[20] Another reason might be that in a traditionally masculine culture, aggressive participation and demanding style
are equated with leadership (although the same style is often deemed unap-
pealing or unnatural for women). Women also tend toward perfectionism,
says a poll from the Financial Women's Association, and do not enjoy
leaving comfort zones that force them to behave inconsistently and
hypocritically.[21]

On the other hand, men may have to wrestle with something researcher
Scott Coltrane calls the "femininity stigma," which equates care giving with
being a less committed worker. In preliminary research Coltrane found that

when men behave in a way that is not stereotypically masculine (such as requesting flexible work), employers perceive them as less-devoted workers and attribute to them such negative traits as weakness and lack of power, penalizing them at first. In a 2013 study, Laurie A. Rudman found that men who requested family leave were viewed as poor organizational "citizens" and ineligible for rewards. Kenneth Matos said men who take substantive paternity leaves "suffer socially, professionally, and financially."[22] They receive worse job evaluations and lower hourly raises and are at greater risk of being laid off or demoted. Matos also says that when men reduced their hours for family reasons, they lost an average of 15.5 percent in earnings over their career.

SUMMARY

Gender stereotyping and accompanying inequities are still controversial issues that affect both men and women and their families in terms of pay, flexibility options, and advancement. While men still hold the lion's share of CEO positions, some women are fashioning different economic alternatives by going entrepreneurial or entering nontraditional fields. Some married men also take leaves or use flextime; others resent their wives' pay inequity because this affects total family budgeting and long-term goals. Gender is not the only contributing factor, however, to lowering WLB. In Chapter 7, readers will see how demographics affect the success or failure to achieve good WLB.

CHAPTER 7

Do Demographics Affect WLB?

We have seen how gender affects WLB, but what about socio-economic class, age, marriage, children, career choice, sexual preference, or ethnicity? In a perfect world, these factors would not affect the quality of any one person's WLB, but income or social equality—i.e., a level playing field—has not yet extended its full reach, which is why every worker's demographic profile has a unique set of assets and liabilities. Compare your profile with the information given here. It will help you evaluate and modify your WLB strategy for maximum benefit.

AGE

Age impacts attitudes about employment. In general, Boomers rate work over personal life. Influenced by 1960s civil rights demonstrations, Viet Nam, and inflation, Boomers generally distrust authority and large organizations although they are more receptive to change and have a sense of entitlement. *Employment Benefit News* (December 2015) states that 50 percent of Boomers want more vacation time, better 401(k) matches, and expanded health care.

Due to the 2008 recession, many Boomers must work at least part-time in retirement, and about 5 percent never plan to retire. According to the *AARP Bulletin*, 39 percent of Boomer women intend to keep working.[1] In fact, according to "Boomer Expectations for Retirement 2016," just 24 percent of Boomers believe their savings will last through retirement.

Next in seniority are the Gen Xers born between the early 1960s and the early 1980s and nicknamed "slackers" due to the twin negative influences of Watergate and the Space Shuttle Challenger disaster—two events that contributed to loss of faith in government and authority. Dual families dominated, and many Gen Xers developed self-reliance as latchkey kids. Today, they work hard but focus on task completion rather than time investment. Instead of worshiping heroes or expecting rewards, they create their own opportunities. Skeptical about attaining WLB, Gen Xers commit to careers but not to one job or one company. In 2007, State University of New York (SUNY) research on 543 alumni showed Gen Xers more apt to use wellness programs because work is not their sole focus. *Employment Benefit News* reported that 47 percent of Gen Xers want better 401(k) matches, more vacation time, and a flexible work schedule; 56 percent intend to work into retirement.[2]

Next in line are the Millennials. One in three workers fits into this age category (18 to 34, as of 2016), according to a Pew Research study. Joshua Grubbs at Case Western Reserve University says Millennials admit they are narcissistic in an "individualistic" way. Their attitudes have been shaped by the Internet and global terrorism, but they work hard, set goals, and expect perks in exchange. However, if a job lacks in professional development and skills acquisitions, according to a 2016 Fidelity survey, Millennials are likely to quit. Research from Willis Towers Watson predicts Millennials will in the near future prioritize benefits such as identity theft protection, critical illness insurance, retirement savings, bonus opportunities, and student loan repayment programs. According to the 2015 Mass Mutual Generations@Work Study, 48 percent of Millennials want more vacation time and flextime. They look for good salaries to pay back student loans, auto loans, and mortgages and are politically liberal, according to the General Social Survey conducted from 1972 to 2012.

Technology company Workfront surveyed Millennials and said 52 percent answered e-mail during dinner and did not believe bosses negatively impacted their WLB, but 29 percent did see incompetent colleagues as career obstacles. *Employment Benefit News* also reported that 35 percent of Millennials desired better 401(k) matches,[3] and *AARP Bulletin* found that seven out of 10 Millennials plan to work during their retirement years.[4]

Harvard Business Review (February 23, 2015) published a survey of 16,637 Millennials; in general, 40 percent aspired to the role of manager or leader (ranging from 8 percent in Japan to 63 percent in India), but high future salaries were the bigger incentive (50 percent of respondents from Central and Eastern Europe prized high wages compared to 17 percent of Africans). Decision making and doing challenging work also rated high, and 40 percent of Millennials in North America, Western Europe, and Africa favored managers who empower their employees.

Millennials across the globe prioritize WLB but regard it more as a "work–me balance." North Americans prefer flexible work hours but accommodate to long hours if the schedule will accelerate their careers. And nearly half of respondents in every region said they would give up a well-paid job for better WLB. Furthermore all respondents prioritized time with family but discounted "working for the betterment of society" as important.

MARITAL STATUS

Traditional marriages (think the 1950s) in which women do not work still offer the most benefits to employed men, according to *Administrative Science Quarterly* (June 2014). Economists found that marriage increases men's wages from 10 percent to 50 percent, and fatherhood inflates it even further. According to Payscale, Inc.'s report ("Inside the Gender Pay Gap"), married men earn the highest overall salaries ($67,900 for men with children; $60,800 for those without).[5] Bella DePaulo, a social scientist, says even when married and single men are equal in education and experience, married men are paid more.[6]

According to the Bureau of Labor Statistics (BLS), singlism—a bias against singles—is rampant even though SWOCs (singles without children) make up 60 percent of the labor force. Some employers expect single people to fill in on holidays, take second-choice vacation times, and cover for married co-workers. Singles also are sometimes expected to work late, take inconvenient shifts, and travel to undesirable places. Furthermore, singles generally receive less compensation and opportunities for flextime, leaves, and health care benefits. According to new research by the Employee Benefit Research Institute, older singles face higher out-of-pocket expenses for non-recurring health care services such as home health care, nursing home stays, overnight hospital stays, and outpatient surgery. For example, in non-recurring health spending by those ages 85 and older, singles spent an average of about $13,355 compared with $8,530 for couples.

Childless singles also pay more for employer-sponsored health insurance premiums due to the lack of dependent children, and while the spouse or child of a deceased married employee receives the decedent's social security benefits, singles' social security benefits revert back to the system. Singles also do not qualify for an earned income tax credit (a refundable tax credit for low- to moderate-income individuals and couples, particularly those with children, and dependent on a recipient's income and number of children).

In an article in *Marie Claire* (June 2013), writer Ayana Byrd tells how a 32-year-old SWOC litigation attorney in a large Philadelphia firm busied her after-work calendar to avoid spending nights working at the office. As it turned out, she and four other SWOC attorneys (out of the 100-plus staff) were pressed into after-hours work. Some companies even pocket part-time dividends that result from (single) employees doing excess work without added compensation.

Furthermore, although single and childless workers both utilize the FMLA to care for a parent, SWOCS cannot take leave to care for someone who, for them, may be as important as a spouse or a child (for instance, a close friend, sibling, extended family member, or someone else's child).

Single parents suffer bias too. For one thing, divorced singles do not always have the flexibility to relocate due to child custody restrictions. Also, a single employee might lack a home caretaker to nurse ill children. Lack of support is one of the biggest disadvantages of singles with children, whose needs range from child care, social life, and flextime schedules to employment at companies which, while not offering perks like tuition reimbursement or profit sharing, might offer "free money" for employees' offspring in the form of summer jobs and tuition reimbursement.

Economic Class

Blue-Collar Workers

In a 2015 study at Kansas State University, researchers learned that blue-collar employees (with vague work–home boundaries and rigid and inflexible work schedules) felt less appreciated than white-collar workers. Their problems can lead to increased work–family conflict and higher levels of sickness and absenteeism. Another blue-collar deficit is fewer benefits programs. In 2009, Linda Haas and C. Philip Hwang found that 34 percent of companies offered blue-collar programs compared to 48 percent for white-collar workers (*Fathering*, vol. 7, no. 3, Fall 2009).

Furthermore, in a Swedish study of blue-collar operators at a paper mill, researchers found blue-collars believed white-collar management took less responsibility for their actions.[7] These tensions were exacerbated by environmental discrepancies such as production planners residing in comfy office buildings adjacent to the mill while production floor employees had to tolerate loud and stressful surroundings.

Australian blue-collars also exhibited stress, poor health, and higher rates of disability and mortality in a cooperative U.K.–Australia study (University of Birmingham and Health Exchange, 2014). Although physical work, especially in construction, partly accounted for this, psychological challenges (unrealistic time frames and irregular work) also stressed these workers. U.K. blue-collars faced similar stresses, among them low levels of job control, work overload, long hours, relationship problems, and alcohol and drug abuse.

White-Collar Workers and Professionals

According to *Employee Benefit News*, white-collar industries traditionally attracting females do not guarantee leave policies.[8] For instance, only 15 percent of teachers and 16 percent of office and administrative support workers get paid family leave. The highest wage earners usually get the most leave. Only 4 percent of the lowest wage earners have paid family leave.

Interactions and life-changing decisions impact white-collar workers, especially health care workers, according to a 2015 study by VITAL WorkLife and Cejka Search. Forty-six percent of physicians are severely stressed today compared to 38 percent in 2011. Overall, 89 percent desire job modifications, ranging from switching careers to leaving medicine entirely. Only 19 percent report good organizational support systems. Mayo Clinic researchers said in a 2011 survey that physicians with the highest burnout rates occurred in the areas of internal, family, and emergency medicine.

In 2012 in the U.K., LawCare conducted a stress survey of 1,000 lawyers. Findings showed that more than 50 percent felt stressed and 19 percent suffered from clinical depression. In 2013, the (British) Law Society interviewed 2,226 solicitors, and 95 percent said they were stressed; 16 percent acknowledged severe stress. Lawrence S. Krieger, a Florida State University law professor, studied contentment in the legal profession and found that of the 6,200 lawyers, those in relatively low-paying public-service positions were happier.[9] The more prestigious jobs apparently did not generate feelings of competence, autonomy, or connection to others. In a 2015 *New York Times* story, Krieger indicated that lawyers suffer greater depression than many other workers and face a 54 percent increased possibility of suicide.[10]

Financial occupations also produce their share of stress. A female respondent to *The Qualitative Report* (2015) summed up banking stress as time-associated risks such as cash balancing and check clearance with responsibilities that negatively affect job security and relationships. The woman employee eventually developed an ulcer, and five years later, left banking for a job in education.

Since the 2008 economic downturn, the suicide rate among financial workers in the United States is 1.51 times higher than the average. In the first three months of 2014, 11 suicides took place within the financial industry, which traders attributed to market plummets. Some firms exacerbate stress by holding commission contests for all-expenses-paid, month-long vacations—huge incentives for traders to work even harder and raise their anxiety levels.

Some work situations turn out positively, though. For instance, at cyber-security firm DigiCert, comptroller Eric Porter took his seven-year-old autistic son to periodic medical appointments and did not get into the office until midmorning. His flextime and paid leave agreement with management flourished, and he reciprocated by working extra hard.

Older women (Boomers and Gen Xers) are much less likely than their male counterparts to work in management, business, and financial occupations (12 percent compared with 21 percent), according to the document "The Status of Women in the States: 2015 Employment and Earnings."[11]

Millennial women, however, are slightly more likely than their male counterparts to work in these areas (10.2 percent of women compared with 9.7 percent of men).

Science and Technology

The American Association for Women in Science (AWIS) surveyed people on work–life integration issues, and respondents acknowledged they lost much potential talent due to the lack of family-friendly flexibility in organizations, according to *Social Currents* (September 21, 2015).

In STEM fields, the National Science Foundation (NSF) found that greater work–life supports correlated with greater gender diversity.[12] According to the 2011 NSF initiative "Balancing the Scale," flexibility in research grant timings, grant supplements for family care, and parental leave (among other provisions) attracted greater academic gender diversity. A survey in *Work and Occupations* reported that STEM faculty have an advantage because they have more freedom or flexibility to rearrange their busy schedules to accommodate family responsibilities although flexibility stigma still can trigger dissatisfaction and turnover, resulting in high academic replacement costs.

Flexibility stigma increased, for instance, when high-tech companies Twitter, Netflix, Etsy, and Facebook recently expanded their parental leave policies. Due to their male-dominated workforce, the costs favored these companies because men tended to avoid paid leave due to cultural stigma. Plus these tech companies have the financial assets, says Bruce Elliot of SHRM. Besides, parental leave is a good public relations tool for recruiting, retention, and gender diversity although it may not satisfy in the long term if company culture and HR personnel do not fully commit to their workers. For instance, sports supplier Patagonia maintains a family care network of trained, in-home care providers, but the company also transmits an environmental philosophy.

Geographic Proximity to Job

A recent *New York Times* article (April 7, 2015) reported that many workers—blue-collar and white-collar alike—believe long commutes and housing prices negatively influence their WLB. Low-wage employees are at a greater disadvantage because they cannot telecommute—in other words, workers cannot clean offices or pour lattes by e-mail!

The *Washington Post* reported in 2015 that District of Columbia legislators and CEOs have significantly shorter commutes than city builders or housekeepers, and a study found that the lowest 25 percent of wage earners in the District of Columbia have the longest commutes.[13] The *Seattle Times* concurred with this, as reporters found that low-income families in the Puget Sound area typically pay a higher percentage of their salaries to commute than their wealthier counterparts. These extended commutes negatively affected family life and personal well-being. In one example, one earner spent a third of his income on transportation because neither of the jobs—packing boxes at FedEx or working security at a bank—could be done remotely. This employee had to commute three hours every day from suburban Seattle to the downtown area.

ETHNICITY

The Hispanic Experience

According to the U.S. Census Bureau (2012), the Latino population grew by more than 1.1 million between 2011 and 2012. By 2050, according to the Pew Research Center, Hispanics will represent nearly 30 percent of the total population. Although some Latinos have little formal education, many do have professional skills. Karina Amaez, born in Peru and now living in the United States, is an exception. She graduated with honors from a U.S. college and spent time working in Argentina and Brazil. Her global skills easily attracted American hirers looking for diverse talent.

Racism and stereotyping are more common for most Hispanic workers. Some company cultures abhor the custom (deemed acceptable in South America) for Latino women to wear fitted clothing and for men and women to embrace, hug, and pat each other on the shoulder or back. Based on 59

interviews with first- and second-generation Mexican-American professionals, results showed that those from poorer backgrounds report more
subtle racism than those in white-collar jobs (*Latino Studies*, 2015).

For many Latino Millennials, family and career fulfillment are more
important than money. Establishing more flexible policies might help companies retain more workers, some of whom, for example, can offer bilin-
gual skills. In a study of 262 Hispanic and white university employees,
researchers examined whether cultural aspects influenced workplace incivility and work and health outcomes. Fifty percent of Hispanic males and
63 percent of females reported incidents of incivility and burnout as well
as job satisfaction. This latter finding on job content, which at first bewil-
dered researchers, suggests that Hispanic employees experience greater
resilience to incivility than other ethnic groups due to strong social skills
and self-reliance (PsycINFO Database Record 2015, APA).

Unfortunately, bias and stereotypical beliefs (such as Hispanic workers
are always late to work and leave early) have interfered with that perception of healthy emotional resilience. Bill Herrera Beardall (half American,
half Panamanian) understands prejudice better than most American managers. Schooled in Panama, he speaks English fluently but considers Spanish his native tongue. Assistant director of facility operations at North
Carolina State University in Raleigh, Beardall supervises 82 people, some
educated, some not. He says if managers want to be effective with Latinos
they must adjust to cultural differences, such as supplying safety information in Spanish, encouraging workers to attend English as a Second Language (ESL) classes, and learning Spanish phrases to facilitate communication
and respect. In-house awareness or diversity training and mentoring also
might encourage employees of all races to self-acknowledge how stereotypes impact decision-making, such as the skepticism that Hispanics lack
leadership abilities even though the facts show they excel at entrepreneurial ventures.

The Asian Experience

The Asian population in the United States increased by 530,000 in 2011,
reaching 18.9 million in 2012. Second-generation Asians live in two different cultures and tend to hyphenate themselves. In the workplace, they
tend to retain the values of both cultures. In fact, according to the Pew
Research Center (2013), 37 percent of second-generation Latinos and
27 percent of Asian Americans identify themselves as simply "American."
Yet Asians, more than Hispanics, are likely to speak English and have
friends and spouses outside their ethnic group.

Another ethnic influence is that Asian- and African-American women are not considered equals in the business community. When Asian women managers attempt to deal with men, they are sometimes shunned or belittled. Local customs—not the company culture itself—may foster company bias. For example, the Chinese culture emphasizes formalities, such as respect for seniors and a hierarchy of greetings, and other cultures may not realize their own behaviors are perceived as anti-ethnic. Other differences are that most Chinese identify themselves by using their last name first, and eye contact can be perceived as rude and disrespectful. Furthermore in Japan, as in other Asian cultures, important behaviors include the bow as a common greeting and the exchange of business cards. Also, touching customs and norms can be associated with religious meanings. For example, many Asian people believe the head houses the soul, so another person touching an area on the head might place the person in danger.

The African-American Experience

According to the *Journal of Organizational Behavior* (2015), minority groups such as African Americans can encounter job discrimination that leads to negative work attitudes as well as physical maladies. Many African Americans remain unemployed (BLS, 2011) since the Great Recession of 2008, which hit that ethnic group especially hard because they were employed disproportionately in physically demanding blue-collar jobs. Another discriminatory practice is wages. African Americans generally earn substantially less than whites but more than Hispanics. In a 2009 Harvard study, sociologists sent African Americans and Anglos to apply for low-wage jobs with identical résumés and similar interview training. White applicants with criminal records were offered jobs at a rate equal to that of African-American applicants with no criminal records. The Economic Policy Institute found that as of 2015, black men living in similar metropolitan areas of the country make 22 percent less than white men with the same education and experience; for black women, the number is 34.2 percent less.

Some African Americans do not participate in the workplace because of organized exclusion, negative stereotypes, and what the nonprofit group Catalyst calls "unconscious bias." African Americans perceive themselves as outsiders and not team players in the workforce. Some black women corporate leaders deal with "microaggressions," according to an article by the APA. (Microaggression is subtle bias undermining intellect, competence, and capabilities.) Black women also receive limited mentoring and sponsorship and face exclusion from work and social meetings because due to the under representation of minority employees, African-American networks and other cultural work groups are hard to develop.

African Americans also sometimes report feeling career pressure to alter their natural hair to fit in, according to a 2013 Deloitte study of 3,129 employees.[14] Many feel conflicted in the natural-versus-straightened hair debate, some arguing that dreadlocks are significant in African-American culture and that banning them equates with unprofessionalism—an accusation that could limit their advancement.

DIVERSITY PROGRAMS

The nonprofit organization Catalyst says companies usually deal with unconscious bias of non-whites with formal training, but this strategy works only if employees set specific goals to change behaviors. Since 2009, Kimberly-Clark has made a special effort and seen a 90 percent increase in the number of women holding leadership positions. Developing diverse talent is important to the company because the executives want to employ talent that looks, thinks, and behaves like the people using their products, says Sue Dodsworth, chief diversity officer for Kimberly-Clark.[15] Another progressive company, Baxter International, which supplies global hospital products, has eight business resource groups to develop skills, strengthen cultural connections, and support key business initiatives. The groups, which include the African American Leadership Council, Asian Leadership Network, Baxter Women Leaders, Latinos@Baxter, and an LGBT group, report directly to the CEO.

Such diversity programs are vital for African Americans, according to the *International Journal of Business and Science* (February 2015) in "Code Switching in Working African Americans" (Southern Illinois University, 2008). Otherwise some African Americans opt for inauthenticity and unwillingly engage in standard English, feeling less committed to the organization. Hiring on at non-diverse organizations can encourage stress as it forces employees to mask their ethnicity, which ultimately leads to burnout.

Some African Americans combat bias with coping strategies already discussed in Chapter 3, but others defer to religion and spirituality (which provides a sense of empowerment, understanding, and forgiveness); pride in self and cultural ancestry; speech monitoring and de-emphasis of racial differences; and perfectionistic standards that contradict negative stereotypes.

One governmental assist for African-American techies (and by extension other ethnic groups) was the Congressional Black Caucus (CBC) TECH 2020 plan launched in May 2015. In major tech companies in Silicon

Valley, African Americans represent 2 percent or less of the workforce, but the CBC has outlined diversity principles, discussed industry best practices, highlighted African-American students and entrepreneurs, and presented legislation focused on increasing STEM. TaskRabbit might be the only company that appointed a black CEO, but it also has committed to increasing the percentage of African-American employees from 11 percent to 13 percent in 2016 to reflect the population of the United States, according to *USA Today*.

Sexual Preference

Diversity in sexual orientation and gender, including homosexual, bisexual, and transgender, is not just guaranteed legally by Title VII, but guaranteed emotionally to prevent discriminatory behaviors. In September 2014, the U.S. government filed its first two transgender discrimination lawsuits against employers. A Florida eye clinic paid $150,000 in April 2015 to settle a lawsuit involving an employee transitioning from male to female, and another lawsuit is pending against a Detroit funeral home involving a fired employee also transitioning. In a third EEOC lawsuit against Shoreview, MN, Deluxe Financial Services—a check-printing company—the owners refused to allow the use of the women's restroom while the employee was transitioning from male to female. The company recently agreed to settle the case for $115,000 and noted that its national health benefit plan no longer excludes medical care based on transgender status. According to the Corporate Equality Index 2016, two-fifths of Fortune 500 businesses offer transgender-inclusive health care coverage (up from zero in 2002 and six times as many as in 2011).

That said, there is no federal law actually protecting the rights of LGBT employees in the United States and no state-level protection for sexual orientation and gender identity protection exists in 29 and 33 states, respectively. Employees can be fired for being lesbian, gay, bisexual, or transgender.

Litigation and heavy damage awards aside, the presence of sexually different people—whether they are gay or transgender—can cause great discomfort for some employees. In 2011, *Business Management Daily* described how transgender persons can frequently be targets for hate crimes, ostracism, and discrimination, especially if they undergo a physical transformation during their employment. According to the Transgender Law Center, transgender employees often face ridicule behind their backs and the intentional use of old names and pronouns. Some employees react negatively to a transgender employee's bathroom choice, and these conflicts can breed tension in the workplace unless employers create an environment of inclusiveness and a culture of respect for differing lifestyles.

The statistics on LGBT diversity indicate substantial discrimination and harassment throughout the U.S. and Europe, where 47 percent of LGBT people feel they experience discrimination while job hunting or in the workplace. As of April 2013, 88 percent of Fortune 500 companies had nondiscrimination policies on sexual orientation, but fear of humiliation often keeps LGBT employees closeted. Because as many as two out of three LGBTs have heard lesbian or gay jokes,[16] many LGBT employees fear losing connections with their co-workers or not receiving advancement opportunities if they reveal their sexual orientation. According to Catalyst in 2015, more than half of LGBT workers hide their sexual orientation in their workplace, and nearly one in 10 leaves a job due to the inhospitable environment.

The transgender population generally faces the most discrimination in the workplace, says www.catalyst.org (June 2015). Nearly half of transgenders said they were not hired, were fired, or not promoted due to their gender identity, and 90 percent experienced harassment or mistreatment on the job or took steps to avoid it.

Insofar as workplace gender issues are concerned, nearly all top 50 federal contractors and top 50 Fortune 500 companies implement nondiscrimination policies, partner benefits, and gender transition-related health benefits and believe these diversity policies improve business. They point to specific economic benefits such as recruitment and retention of the best talent. For example, the University of Tennessee (a top-50 federal contractor) provost said administrators previously had deceived themselves into thinking that lack of a LGBT policy did not harm the university, but gay and lesbian candidates preferred to go elsewhere, and some heterosexuals were turned off by the overt prejudice.

Then too, power brokers and provosts have discovered that companies with diverse backgrounds and experiences are more apt to reap creative ideas and innovations. For example, the head of global diversity for IBM says LGBT employees contribute heavily to the bottom line. In addition, diversity policies also improve customer service because a varied workforce attracts and better serves a diverse customer base.

LGBT policies also enhance employee productivity by confirming the value and right to authenticity. When several public sector clients requested LBGT policy changes as a contract requirement, companies like top-50 federal contractor Bechtel complied. The company added sexual orientation to its nondiscrimination policy and extended domestic partner benefits after the city of San Francisco passed a requirement. Moreover, businesses such as the "Big 3" auto companies (Ford, GM, and DaimlerChrysler) all agreed to offer domestic partner benefits in response to union requests.

SUMMARY

Although gender has long been identified as having a major impact on WLB, cultural and other demographic factors also impact workers and their WLB due, in part, to biases and discrimination. HR directors and organizational cultures must work to guarantee good diversity programs to balance the scales of success for individual workers and assure them of greater fairness. What also helps attain equity and better WLB is a strong relationship between employees and employers, as readers will learn in Chapter 8.

CHAPTER 8

Are Employees and Employers on the Same Page?

Another debated issue with no instant solution is the disconnect between employers and employees. Without affixing blame to either group, this chapter objectively explores how labor and management both struggle for optimum WLBs in an often disharmonious environment in which employees and employers sometimes have totally different perspectives in such areas as what constitute good management, helpful feedback, and triggers for worker stress.

The result is often employees receiving features such as financial health, strong management, and good training when they really value salary, benefits, job stability, and a pleasant work atmosphere, according to *Employment Benefit News* (July 2016). Says Jim Link, the chief human resources officer of Randstad North America: "Employers are realizing that if they want to attract and keep talent, they're going to have to pay a competitive wage, one that is fair and hard to replicate." In the meantime the disconnect breeds discontent.

DISCONNECT ABOUT CAUSES OF WORK STRESS

Some employers and employees view the causes of workplace stress differently, according to *Employee Benefit News* (February 2016). Although employees maintain that company culture, low pay, and inadequate staffing (for example, lack of support or uneven workloads) contribute to stress, employers cite lack of WLB, inadequate staffing, and 24/7 technologies, according to the 2015/2016 Global Staying@Work Survey and the 2015/2016 Global Benefits Attitudes Survey. The only area on which both groups agree is inadequate staffing, writes Tom Davenport of Willis Towers Watson. As an example, Davenport describes a woman employee who sometimes worked 36 hours straight, driving to various cities for multiple appointments (she averaged 100,000 miles a year). Upon learning she had chronic fatigue syndrome, she switched jobs and got medical help. Here both employer and employee missed the obvious stressor—overwork—until it was too late.

Rose Stanley, a senior practice leader at WorldatWork, says employers think they know what the employee wants or needs but their assumptions may be wrong. Employers need to use frequent surveys to find out how employees perceive stress. For example, she says employees consider company culture to be the third-highest stressor, and that can be improved by allowing time for lunch breaks outside and casual conversation among employees.

Victor Lipman, author of *The Type B Manager: Leading Successfully in a Type A World* (Prentice Hall, 2015), recommends employers devise programs that ensure that all leadership levels learn to recognize employee stress and its triggers and encourage employees to take vacations, do physical activities, and participate in resilience programs.

In another study, many employers attributed employee stress to lack of work–life balance, inadequate staffing, and expanded technology (managers having to be "on call"), but many employees pointed to inadequate staffing, low pay or minimal increases, and unclear job expectations (Workforce Stress 2014 study). Here again the only point of agreement is with staffing. According to *Forbes* (July 2014), employees also view the organizational culture (specifically lack of teamwork and blame-game accountability) as significant problems. Researchers concluded that the disconnect in these stressors might lead to employers trying to fix the wrong problems, thus alienating employees and leading to business problems such as absenteeism, presenteeism, and unwanted turnover.

DISCONNECT IN COMMUNICATION PREFERENCES

According to some employees, managers sometime communicate poorly, missing the opportunity to give appropriate feedback. This can sometimes be due to choice of media. Choices often correlate with generational habits. A recent University of Minnesota study revealed certain general findings that do not necessarily apply to everyone but may give some insight into the communication clash between employees and employers: Boomers like to hear information face to face; Gen Xers prefer e-mail; and Millennials lean toward texting.

One caveat to managers might be to consider all media formats, beginning with face-to-face communication and then following up with e-mail reminders. Prudential's 2013 "Eighth Annual Study of Employee Benefits: Today & Beyond" appears to confirm the importance of digital media, but also emphasizes the fact that face-to-face interactions rate more highly with employees than managers.

A recent State of Employee Feedback study says employees prefer more frequent, informal one-on-ones with managers rather than the more common annual performance reviews that managers lean toward. Employees dislike these discussions because they are apt to be more ambiguous, inconsistent, or one-sided. In fact, Quantum Workplace recommends that one-on-ones should be held at least monthly to provide constructive feedback for coaching or mentoring. The more feedback the better, says Dr. Kenneth Nowack of Envisa Learning Inc., as long as managers supply good follow up with realistic expectations and the feedback does not drastically demoralize an employee's self-perceptions. Nowack's managerial model strives to enlighten employees about their development opportunities, encourages them to implement behavioral change, and enables them to do this by empowering them with techniques and skills that track their progress and cultivate sustained change. Gallup's latest "State of the American Manager" report says employees value this kind of consistent feedback or communication about work roles and responsibilities but would also like more frequent chats with their supervisors about their personal lives.

Disconnect in Perception of Employee WLB

In the national 2015 Workplace Flexibility Study survey of 1,087 working professionals and 116 HR professionals, HR professionals' views on WLB conflicted with those of employees. While 67 percent of HR professionals believed employees led a balanced life, almost half of employees and a third of job seekers felt they had a shortage of personal time. The reason for the differences in perspectives may be overtime: One in five employees spends more than 20 hours per week working outside the office. A second reason is the "umbilical cord" phenomenon. Sixty-five percent of employees say their manager expects them to be reachable outside of the office—either by e-mail or phone during personal time—as do the majority of HR professionals and managers. Some employees may not perceive this as too controlling or intrusive, but others do.

Although flexibility programs are a major component of WLB, employees and employers even show a disconnect on this: While half the employers in the www.workplacetrends.com survey say they think workers consider flexibility their most important benefit, an overwhelming 75 percent rank it as number one.

DISCONNECT IN ENGAGEMENT OR MOTIVATIONAL STRATEGIES

Two recent surveys spotlight employees' and employers' different attitudes on motivation. In the 2012 Randstad Engagement Index, which polled more than 2,000 employed adults and more than 500 employers, 36 percent of workers indicated that bonuses, promotions, and other incentives were effective in engaging employees.[1] However, only 27 percent of employers actually use incentives. Furthermore 28 percent of workers said their companies had a formal system to recognize and reward employees, but 46 percent of employers defaulted to performance reviews. It appears that workers want more motivation than just a great performance evaluation and a "Well done" from the boss. Jim Link, managing director of human resources for Randstad, says employers should not rely only on annual performance reviews to help boost morale and decrease turnover.

Employees and employers also clashed on the "Am I doing my best?" question. Although 72 percent of workers attested they did their best work, about 81 percent of employers believed the percentage was greater. It might seem that employers are either naïve or being overly optimistic about their engagement strategies.

Motivation often comes from good feedback. According to a study by Towers Watson, more than 60 percent of employees maintain they get inadequate feedback to improve performance, says Minu Ipe, associate professor of management at Arizona State University's School of Business. It may be because some managers are actually unable to recognize their workers' strengths or talents or fail to give the necessary feedback. Thus, according to Gallup writer Marco Nink, some employees discover their strengths only through an arduous trial and error process. Managers might speed up this process by supplying strengths feedback (which two-thirds of surveyed employees said encouraged them to become more excited about their job and do better work). Gallup says most high-talent supervisory managers (61 percent) use this strengths-based approach, which appears to reiterate the old psychological axiom that positive reinforcement leads to a vitalizing cycle that achieves peak performance. Gallup describes this as a "cascade effect," when engaged managers influence their employees with helpful "strengths" feedback, which in turn promotes engagement. Of course managers need to know how to give proper feedback. Feedback needs to be specific (based on observable behavior), timely (close to the event or project the employee coordinated), actionable (implemented into an action plan), accurate, and meaningful (for example, saying "a great job" is too vague and requires qualification).

Groups like Stryker Medical hold workgroup feedback sessions many times a year, says Jerry Rudzinski, sales director.[2] He says managers explain the purpose is to improve the organization, which is why they encourage everyone to speak up. Rudzinski says feedback is perceived as "harmless" or safe in these sessions, and everyone considers it part of the positive communication cycle.

DISCONNECT ON TRUST ISSUE

Employees and employers also divide on the subject of trust. Only 62 percent of employees felt they were in good leadership hands (employers' rating was 78 percent), and just 44 percent of employees aspired to their boss' position. This Randstad data also shows that while 92 percent of employers feel they help employees promote their careers, only 59 percent of workers agree. These results might indicate lack of engagement and faith in company operations as well as a sense of devaluation and an unclear career path.

Trust can help or hurt people, according to Michael Baer, a management professor at Arizona State University's business school. In a study of 200 London bus drivers, Baer found that trusted employees became stressed by higher expectations and fear of failure (*2015 Academy of Management Journal*). When a boss initially gave the employees more tasks, the workers felt proud, but upon realizing they would have a lot of work, they began to feel stressed and worry their reputations would suffer. This attitude relates to the "conservation of resources" business theory, which denotes that workers react well to free time, good pay, and recognition, but when a heavy workload threatens those resources, they experience stress.

The 2016 Edelman Trust Barometer executive summary also spells out the disconnect between employees and leaders. The report shows that one in three employees does not trust his or her company, and more than two-thirds feel that CEOs are too focused on short-term performance. Furthermore, 64 percent of executives trust their company while only 48 percent of non-management employees feel the same.

So, based on these studies, it is apparent that obedient employees who automatically extol the virtues of their employers are dinosaurs. Unless CEOs build trust by responding ethically to crises and build motivation with more than profit figures, employees may feel less loyal and be more inclined to bad-mouth their employer or quit.

DISCONNECT ON CULTURE (IDEAL WORKER VS. FLEXTIME)

Although some articles report on the obsolescence of the "ideal worker," a great many organizational cultures still cling to this theory and do not necessarily support work flexibility programs. (The definition of "ideal worker," sometimes called the "zero-drag" worker, refers to an employee with no substantial responsibilities outside the workplace, according to *Gender and the Work-Family Experience* [2014]. Companies that cling to this notion usually prefer both white-collar and blue-collar "ideals.")

Under these circumstances employees' needs are in constant conflict with employers' prevailing philosophies of business. Anne Weisberg, senior vice president of the Families and Work Institute, who believes the ideal worker myth is still firmly entrenched, says perks like unlimited vacations and yoga sessions lure workers, but if a disconnect exists between these programs and the work culture, employees default to the behavior the culture favors.[3] This might mean posing as an ideal worker if the alternative might be missing out on a non-leadership role. Thus employees sometimes fake certain roles and behaviors for the sake of the job.

In a 2012 University College Cork (Ireland) doctoral thesis, the researcher tells how freelancers revolted against the "always-on" mandate of the ideal worker. Some telecommuters used overtime as a bargaining chip with employers, justifying that their overwork was necessary in order to "earn points" for employer negotiations and more secure employment. One employee signed a contract for a 40-hour week although employers knew the job required more.

Weisberg suggests redefining the concepts of leadership so the ideal worker is not perceived as the person who stays the latest at the office but rather the person with the leadership potential to get the work done and still leave at a reasonable hour.

Women often experience even greater disconnects due to gender. In a 2015 issue of the *Fordham Law Review*, Savita Kumra of Brunei University in London says that managers of law firms in Britain disbelieve that an "ideal worker" can be female. As a result, women attorneys gain fewer rewards and higher status and are usually limited to family and tax law areas (unlike male colleagues, who deal in mergers and acquisitions requiring irregular hours and high client demands). Without access to mentors and influential business networks, women cannot advance to more challenging areas. In these organizations, says GloboForce, the majority of employees report feeling disconnected from management and its vision.

An unwritten psychological contract between employer and employee includes informal arrangements, mutual beliefs, common ground, and perceptions, according to organizational scholar Denise Rousseau and www.hrzone.com. When managers who supposedly implement flextime practices do not actually support them, they misinform employees and invite further estrangement.

Disconnect on Bonding

Gallup also found employees appear to have a higher regard for relationship bonding than managers, says an article titled "Creating a Culture of Inclusion to Attain Organizational Success," published in *Employment Relations Today* (2015). It appears that some employees feel they achieve a better sense of value and respect through more intimate contact with supervisors. In a national survey conducted by MSW-ARS Research, results revealed that verbal interactions lead to more employee-friendly, open and inclusive communication. In particular, managerial conversations promoted women's confidence and helped develop skills more than if the exchange merely reviewed tasks (*Business Management Daily*, December 2015).

Senior leaders were more likely to give positive reviews in areas such as valuing employee involvement, WLB, and recognition. In fact, about 70 percent of senior leaders said they felt valued, compared to just over half of front-line workers, according to the American Psychological Association (APA) 2015 Work and Well-Being Survey. David Ballard, PsyD and head of APA's center for Organizational Excellence, says leaders need to realize their perceptions may differ dramatically from those of their employees.

Another contributor to relationship disconnect might be the dramatic shortage of excellent managers. According to Gallup writer Amy Adkins, only one in 10 people possesses the high talent to manage, and companies have a notoriously poor record for spotting managerial talent; they choose the wrong candidate 82 percent of the time. Feedback from current available data may indicate that women managers fare better than males at supervision. They are more likely not only to encourage their subordinates' development but they may also be innately talented as managers.

Playing dumb or giving the cold shoulder may sound like poor relationship technique, but according to the *Journal of Experimental and Social Psychology* (2016), managers sometimes behave that way, minimizing their competence to appear warmer to their subordinates. Some employees also fake things, disguising their own warmth to appear more competent. Sound counterintuitive? Data backs it up, however, as a successful strategy. Four experiments, each with 180 to 200 participants, showed that status or social class stereotypes can lead people to appear differently than they really are. Mirroring or matching the expected behavior of another person is a deceptive behavioral technique that happens frequently in evaluations or interviews, says Princeton professor Susan Fiske. She cautions HR managers, job applicants, reference letter writers, organizational managers, and candidate image handlers to look out for these insincere behaviors that ultimately work against both labor and management.

According to *Employment Relations Today* and Dale Carnegie Training, the best supervisory relationships involve effective managers who provide individual guidance and support—the "critical drivers" of employee engagement.

DISCONNECT WITH HR DEPARTMENT

A huge gulf separates employee and HR perceptions, according to ADP Research Institute's 2013 global "Human Capital Management's Employee Disconnect." The discrepancies involve benefits administration, talent management, and responses to HR inquiries. Employees consistently give lower marks to rate compensation, benefits, and professional growth than HR people do.

For example, take professional growth. HR appears to need a better communications plan with employees interested in mobility or foreign assignments. In a recent global PwC study researchers learned that some HR personnel falsely assume that women with children do not want to work abroad. Yet when 41 percent of females with children were surveyed, the results indicated that these women wanted to undertake international assignments. Regardless, women represented only 20 percent of the internationally mobile population. HR departments, says Mercer Central Market Mobility Leader Daniel Hayot, need to closely target mobility groups in both genders, offering cultural training not only for assignees but for spouses and children and providing spousal allowances for certification in host countries.

Employees also heavily dispute HR performance evaluations and are dissatisfied about getting answers to questions addressed to HR. Only about half of employees find it extremely easy to obtain answers from HR, and senior leadership is rated even less positively than HR. HR directors also seem to have a more positive perception of how their companies are managing employees than employees do. The report showed that employees, with the exception of the U.S. workforce, rate WLB "significantly" lower than HR does. Another head-butting conflict with HR is the subtle discrimination, racism, bullying, and harassment that some HR departments and upper management tolerate.

DISCONNECT IN VALUES

Working for a company that shares your environmental values increases employees' job satisfaction and creativity, says Jelena Spanjol, a marketing professor at the University of Illinois. According to her research on 3,000 employees from a variety of size companies (*Journal of Business Ethics,* 2015), the positive effect is enormously multiplied if companies have balanced portfolios in which they act environmentally responsible to their customers and treat employees with fairness in evaluations, diversity, and health care. If, however, their values are not congruent with their activities, employees will not benefit in the long term and this situation can lead to a further disconnect.

Known as "green washing," (a corporation posing as environmentally progressive but really not), employees usually see through the hypocrisy, become disengaged, and sometimes do not want to stay with the company for long. As an example, Spanjol mentions Walmart, which she says is externally focused and all show, as opposed to Fannie Mae, which provides home mortgage funding to low- and middle-class families and allows employees to volunteer in schools and other nonprofits up to ten hours each month.

Some environmentally progressive companies are sincere in their values, but primarily implement them to reduce employee stress and prevent health problems. They include 3M, DuPont, Allied Signal, Amoco, and Monsanto, according to "Green Human Resource Management Practices" in the *Sri Lankan Journal of Human Resource Management* (2015).

Recently Wells Fargo released a set of environmental commitments for 2020, including reducing environmental impact; financing the transition to a greener economy; and encouraging more sustainable communities. Author Krista Van Tassel worked on Wells Fargo's GRID Alternatives, a California-based nonprofit that installs solar electric systems for low-income families. Employees have volunteered for GRID Alternatives since 2005. By 2012, GRID Alternatives had trained more than 3,000 volunteers and job seekers in solar installation and installed systems for more than 1,200 low-income families in California and Colorado.

Four-fifths of Gen X workers said they would prefer to work for a company with environmental responsibility, according to Tandberg's Corporate

Environmental Behavior and Impact on Brand Values (2010), and this finding predates a Cox Conserves Sustainability Survey in 2015, which found that many Millennials advocate sustainability values. Differences among generations and employee positions abound, however. Global Tolerance in the U.K. says that managers' views on sustainability and other values contrast drastically with Millennials—10 percent of managers said meaningful work was important compared to 30 percent of Millennials, and 48 percent of managers versus 27 percent of Millennials said high pay connotes career success. Furthermore, 11 percent of managers said a sense of accomplishment ranked high compared with 24 percent of Millennials.

In time, Millennials may avoid this disconnect by transitioning to managerial positions and leading the way in national conservation, energy efficiency, and environmental stewardship. The Cox study shows that 60 percent of Millennials are committed to increasing sustainable activities, and more than half say top management impedes their company's sustainability proposals. With only 62 percent of small and medium businesses (less than 1,000 employees) actually implementing employee-based environmental programs (such as reducing energy, composting, or recycling), Millennials definitely see a disconnect in their eco-values compared with those of their employers. According to "The Evolution of Employee Engagement" (May 2015) by WeSpire, which collected 413 responses from a web survey, 62 percent of employees want to know about the sustainability efforts of their employers. Also, the 2016 Deloitte Millennial Survey notes that Millennials think companies are underperforming by 12 percentage points in social-environmental areas and believe long-term sustainability trumps short-term profits.

Congruent values with employers may hasten WLB, says *The Harvard Business Review*, which states that employees satisfied with their job's psycho-social values have a 16 percent higher performance rate. Revenues were also higher in companies active in sustainability activities, says a University of Guelph study.

Almost half the British workforce want to work for an organization with a positive impact on the world, according to *The Guardian* (May 15, 2015) and research by Global Tolerance. Take, for example, Simon Cohen, who abandoned a high-paying advertising career to set up Global Tolerance. His values are consistent with home and office, and Cohen says more companies may end up paying a higher price if compassionate goals fail to win out over productivity. Another example is Australia's Westpac, a bank going to great lengths to fulfill its profitability and social objectives through the bank's Organizational Mentoring Program, where employees volunteer their skills and expertise to support community organizations. Eighty-seven percent of employees believe they are making a meaningful difference and the company's authenticity is meeting the long-term needs of stakeholders, says Westpac CEO Gail Kelly in "The Values Revolution."[4]

Sharon Goymer, resourcing manager for the educational company National Grid, says there is a growing trend for as well as penalties for green washing.[5] In July 2015, *The Guardian* cited the global PR firm Edelman for green washing. Edelman's Business and Social Purpose clashed with their PR culture, authenticity was lacking, and as a result, some employees flaunted their "disconnect" and quit, along with top clients like Nike. According to the Cone Millennial Cause report, one reason Millennials identify their values with those of corporations has to do with psychologist Abraham Maslow's Hierarchy of Needs theory, which holds that self-actualization is the highest spot on the needs pyramid. Millennials are transferring self-actualization into the workforce, says the Brookings Institute report "How Millennials Could Upend Wall Street and Corporate America (May 2014). The recent Intelligence Group study found that 64 percent of Millennials said they would rather make $40,000 a year at a job they love than $100,000 at a job they think is dull. Some Millennials and younger workers will not hire on with organizations who do not strive for social good. Global Tolerance says the challenge for companies will be to adapt quickly and not fall behind.

SUMMARY

Studies point to a pronounced gulf between workers and employers. Corporate America still holds to a belief in the ideal worker, and managers, leaders, and HR personnel court overly optimistic perceptions of employee attitudes and productivity. On the part of employees, their weak relationships with managers and once-a-year personnel reviews with insufficient feedback on employee strengths can depress employee morale and exacerbate lack of engagement. Moreover, discrepancies in environmental and social values can disturb some employees, affecting WLB even more than salary. In Chapter 9, readers confront another employee–employer disconnect—differing attitudes regarding flextime, shift schedules, and face time.

CHAPTER 9

Do Benefits Close the Salary Gap?

In Chapter 8 we learned about the chasm that often exists between employers and employees. Estrangement can also be caused or exacerbated by dissatisfaction over benefits. Not every employee can take advantage of flexible scheduling, for example, because not every employer offers it, and unfairness can exist on both sides—for flextime users and nonusers. Furthermore, job security can short circuit any use of flextime because employees worry that they might be the last in line for promotions or the first in line for layoffs.

The costs and confusing array of benefits such as health care can challenge employees and employers alike, and confusion over the number and type of plans can frustrate even the most discerning worker. Furthermore, not every perk gets the wholehearted support of employees, as we shall see with financial literacy programs and breastfeeding. In presenting the facts objectively we also question whether flexibility is incompatible with face time and whether employers—both small companies and larger organizations—can afford to offer the benefits they feel are vital to attracting talented workers.

OBJECTIONS TO BREASTFEEDING AND PUMPING BREAKS

Employees and managers often have to negotiate breastfeeding or lactation breaks in the workplace. Depending on the managerial relationship, employees may or may not gain access to special rooms suitable for lactation or breastfeeding. Employers who do not support breastfeeding sometimes resent the use of physical space or worry that overall productivity might suffer. Furthermore, some employers believe not all employees are comfortable interacting with breastfeeding mothers. The irony is the cost of supporting breastfeeding mothers is relatively low compared to the payout for family leave.

Global progress in this area has been modest considering that only four countries provide unpaid breaks or breaks less than six months. In 2014 the overwhelming number of countries—55 to be exact—did not guarantee paid breastfeeding breaks for the first six months of a child's life (*Journal of Human Lactation,* February 2015). The United States advanced more rapidly in this area than many countries. According to the SHRM, one-third of information science employers offer an on-site lactation room; that is up from 25 percent in 2009. Private equity firm KKR makes certain that private spaces are available globally and provides for nannies or comparable caretakers to accompany traveling employees who wish to bring infants along. Credit Suisse Bank supports a "flying nanny" policy, says *Employee Benefits News* (January 26, 2016), although special mother rooms and nanny provisions can nurture resentment from colleagues. Childless employees or those with older children may feel that this is just another instance of greater accommodation to mothers. Actress and author Vanessa de Largie expresses this sentiment in *HuffPost Women* (July 24, 2015), complaining that early shifts are reserved for mothers whereas childless women often have to take later or less desirable shifts.

In general, universities support female faculty members in breastfeeding when the latter use their own offices for pumping, but a 2010 Penn State study on work–family balance says status is the great divider: For those who inhabit shared office space, co-employees often perceive the experience as unpleasant and unhygienic, or the lactating mothers are forced to use a bathroom or find a spare room. On the other hand, if a staff member has her own office, the problem disappears. The process can become even more complicated if staff members are required to walk to campus lactation stations—more time and logistical problems result.

Minnesota researcher Tawni Jaakola found a similar correlation between social and educational status and workplace support for breastfeeding. Only 38.5 percent of high school-educated mothers conceded that their employer supported and accommodated breastfeeding, but the figure jumped significantly to 75 percent for college-educated women. The same percentages applied to support and encouragement from co-workers. Jaakola believes that American mothers at smaller companies face an even larger disadvantage with breastfeeding support than those employed by larger organizations.[1]

Another confusion rose when some staff at universities were confused as to whether pumping counted as time working or not working, although the law is sufficiently clear on this aspect. (Section 7 of the FLSA guarantees unpaid "reasonable break time" for breastfeeding mothers.) However, the legislation also stipulates that employers with fewer than 50 workers are exempt if allowing lactation breaks would "impose an undue hardship."

Obviously, not all women have the same legal protections. Although the 2010 FLSA addition to the ACA mandates lactation breaks, a larger number of women employees breastfeed their children in states with supplementary laws supportive of breastfeeding (such as states exempting mothers from jury duty, encouraging breastfeeding awareness campaigns, excluding breastfeeding women from indecent exposure charges, or enforcing workplace pumping laws). Thanks to Jaakola's findings, the enforcement of workplace pumping laws has increased the employee breastfeeding rate by 225 percent.

Duquesne Law professor Gabriela Steier wrote in the *Buffalo Journal of Gender, Law and Social Policy* (2013) that if workplaces do not accommodate breastfeeding mothers, workers often give up breastfeeding or give up the job. Take the case of the third-year Boston neurology resident who had access to only one room with a single chair and no screens or curtains— an accommodation that only one person could use at a time. Eventually the neurologist opted for formula feedings.

LACK OF FINANCIAL LITERACY

Although as many as 24 percent of American workers (including 60 percent of Millennials earning $100,000 or more a year) say they experience stress at their job due to personal financial issues (according to a 2014 Price Waterhouse Coopers survey), only 36 percent of workers say their employers offer financial wellness programs. In fact, half of all respondents reported using work time to review financial statements or pay bills, reports Lockton Retirement Services.

Women, in particular, have been shortchanged, according to the nonprofit National Institute on Retirement Security. Instead of women relying primarily on technology, such as online retirement planners and "robo-advisors," the Financial Finesse study suggests closing the financial gender gap with person-to-person coaching. The gender gap is especially significant in areas like debt and managing competing financial priorities, says Liz Davidson, CEO of Financial Finesse, an education provider.[2] For instance in response to the statement "I have a general knowledge of stocks, bonds, and mutual funds," 78 percent of men responded affirmatively compared to only 60 percent of women. Women also lag behind men in terms of saving and planning for retirement, partly because women's higher rates of part-time employment and shorter job tenure make it harder for them to meet employers' eligibility requirements for retirement plans. Also, because women statistically tend to live longer than men, their retirement nest egg should ideally be bigger, but according to data from investment firm Vanguard, in 2014 the median amount in 401(k)s and similar retirement plans was $36,875 for men and $24,446 for women.

Other contributing obstacles to women's retirement programs include lower pay and more time out of the workforce for parenting or care giving as well as the need for more individual counseling. Less-educated women or those who earned incomes below $50,000 felt more financially stressed and worried about their futures to the detriment of their work productivity.

Another controversial area is the generational imbalance. According to *Employee Benefit News* (June 2016), despite the high levels of education and income of Millennials, these employees tend to have low levels of financial literacy and could conceivably outlive their retirement savings. Some employers are taking personalized approaches—providing education in languages other than English and basing it on age or income—but still some employees are falling through the cracks and not receiving the education they need.

A third area of money conflict deals with providing more financial information than just data on retirement plans. *Benefit News* recommends employers provide educational programs that advise on immediate and long-term issues, such as developing and initiating savings plans early in life as well as balancing your credit and debt wisely and managing health care costs with health savings accounts. Because just 10 percent of Americans have discussed health care with a financial adviser, experts believe linking HSA savings with 401(k) retirement planning would simplify the dilemma of how much to save for health costs, which probably is the employees' most valued and coveted benefit.

HEALTH CARE PROGRAMS: COST EFFICIENCY AND ACCESSIBILITY

The most popular EAPs are health and wellness programs due to rising health-care costs and obesity rates. In 2016, according to the Congressional Budget Office, most Americans ages 18 to 65 got their health insurance from their employer due to $266 billion in tax breaks from the federal government. The problem for employees is that employers are forcing them to assume a larger share of the costs through co-insurance and high deductible plans.

In 2015, out-of-pocket costs rose to $3,470 and the average deductible was $1,279, according to *Employee Benefit News* (July 2016).

Wellness programs include health screenings and bonuses or other rewards for health program completions and are more popular with employees than managers, probably because non-HR managers are focused on the bottom line or ROI, so they tend to think the population is healthier than HR departments do. According to Optum's seventh workplace study on wellness budgets, 17 percent of HR (versus 30 percent of business leaders) think employee well-being is good. Also, 41 percent of HR executives (versus 32 percent of business leaders) say wellness solutions are important.

Another controversy surrounding wellness programs is whether or not they succeed in keeping down health care costs. According to "Is Your Onsite Clinic Delivering Value?" in *Employee Benefits News* (January 13, 2016), no one really knows if health care programs and initiatives actually keep people out of the hospitals. Optimists say the wellness industry is in its beginning stages and will continue to improve, but statistics from the Centers for Disease Control and Prevention (CDC) and HealthMine seem to contradict the health gains that HR leaders tout. *Benefit News* also seems to doubt if wellness programs are living up to their expectations, noting that critics say Americans are not getting any healthier or smarter about their health. Total health costs have soared to $2.2 trillion, which includes lost productivity, chronic disease, work-related injuries and illnesses, and work-related stress, according to Global Wellness Institute.[3]

The participation rate is also at issue. Some experts say greater participation in wellness programs depends on individualizing communication techniques, such as using paycheck stuffers (instead of sending e-mails to warehouse employees) and using creative incentives such as hanging posters in elevator lobbies or writing blogs and social media posts.

Another equally controversial problem is employers dealing with the extreme costs of specialty drugs—for example, Hepatitis C drugs Sovaldi and Harvoni. At 84 Lumber Co. in Pennsylvania, specialty drug spending rose to $159,000 for one employee, said Mark Mollico, company president.[4] As more people (primarily Boomers) get tested for Hepatitis C, companies worry over increasing demands for treatment and spiraling costs.

Because expensive pharmaceuticals account for more than 9 percent of an employer's overall health cost, almost 46 percent of employers are adopting a telehealth plan, says Jake Cleer, director for New Benefits.[5] Seventy percent are expected to adopt one by the end of 2016 and 90 percent by 2018. Rand Corporation confirms that telemedicine can save an employer about $117 every time a patient is redirected from a doctor's office or ER to a telehealth plan and, in certain organizations such as Jet Blue Airways and Palm Beach County School District, to worksite telehealth kiosks. Also, according to *Employer Benefit News* (March 2016), rising health care premiums have motivated employers to consider cost-saving solutions such as self-funding, captives, and PEOs.[6] *Employer Benefit News* (July 2016) says the majority of employers with 50 to 1,000 employees are missing out on opportunities to manage health costs more effectively due to pharmacy carve-outs (dispensing of specialty drugs through a pharmacy that specializes in that disease) and narrow network plans (that limit the doctors and hospitals their customers can use). Another cost brouhaha for employers is avoiding the Cadillac Tax of the ACA, which has been delayed until 2020.

Difficulty accessing the health care systems is another employee gripe as evidenced in a Harris Poll of 1,536 Americans. Andrea Davis, editor-in-chief of *Employee Benefits News*, says employees want one-on-one benefits support with a health care concierge who works with employees and health plans. Aflac, the largest provider of supplemental insurance in the United States, reports that 60 percent of employees do not feel that they understand their benefit options and that the cause is a lack of human communication.

FLEXIBILITY "UNFAIRNESS": THE BENEFIT NOT EVERYONE GETS

The most significant issue associated with flexibility is its unfair distribution. Flexible programs are not available to most of the workforce, a Boston College study of 545 U.S. employers reported. Furthermore, only one in five companies offers more than one approach to flexibility. In a 2014 SHRM survey, researchers found that companies offered flexible arrangements to less than half of their staff. Employers were most likely to say that only 1 percent to 25 percent of eligible workers used flextime. According to an article by Vickie Elmer in *SAGE Business Researcher*, blue-collar, retail, and service workers were among the employees usually excluded from flexibility options because their jobs required them to be physically present at the job site. Quantum Workplace reports that nearly 75 percent of U.S. employees want flexible work hours yet only 45 percent of employers offer them. Additional research by Censuswide says more than a third of British workers claim their companies do not offer flexible working arrangements despite law changes that allow everyone to request it.

A further controversial aspect of flexible scheduling is that it can raise the ire of co-workers who feel they must pick up the slack of telecommuters or colleagues who leave the office at 3 p.m. instead of the traditional 5 p.m. This perceived unfairness in allotting flexibility can breed backlash. One employee wrote to an *Inc.com* columnist that her colleague "Mary" worked only 60 percent, clocking in at 10 a.m. and leaving at 3 p.m. five days a week. The co-worker complained Mary did not answer e-mails or do online research after leaving the office and the colleague had to deal with Mary's clients, who phoned in after Mary clocked out. The co-worker also complained she worked through lunch and left by 8 p.m. at the earliest, which doubled her travel time.

Other non-flexibility workers do not gripe but miss the in-person interactions with colleagues and resent the increased e-mails. Non-users sometimes retaliate by ignoring e-communication from their remote-situated colleagues. And resentment can work the other way, too. One reduced-hour worker said she felt marginalized by her colleagues after the birth of her child; she disliked hearing comments about "leaving early." Virtual employees can also feel isolated when they do not feel they are part of the team. In one instance, according to Kossek, two employees in a job share arrangement ran into a conflict when they found out only one could be promoted. Kossek says the job share broke up; the individual without the promotion felt stigmatized and eventually left the company.

Face-Time Culture Breeds Lack of Trust

Another impediment and problem surrounding flextime is some companies cling to a high face-time culture due to lack of trust in their employees. Whether face time and flexibility are incompatible is the "Great Debate," say experts, because it comes down to trust. Managers' pressure for face time stems from the feeling that if I can't see you, then you're not working. Some telecommuters, a large part of them women, have even faked face time by leaving office lights on and coats on the backs of chairs. Despite these ploys, as well as getting digital assistance from e-mails, instant messaging, and voicemails, this brand of face time does not necessarily lead to top performance outcomes. "Ideal workers" may still be the prevailing model because studies confirm that managers and supervisors evaluate employees with more face time more positively than those on flextime or who work remotely.

In one firm studied by Ellen Kossek and colleagues, the IT workers were expected to attend virtual meetings overseas when they would normally be asleep and still clock in for work the next morning at the usual time. Face time's value in certain organizations can engender resentment among staff as well as confusion and mismanagement of flextime schedules. Employers need to trust their employees but also take advantage of new communication technologies like Skype in order to maintain camaraderie and culture. Bringing the team together once a month for coffee,

lunch, or brainstorming may allow remote workers to deal with any conflicts or glitches with their co-workers.

Face time is even a factor in the field of sports. In a 2015 dissertation on
male coaches, Jeffrey Alexander Graham at the University of Texas, Austin, learned that coaches were expected to be visibly working in their offices,
especially at odd hours. To management, that proved these coaches were
willing to sacrifice for a winning program. However, the many hours and
large amounts of face time severely restricted the WLB of coaches. Fathers,
in particular, faced increased stress and levels of work–family conflict.

"Gatekeepers of Flexibility" Barter with Bias

Another unfairness in flextime relates to reduced-load work (RLW).
According to a 2015 article by Ellen Kossek and others in *Human Resource
Management*, interviews with 42 managers in 20 North American organizations suggest that managers are more likely to support RLW for employees whom they perceive as high performers. Managers retain reservations
about flexibility as some find it difficult to schedule meetings, meet performance objectives, and manage teams of virtual employees. In a summer 2015 article in *California Management Review*, Kossek identifies other
supervisory unfairness traps such as awarding flexibility only to employees with visible family and caretaking needs. These supervisors also tend
to shortchange employees on information as to how non-flexibility users
should work with flexibility users. Furthermore, managers sometimes exacerbate flexibility stigma by attributing employees' use of flexibility to low
job commitment and by showing a preference for physically supervising
employees' work and requiring face-to-face meetings. Unfortunately, says
Kossek in "Balanced Workplace Flexibility: Avoiding the Traps," some
managers also lack the leadership skills to motivate and supervise employees working away from the central site.

Corporate Costs: Do Benefits Hurt the Bottom Line?

Position 1: Perks Pay for Themselves in ROI

According to FindLaw, a free legal website, a good benefits packages
helps attract and retain talented employees, decreases absenteeism, and
improves employee health and morale, all of which save money. Businesses
also get the tax advantage of deducting their plan contributions (eligible
employers must have no more than 25 full-time employees and full-time-
equivalent employees). Fringe benefits, according to Rea & Associates,
also are tax exempt—for example, achievement awards, athletic facilities,

employee discounts, employer-provided cell phones, and meals on work premises.

Also, employees sometimes accept better benefits in lieu of higher salaries, and some business owners can then get their own personal benefits for less because they are purchasing for a large group. Some benefits can be low-cost or even free. In a study on tuition waivers by Deniz Gevrek (June 2015) at Texas A&M University–Corpus Christi, Gevrek found that offering dependent college tuition waivers is a relatively low-cost benefit if the intention is to retain employees and stimulate productivity. Another benefit, according to a Willis Towers Watson analysis, is to offer free telemedicine visits (approximately $45 each) because with no co-pay, utilization is higher for ailments such as bronchitis, colds, urinary tract infections, skin rashes, and allergic reactions. According to *Benefit News*, even if employers cover the full cost, they can save a lot of money—between $70 and $855 per visit—when compared to the ER or urgent care facilities. Besides, 67 percent of employers offer telemedicine currently and by 2018, 90 percent of employers are expected to commit. Apps are being developed for smart phones and other hand-held devices to help employees consult with doctors or have video chats. A telehealth app charges employers a per-employee-per-month fee, which can realize huge savings for employers, says Scott Sanford of HealthiestYou, a telehealth network of doctors.

Business owners must weigh these flextime benefit costs with high real estate costs for office space, the need for business-as-usual in nasty weather, corporate cutbacks, and demand for specialized professionals. Company overhead—in the form of real estate and utility fees—declines when workers no longer need space in corporate offices.

According to IBM, the company estimates it saves $200 million a year in U.S. and European office and real estate costs on top of the $1.9 billion the company makes from selling property by supporting the teleworking programs the company started twenty years ago. Flexibility also may build shareholder value on Wall Street; companies that made it onto *Fortune Magazine*'s "best places to work" list gained two to three times in value. According to Sarah Jane Glynn, a sociologist, and Heather Boushey, executive director and chief economist at the Washington Center for Equitable Growth Committee of the Whole, good benefits keep people on the job, and this saves firms money because businesses spend about one-fifth of a worker's salary to replace that worker (Testimony of Heather Boushey before Council of the District of Columbia, January 14, 2016). The typical cost of turnover for an employee salaried at $30,000 or less is about 16 percent.

One of the best and most attractive benefits—paid leave policies—has had either no effect or positive effects on corporate profitability or performance in California, say sociologist Ruth Milman and economist Eileen Appelbaum. Also, the National Institute of Health (NIH) recently stated that paid sick leave for cancer patients comforts them and doubles the likelihood they will retain their jobs, says Christine Veenstra, MD, of the University of Michigan Medical School. Job retention converts to saved dollars.

Another medical finding in *Injury Prevention* indicates that paid family leave might lead to reduced risk of abuse-related head injuries in children ages two and under. The CDC and the National Center for Injury Prevention and Control compared data from 1995 through 2011 in California (which introduced paid family leave in 2004) and found that seven states without such a policy (among them Arizona, Florida, and Massachusetts) saw increases in hospital admission rates between 2007 and 2009.

Procuring talent is another positive. Yeo & Yeo, an accounting and consulting firm with nine offices in Michigan, may not be small by non-industry standards, but it competes with larger accounting firms for talent by offering a 40-hour week, an overtime bonus (in money or time off), and a customized flexibility plan. The firm's turnover rate remains at about 7 percent annually compared with 25 percent for the overall accounting field.

Position 2: Costs Are Too High for the ROI

That being said, small businesses face a greater financial challenge paying for flextime and other perks than larger companies. The negatives to benefit packages must be weighed carefully. For one thing, the cost of health insurance has steadily risen, making it less affordable for employers and complicating financial planning. Prices are higher for small businesses due to less buying power and higher rates of administration, although some smaller businesses can purchase through trade associations, which are able to negotiate lower rates and improved coverage. On the other hand, Linda Keller, national operating officer for Hub International, says although self-funding health benefits was once uneconomical for smaller employers, today 100 percent of companies can self-fund and use narrow networks and derive savings. Small businesses also have less choice in designing retirement plans due to administrative costs—the more benefits a business offers, the more administrative costs it must bear.

Then, too, businesses lack research on how to reduce associated costs for supportive care giving policies. A significant number of employees are family care givers. Of those, one in four is a Millennial working about 35 hours per week. Future work is needed to test the ROI and arrive at a best practices approach (AARP and Respect a Caregiver's Time ReACT).

Furthermore, workplace flexibility adds costs, especially when the programs are new, says *SAGE Business Researcher*. Planning and execution can consume many staff hours as can management training. Mistakes can be costly too, such as the U.S. Patent and Trademark Office's fiasco when employees based in their homes lied about their hours and received bonuses for work they did not do.

The U.S. Bureau of Labor Statistics recently released a chart citing the high costs of employee compensation (September 2015) among employees in private industry and those in state and local government. The percentages of employer costs for benefits were 30.3 percent and 36.3, respectively. These percentages include benefits such as paid leave, health insurance, and retirement. Thomson Online Benefits states that some enterprises spend the equivalent of 30 percent of employees' salaries on benefits (2015 Global Employee Benefits Watch).

Small businesses and start-ups have the hardest challenge financing low-cost benefits. Chase Garbarino, CEO and co-founder of VENTUREAPP, said in *Business News Daily* (January 4, 2016) that small businesses may have to add better benefits as they grow, such as full health coverage. Garbarino advises considering cost-conscious options like work from home, dog-friendly days, and weekly learning sessions. A few companies offer unlimited vacation days, summer hours, workouts, ski breaks, or Friday afternoon bike rides. Evren Esen of SHRM says companies are putting a little more money into benefits and bonuses rather than salaries to attract talent without driving up fixed costs.

Furthermore, offering benefits creates concerns regarding legal compliance, which can lead to companies incurring legal fees; mistakes made in benefit plans can trigger costly lawsuits or regulatory fees.

SUMMARY

Experts claim perks attract and retain talented, engaged workers and serve as trade-offs on higher salaries. The jury may still be out on this issue, but WLB may have more to do with intangible benefits than people realize. Some potential solutions for improving WLB might be as cost-efficient and simple to execute as certain revisions to company culture and leadership and the willingness to change structural organization, as we will see in Chapter 10.

CHAPTER 10

Are There Better Solutions for a Better WLB?

For the past few decades controversy has raged over what is the "best" method to improve WLB. Everyone has a different and better solution. In this chapter we objectively examine organizational models, which fall into one of three categories: those that alter the structure or model of work; those that change the company or organizational culture; and those based on governmental legislation and proactive strategies.

Which model(s) do you think is/are best? As we have seen in past chapters, a one-size-fits-all philosophy does not define WLB, but is there a one-size-fits-all solution to your organizational complaints?

OCCUPATION-SPECIFIC STRUCTURAL MODELS

According to Joan Williams and others, new organizations are emerging in which WLB is integral to the business model. In Williams' "New Models of Legal Practice" (2015), she identifies more than 50 organizations with five new and distinct business models for practicing law in a more flexible way than the traditional model. For instance, she reports on 11 virtual law firms where attorneys work from their homes and earn as little or as much as they wish. Another model provides legal services in return for a monthly subscription fee.

Another special intervention is aimed at health care workers. CARE (an acronym for Compassion, Awareness, Resilient Responding, and Empowerment) focuses on nursing burnout (*Journal of Nursing Education and Practice*, 2015). Training programs and exercises target four major components: compassion for self and others; awareness of options, resources, external events, and inner experiences; resilience through supportive mentoring, positivity, emotional insight, and spirituality; and autonomy in shaping the work environment to reflect employees' personal values. The intervention requires five one-hour, face-to-face training sessions once a week with a facilitator who introduces each phase and helps nurses practice related exercises. This proposed model, or curriculum, is yet to be tested in the field, but it is hypothesized that nurses who complete this program would demonstrate reduced burnout scores. This study is in the planning stages for a future research project.

GENERAL MODELS ALTERING WORK STRUCTURE

Predictability, Teaming, and Open Communication (PTO)

The PTO model was first introduced in about 2005 as part of an experiment conducted by Leslie A. Perlow at BCG in Boston, where schedule predictability was a common problem. Many employees were so conflicted between flextime (and the price they paid with flexibility stigma) and the ideal-worker culture that they devoted extra time to the job, defeating the whole stress-relieving purpose of flextime.

Perlow proposed a work redesign in which team members took the same day off each week but met weekly to discuss their progress. This format succeeded so well that within four years, 2,000 teams sprang up in 66 BCG offices in 35 countries. To qualify as a PTO team, members had to set a collective goal to meet weekly with full participation to establish trust and openness. Supportive managers asserted authority, and PTO teams were encouraged to establish new ways of prioritizing work. As a result, team members gained confidence in their ability to promote change, manage complex projects, connect with colleagues and clients, and build the teamwork and leadership skills needed to advance. BCGers reported improvements in both personal satisfaction and project performance, including an average 35 percent increase in teamwork and collaboration, a 35 percent increase in value delivered to clients, and a 100 percent increase in team effectiveness. According to investorplace.com (March 2016), PTO has resulted in a 74 percent increase in retention rate among workers interested in remaining at BCG for the long term. Other perks include fully-paid sabbaticals, discounted gym memberships, and 100 percent compensation for health care costs. Japan's Bridge Group, an executive search company, also uses PTO.

Results Only Work Environment (ROWE)

ROWE is another innovative work design model. Initially supported by Best Buy's HR department as well as sociologists Phyllis Moen and Erin Kelly, ROWE functions at the departmental level so that teams report to the same director or senior manager. ROWE trades traditional work structures for employee strategies that prioritize WLB and allow employees to complete the work in any manner they choose. ROWE also emphasizes moving from a face-time, person-to-person interaction to an environment focused on work outcomes. Results have shown that ROWE reduces turnover, increases schedule control, and decreases work–family conflict as well as promotes health benefits such as sleep, exercise, and less drinking and smoking.

Although Best Buy acknowledged this success, the company dropped the model after a new CEO was appointed. Since 2008, however, ROWE has been used as a model in more than 30 organizations (see gorowe.com for examples such as Gap Corporate and Banana Republic). Implicit in ROWE's achievement is support from top management and senior leaders with confident leadership abilities. According to the aforementioned website, ROWE Certified Organizations balance freedom and responsibility, autonomy, and accountability with high levels of employee engagement, low attrition rates, increased efficiency, and reduction in real estate costs.

Support, Transform, Achieve, Results (STAR)

Sociologist Erin L. Kelly says the organizational model of STAR exemplifies how workplace restructuring can influence WLB. Her data is based on information technology employees in a Fortune 500 organization where the objective was to train workers to control work time and deprioritize face time.

Facilitators oriented managers to the project, and then reinforced that with computer-based training. Managers learned how work–family conflict impacts business outcomes and how managerial support for employees' personal and family life could benefit. According to researchers, who acknowledge the project improvements were "modest," STAR legitimized flextime by decreasing flexibility stigma and making it more routine and acceptable. It also minimized the "ideal worker" standard while helping employees to improve schedule control and family time and lessen family conflicts.

Boundary Management

According to Ellen Kossek at Purdue University (in her 2016 paper "Managing Work Life Boundaries in the Digital Age"), people can improve how they manage their work–life boundaries by interpreting and identifying their past actions. For instance, employees identified as "integrators" blend employment with personal commitments, consciously allowing work and personal activities to compete for time. They may return e-mails on vacations or at sports events or plan a barbecue while in the office. "Separators," however, are employees who compartmentalize work and personal tasks. They prefer to schedule personal appointments like a teacher conference at the start or end of the day or around a lunch hour. "Cyclers," says Kossek, are employees who combine integrating with separating. An example is the divorced parent who travels a lot and behaves like a separator on the road, but at home, catches up with his child and focuses on the family role as an integrator. Cyclers often have jobs with seasonal highs and lows such as accountants, teachers, or retailers.

Organizations structured to allow employees to pursue one of these three different roles usually flourish because workers are more engaged, says Kossek. (Workers with low boundary control due to flexibility stigma or "ideal worker" pressure usually are less engaged and deficient in WLB.) Finnish psychologists identified different boundary styles among their university staff and nurses. They discovered that worker-segmentors (separators) and those favoring family over work were less satisfied with their WLB than individuals who integrated work and family. According to psychologists, integrators experience lower work-to-family conflict and more enrichment than segmentors.

The model of maintaining different-style boundaries between home and work came to attention in a national U.K. study in which researcher Rowanne Fleck discovered that people who use multiple electronic communication devices, such as tablets and laptops, were more likely to use separate devices for home and work and fit into the category of "segmentors." The obvious inference from that study is that people dissatisfied with their WLB might want to purchase separate devices to help them better control their boundaries (CHI, April 16–23, 2015, publication rights licensed to ACM).

Another structural way to assist workers is categorizing styles as work-centric, family-centric, dual-centric, or non-work-centric (person identifies highly with a hobby or nonprofit rather than a job or family). Experts claim that people need to understand their predilections because they reap most of their life validation from excelling in whatever role suits their style. So are you work-centric or family-centric?

Managers can help support these different boundary styles using structural aids such as the creation of a results-oriented work environment (ROWE), a menu of flexible work options, and the provision of social support. Leaders who see diverse work styles as necessary structural elements rather than as mere accommodations can help create healthy WLBs.

COMPANY CULTURE SOLUTIONS

According to psychologist-author Daniel Goleman, some researchers think emotional intelligence (EI) is more important than technical expertise because it incorporates insight and management skills to balance emotion and reason and may maximize happiness or WLB. EI falls into five categories: 1) the self awareness of drives, emotions, and moods and their effects on others; 2) the self regulation (or ability to control or suspend judgment of negative moods or impulses before acting); 3) the motivation (or passion to work for more than money or status); 4) the empathy (or ability to understand the emotions of others and react appropriately to others' emotional responses); and 5) the social skills (or expertise to manage relationships, build networks, find common ground, and create rapport. Some emotionally intelligent individuals may exude self-confidence, ease with ambiguity, optimism in the face of failure, cross-cultural sensitivity, and effective leadership—all highly powerful organizational tools.

According to HR Director Syed J. Hyder (*International Journal of Advanced Research in Management and Social Sciences,* January 2016), his findings suggest that high EI individuals cope better with work stress than those with low EI. High EIs excel at recognizing their own emotions and those of their colleagues, which leads to greater job satisfaction and productivity. Hyder says managers especially need to develop EI to supervise subordinates. In another article in the same journal, Parul Deshwal, assistant professor at Maharaja Surajmal Institute in New Delhi, India, calls EI essential for optimum organizational performance and says EI programs can be introduced at any time because EI improves with age, education, and experience. Furthermore, in *The IUP Journal of Organizational Behavior* (April 2015), Monoshree Mahanta at Gauhati University evaluated the WLB of employees of high, moderate, and low EI and concluded that those with high EIs appear to have better WLBs then those with low EIs.

Organizational cultures deficient in EI among executives might be unable to maximize employee productivity and thus WLB, says R. Sadia at Shenkar College of Engineering and Design, Israel. Sadia believes interactions between employee health and a quality culture yield more productivity. Three important benefits stem from creating an EI team-oriented culture, says psychologist Daniel Goleman. First, honest, open evaluations of the behavioral and emotional aspects of the culture lead to healthier employee relationships; second, head managers who model EI behaviors encourage employees to adopt these habits and develop more respect toward their co-workers; and third, employees take more risks in creativity when head managers demonstrate integrity. Integrity in managers is considered the building block of trust and triggers the capacity and willingness to understand co-workers, says Svetlana Lazovic of the International School for Social and Business Studies in Slovenia ("Management, Knowledge and Learning International Conference 2012"). She says managers should use EI to become "synergistic" leaders. Upon interviewing 10 key managers from different organizations, she found that employee trust in a manager's leadership induced employees to acquire new knowledge and professional development and share that knowledge with others. Lazovic also said that managers with low esteem and confidence should not accumulate vital knowledge because they cannot transmit it beneficially to promote a healthy work culture. Upper and lower managers with communication or information gaps decrease productivity, says Madiha Sahdat at the University Islamabad, Pakistan (in a 2011 paper in *World Applied Sciences Journal*), but managers with healthy EIs and good relationships with their subordinates can become company standouts.

That is why most successful business executives have high EI levels, according to global speaker Bryan Kramer's blog *Human Conversations*.[1] The Carnegie Institute of Technology also agrees, averring that financial success is linked to good communication, negotiation, and leadership. Practically speaking, this translates to allowing managers to lead by example; treating the public fairly by listening and extending kindness; accepting diverse opinions and accountability; and encouraging employees to envision how professional success can enhance their family life and provide a good WLB.

Jim Knight, who spent years training at Hard Rock Café and authored *Culture That Rocks* (Knight Speaker, 2014), says leaders are starting to understand that culture is the most important element in WLB and organizational productivity. For instance, Chili's Grill & Bar's culture focuses on promoting WLB through financial, social, career, community, and physical elements. Company leaders hold field town halls weekly and Chili's sends messages to its 50,000 team members through its digital HotSchedules platform as well as through employee surveys. Their goal is to connect with team members so that despite the immense size of the company, each employee feels special and is known by his or her colleagues.

EI is considered a proactive strategy due to its self-initiated, change-inducing, and feedback-seeking behaviors that can benefit individuals, teams, and organizations, according to Wu Liu at the Hong Kong Polytechnic

University.[2] EI may spread due to the increasing number of relationship-oriented Millennial managers, wrote Lisa Evans in *Fast Company Magazine.* Chip Espinoza, author of *Millennials Who Manage Companies* (Pearson FT Press, 2015), agrees and emphasizes that EI helps people to nurture relationships.

For example, in a 2015 study of computer employees (*International Journal of Computer Applications*), the results showed that employees who recognize their own emotions manage their work more efficiently, thus navigating the boundaries between work and home more easily. Although hard data on EI's effect on WLB is scanty, a 2010 study of Nigerian policemen in the *Journal of Social Sciences* shows a positive correlation between EI and job satisfaction. Teacher education also documents this. When Loughborough University, U.K., teacher trainees were observed on their degree of self-awareness, experts found that WLB-focused trainees needed to reflect critically on their strengths, core values, and performances. They also needed to organize their time and create proactive strategies to solve problems and conflicts.

Proactive Strategies to Alter Culture

Resilience Training

Another proactive strategy is resilience training to reinforce hardiness, emotional insight, and optimism. For example, in an Australian study of nurses and midwives (*Journal of Nursing Management*, 2015), resilience training helped them improve their ability to cope with adversity. However researchers found much of the credit was due to support networks, mentoring, and the person's sense of autonomy and control of responsibilities. Another innovative resilience program at Wellesley College in Massachusetts substituted a digital coach called meQuilibrium for telephoning a counselor. Employees like Marmee Saltalamacchia got emotional support from meQuilibrium through a smart phone or computer that provided a mix of self-help, therapy, and positive affirmations. Employees showed a 15 percent overall decrease in anxiety along with greater resilience. Another proactive engagement strategy that works is expressing gratitude. Recognition can be as simple and effective as a thank-you note or e-mail because it builds resilience.

Professor Fred Luthans, editor of the *Journal of Leadership and Organization Studies,* has applied positive psychology to the workplace, examining how human strengths and psychological capacities can be measured, developed, and effectively managed for performance improvement in today's workplace. He says four characteristics are most important: self-efficacy or the confidence to take on challenges; optimism or maintaining the expectation of success now and in the future; hope or persevering and redirecting efforts in order to succeed; and resilience or bouncing back from adversity.

Trust Nurturance

Nothing tests the bonds of trust more between managers and employees than telecommuting, according to Courtney Brown and others in their 2016 report "Trusting Telework in the Federal Government" (*The Qualitative Report*). Brown says lack of trust in employees is why Yahoo CEO Melissa Mayer ultimately decided to ban telework. The federal government's slow adoption of telework is another example of failed trust—all because managers lack confidence in "invisible" workers (employees working at home or at another venue). A 2009 Bureau of Labor Statistics (BLS) study showed trust plays a factor in implementing or approving telework and that high-performing employees are more apt to win approval for telework than those perceived as lazy. Also, a Canadian study concluded that managers dislike telework due to the supervisory need for good communication, balance between employee autonomy and managerial micromanaging, and the demand for trust.

Results from 409 employee questionnaires revealed that trust is the most important factor in instilling a sense of leadership, say Gus Gordon and colleagues at the University of Texas at Tyler.[3]

Managers and leaders develop trust in employees when they act in ways that build respect and confidence, communicate clearly, understand the importance of personal commitments, share common values with employees, and encourage growth and development. For these managers, WLB is not a duty but a means toward productivity.

Marisa Stoltzfus, a talent development partner with Great Place to Work, endorses trust as a two-way street attained via transparency, and Blake Irving, CEO of GoDaddy, says transparency allows employees to feel confident in their aims so they can forge ahead and meet their goals.[4] Irving says promoting face time with leaders and pairing that with the use of employee engagement surveys promotes transparency.

Employers should stop worrying whether remote workers are being productive, says Dora Wang, managing editor of the TINYpulse Institute. A poll the Institute took of 509 employees who work remotely 100 percent of the time revealed that 91 percent of the workers are more productive due to this nontraditional work arrangement.

Cooperative Engagement Alters Culture

According to Quantum Workplace, employee engagement is not just any one department's responsibility. Top-level leaders need to set the tone and walk the walk, listing attainable goals and updating them frequently. HR also needs to pitch in by ensuring the smoothness of everyday happenings and managing the organization's employee engagement initiative. Research shows that when HR treats employee engagement with transparent accountability and as a year-long initiative—instead of as a short-term project or another item on the agenda—employees are more likely to be engaged.

Futhermore for engagement to succeed, team managers must function as liaisons between employees and leaders, acting as both the voice and representative of employee concerns and suggestions. Employees also must supply honest insights to improve the work experience and participate in focus groups to brainstorm new, creative solutions. Employees will self-engage when they trust they are being heard.

Governmental Interventions to Alter WLB

Current WLB Laws

Globally, work–life balance laws differ dramatically. In European Union countries, for example, WLB programs stem from state legislation and corporate social responsibilities. In the United States, flextime and EAPs are the primary means to retain talented employees; federal mandates play a meager role. In a 2016 paper in the *Handbook on Well-Being of Working Women*, the authors discuss how the U.S. government might accelerate WLB by enacting laws common in other industrialized countries—for example, paid sick and parental leave, protected leave, and universal access to affordable child care.

Currently only 12 percent of U.S. private sector workers have access to paid family leave, and just two in five U.S. companies—about 15 percent of midsize to large employers—offer paid maternity or family leave. Access to paid leave is most available to high-income employees in managerial or professional roles at companies with 100 employees or more. Furthermore, according to the U.S. Department of Labor, only 59 percent of Americans are currently covered by the FMLA law (unpaid leave from organizations with 50-plus employees).

In the *Handbook on Well-Being of Working Women*, Laura Sabattini and Faye J. Crosby conclude that the beginnings of real progress in WLB took place when California in 2002 became the first state to pass a paid family leave act to allow employees to take six weeks leave up to 55 percent of their weekly wages. Rhode Island and New Jersey passed their own family paid leave laws.[5] In July 2014, the EEOC also weighed in on the leave issue, mandating that any parental leave provided by businesses must apply equally to men and women. Furthermore, a handful of states have increased the length of time fathers may stay home and collect paychecks. California established an insurance fund in 2004 to provide paid caregiver leaves, and since then, the number of men taking leaves increased more than 400 percent; by 2012–13, men accounted for 30.2 percent of paid parental leaves. Another advance came in 2016 when New York City Mayor Bill de Blasio signed an executive order that gave 20,000 city employees six weeks of paid leave after the birth or adoption of a child. New York Governor Andrew Cuomo passed a similar statewide law in April 2016.

Also, in February 2016 the Department of Defense (DoD) backed better WLB for service men and women by increasing paid maternity leave to 12 continuous weeks; paternity leave expanded from 10 to 14 nonconsecutive days; and DoD child development center hours remain open for a 14-hour minimum. Additionally, military bases where 50 or more women are regularly assigned are committing to installing or modifying mothers' rooms to assist with breastfeeding. Service members also can delay moves to different duty stations if family members feel it is in the family's best interests; adoption leave will be expanded for dual military couples; and the DoD will cover the cost for active-duty members to freeze sperm or eggs.

Shift scheduling has also come under the microscope because last-minute shuffling makes it difficult for working parents or others who juggle multiple roles, such as caring for children, holding jobs, or going to school. Workers in San Francisco and Vermont now have the legal right to predictable shift hours.

An emerging area in flextime is the assurance that these opportunities should not harm workers, deprive them of pay, or subject them to any retaliation. San Francisco and Vermont have mandated such "right to request" laws, and more are being considered elsewhere.

Also, the U.S. Labor Department has actively prosecuted companies that "misclassify" workers as exempt from overtime or misidentify them as independent contractors instead of employees; class-action lawsuits have increased over the past seven years, and the department has collected millions of dollars in back pay for workers at banks and utility companies. Clothing maker Levi Strauss was targeted because the company required assistant managers to attend off-the-clock meetings during staff shortages.

Overtime rules have recently been redefined, entitling an additional 13.5 million workers to additional pay under the Fair Labor Standards Act. The EPI reports that slightly more than half of those workers are women, and a disproportionate share are African Americans and Hispanics.

The Associated Press reported in May 2016 that "living wage" laws are tough to enforce—this includes minimum wages, back wages, and overtime—but the newer amendments will strengthen governmental clout by doubling the threshold of salaried workers to $47,476, guaranteeing overtime rights for workers earning less than that. Labor advocates say that one in four businesses nationwide cheats workers out of minimum wages. Haeyoung Yoon of the National Employment Law Project says the violations are "rampant."[6] Although many businesses were not aware of the mistakes, others were taking advantage of employees, many of them immigrants. The new rules go into effect on December 1, 2016, but many businesses say there will be negative consequences such as salaried workers transitioned to hourly wages, which means they might lose certain benefits and prestige.

WLB Legislative Recommendations

More legislation is warranted, says Purdue's Ellen Kossek and others. Whether paid family leave becomes the nation's law depends on pressure from employees, the state of the economy, local and regional agencies, and the political climate. Some states seem to be more progressive than others. For instance, California's Fair Pay law took effect January 1, 2016, to close the gap in wages between women and men.

Experts also recommend changing federal social security policies to award credits to women caregivers who receive either no pay or low pay. One indicator that the wage issue is approaching critical mass is the nation's growing armies of contingent workers, such as Uber drivers, who are debating the formation of unions. Adjunct faculty also are pressing for pay hikes, as are warehouse workers. Workers are starting to claim a larger share of the profits that their labor generates, says Sarah Leberstein, attorney for the National Employment Law Project. According to Susan Houseman, economist for the Upjohn Institute, employers may start having trouble finding workers at the current wages. Moreover, in September 2017, the EEOC will require businesses with more than 100 workers to furnish more information on pay practices regarding gender, race, and ethnicity.

Because employee needs and the organizational structures of companies vary tremendously, not every "fix" is appropriate, but the first step toward WLB improvement is considering all the available options.

Summary

The models and modalities covered here for improving WLB may not furnish all the answers, but in closer analysis, each approach emphasizes five aspects: control, support, flexibility, leadership, and intelligent boundaries. Focusing on these common points might help employees, employers, public officials, and HR departments strategize innovative structural and culture redesigns. A holistic approach may yield the best results, changing structures of organizations while utilizing proactive strategies such as trust, emotional intelligence, and resilience that can change organizational cultures and reduce work–life stress, especially if employees have the option to join companies whose values are congruent with their own. Workers may ultimately need increased government legislation as legal support, but they also need to reassess and reshuffle their commitments and priorities to work and family as they age and their circumstances change. By constantly redefining boundaries as different challenges appear, workers can orchestrate a WLB that satisfies their personal needs while making them productive, appreciated employees.

SECTION III

Resources

Primary Documents

Jonathan Foley: Testimony before Congress on ROWE and Other Work–Life Balance Programs (2010)

As Senior Adviser to the U.S. Office of Personnel Management (OPM), Jonathan Foley addressed a federal subcommittee on May 4, 2010, regarding ROWE (see Chapter 10 for more) and other flexible programs. ROWE is an acronym for a Results Only Work Environment pilot program of nearly 400 OPM (Office of Personnel Management) employees carried out in Washington, DC, and Boyers, PA. Telework (especially implemented in emergency situations) and campus wellness pilot programs (similar to those addressed in Chapter 4) are other WLB programs for federal workers. Foley explained that Deloitte will assess the ROWE project as it did for the Campus Wellness Pilot Project, which referred employees to on-site programs such as stress management and smoking cessation. One OPM goal was to establish wellness programs by helping agency work–life coordinators to promote wider use of on-site programs. For example, OPM launched the Feds Get Fit program in 2009 to highlight the importance of physical activity, nutrition, healthy choices, and prevention.

Good afternoon Chairman Akaka, Ranking Member Voinovich, and distinguished members of the Subcommittee.

I am pleased to be here today on behalf of John Berry, Director of the Office of Personnel Management (OPM), to discuss the work we have been doing at OPM in the areas of work-life balance and wellness for attracting, retaining and empowering a 21st-century Federal workforce.

I commend the Subcommittee for your leadership in supporting and honoring the important work of our nation's public servants by holding this timely hearing during our annual Public Service Recognition Week. This year's theme, "Innovation and Opportunity," gives OPM the opportunity to highlight our new Results Only Work Environment (ROWE) and campus wellness pilot programs.

We all understand that work is a fact of life. For most of us, this will never change. What is changing, however, is the **way** we work—i.e., **when, where, and how** we work. Technology has provided us with options we never imagined 20 years ago. Who would have ever guessed that you could carry with you everything you need for your job in a piece of equipment the size of a small notepad?

Not only is it easier for us to do our work almost anywhere, it is easier for us to do our work any time. This means that we can schedule our work around responsibilities and events that in the past would have required us to take time off from work. The Federal government offers a variety of flexible work arrangements that, when fully integrated into the day-to-day way of doing business, allow employees to continue making productive contributions to the workforce while also attending to family, pursuing higher education, and taking care of other responsibilities. These flexibilities include alternative work schedules (AWS), part-time schedules, and job sharing. As part of the ROWE program, OPM is reviewing its current regulations and guidance on AWS to provide maximum flexibility to Federal agencies to assist them in implementing these flexible arrangements. The availability of these flexible work options makes the Federal government a key player in a competitive market looking to attract and retain the best and the brightest employees, a win–win situation for the American taxpayers.

Telework

Telework is one of the many flexibilities offered by the Federal government. We know that telework is vital for the recruitment and retention of Federal employees. We are aware that it mitigates environmental damage from commuter traffic and it can help employees balance work and other life responsibilities. Unless telework is viewed as a good business practice by incorporating it as an integral part of doing business in the Federal government, we will continue to ignore an important tool. If implemented effectively government-wide, telework can make the difference between shutting down Federal government services in emergency situations and continuing to operate with minimal interruption. Telework enables agencies and businesses to continue services and operations without jeopardizing the safety of its employees.

For example, while Federal offices in the Washington metro area were closed during this past February's storms, we believe that at least 30 percent of Federal employees worked during the snow days, mostly from outside the office. During the snow event, 30 percent of OPM and General Services Administration (GSA) employees logged on to their respective networks. OPM's request for information on remote access during the February storms to the Chief Information Officers of executive branch agencies revealed similar employee logon rates. In addition, OPM's data analysis team estimated that the Federal government offset approximately $30 million per day in lost productivity during the February storms as a result of telework.

These past winter storms have demonstrated not only the need for teleworking, but also the incredible potential of telework to support the Federal government's operations. Therefore, I want to take this opportunity to reaffirm Director Berry's commitment to advancing telework in the Federal government. OPM has set a strategic goal of increasing the number of eligible Federal employees who telework by 50 percent by fiscal year 2011. To meet this goal, we continue to work on the telework initiative Director Berry introduced on Capitol Hill last year. Although we recognize that we have many obstacles to overcome, we are optimistic that given the right support and resources, teleworking will become a commonplace practice in the Federal government. The results from the 2008 government-wide, annual call for telework data showed that 49 percent of agencies reported that management resistance remains a major barrier to telework. In addition, 32 percent reported that information technology (IT) security and IT funding are each significant barriers to the use of telework.

With the importance of overcoming these barriers in mind, OPM, in partnership with GSA and the U.S. Patent and Trademark Office, held a Federal Telework Leadership Thought Forum on March 10. This forum was sponsored by an interagency White House Task Force on Telework of which Director Berry is the chair. This task force is analyzing barriers to the adoption and promotion of telework programs in the Federal sector. The Forum had more than 60 participants government-wide, which included representatives from labor. It was designed to solicit from the participants solutions to agency barriers frequently identified in research and practice. Results will be used to guide and model effective telework strategies government-wide.

We believe that we can move telework to where we never again need to close the Federal government for an emergency. By creating a mobile workforce, employees will always be able to work no matter where they are located. With the proper training, equipment, and the right emergency planning, we need only to declare a mobile workday and the Federal government will be able to seamlessly conduct business as usual.

Workforce Flexibility Initiative Pilot Program

As part of our mission to be a model employer for the 21st century, on March 31st, Director Berry announced OPM's new ROWE pilot program, the "Workforce Flexibility Initiative," that will go beyond existing telework and workplace flexibility programs. We hope that it will be successful and serve as a model for the rest of the Federal government. I am pleased to give you more details today on this new initiative.

OPM has hired two groups of contractors to implement and independently evaluate the pilot project. ICF International will lead the project implementation, and they have subcontracted with CultureRx, a company founded by Cali Ressler and Jody Thompson, co-creators of the ROWE and authors of the book, *Why Work Sucks and How to Fix It*. This is the first attempt to implement a version of ROWE in the Federal government, although a successful project is underway with more than 2,000 participating employees at a county agency in Hennepin County, Minnesota.

Nearly 400 OPM employees ranging from retirement and benefits claims processors to policy makers, including union and non-union employees, are in the pilot and were selected to represent the whole spectrum of positions available in the Federal government. Approximately half of the participating employees are based in Boyers, Pennsylvania, and the other half are based in Washington, DC. OPM components involved include Retirement and Benefits, HR Solutions, Communications, and the Director's Office.

In general, ROWE allows employees to work whenever they want and wherever they want, as long as the work gets done. Managers are expected to manage for results rather than process. Employees are trusted to get the work done. This is a shift in culture from permission granting (e.g., granting leave, permission to telework, etc.) to performance guiding.

A major principle of the project is that all employees in a participating group are included in the pilot without exception. ROWE is not a perk given to some employees and not to others. It is a management strategy that is applied to all members of a coherent work team. Employees who must be physically present to do their jobs now must be physically present when working in ROWE. Remember the guiding principle: "as long as the work gets done."

Implementing ROWE is more challenging in the Federal government than in a private corporation because of the restrictions that Federal law places on some aspects of the workplace flexibilities that are usually implemented under ROWE. ICF and CultureRx will work with OPM management and our unions to implement a version of the Results Only Work Environment that is consistent with all current Federal laws. Any changes to existing practices will be agreed upon by labor and management representatives, and the design of the program will be reviewed by OPM's General Counsel to ensure its consistency with Federal law.

This pilot program will be implemented in various phases consisting of assessment in April, education in May, commencement of the pilot in June (lasting through the end of the year), and beginning of evaluation in July with final evaluation in February 2011.

Assessment in April

During this month of April, the contractors have been visible in the pilot areas in both Washington, DC, and Boyers, PA. ICF and CultureRX are assessing the current work climate and attitudes toward work in the participating offices. This involves surveys, focus groups, and job shadowing.

Education in May

In May and June, ICF and CultureRX will work with OPM labor and management to shift our culture toward the general principles of ROWE. There will be much more information developed as the pilot project progresses, including a password-protected website for participating employees and managers, as well as a general webpage for all OPM employees and the general public.

Start of Pilot in June

The shift to ROWE really begins in the summer in June and it will continue through the end of the year. The heart of the training is aimed at equipping employees and managers to change how they spend their time and how they communicate with one another to produce results.

Evaluation by Deloitte

The project will be independently evaluated by Deloitte, who will assess the project on the basis of its effect on employee performance and morale. Currently, Deloitte is studying available data and using surveys and focus groups to establish a baseline for employee performance and morale among the participating offices. The metrics used to determine those elements will not change throughout the pilot project. Their evaluation will help OPM determine how performance metrics could be improved.

Deloitte will begin assessing the effect of the pilot in late July and will periodically evaluate its effects. A final report is expected in February 2011.

The evaluation will include recommendations for making ROWE more effective in the Federal sector, including potential changes to laws and regulations and improvements to internal policies, training and IT infrastructure.

If the pilot project increases employee performance and morale, as we hope, OPM will expand it within our own agency and encourage Federal agencies to adopt this system across the government.

Wellness

OPM has recognized that worksite wellness programs are also another way of attracting and retaining a strong Federal workforce. As you know, on May 12, 2009, President Obama met with CEOs from several major corporations to discuss their initiatives to improve employee health and reduce health care costs through worksite wellness and other initiatives. Following this meeting, he requested that OPM, the Office of Management and Budget (OMB), the National Economic Council, and the Department of Health and Human Services (HHS) explore the development of similar programs for the Federal workforce.

Campus Wellness Pilot Project

As a result, in the summer of 2009, OPM, GSA, and the Department of Interior (Interior) agreed to operate as a combined "campus" with respect to several work–life initiatives, including a comprehensive health and wellness program, at their downtown Washington headquarter locations. OPM received funding within its FY 2010 appropriation to implement this health and wellness prototype and was authorized to spend these funds on behalf of GSA and Interior employees for the purposes of this demonstration. The President's FY 2011 budget includes a $10 million appropriation request at HHS for continuation of the GSA/OPM/Interior campus program, the funding of two additional prototypes, and a rigorous evaluation of all three prototypes. This evaluation will be used to determine if the prototypes represent a viable approach for the government as a whole.

In advance of the implementation of the prototype, the OPM/GSA/Interior campus currently offers limited on-site health and wellness services, including urgent care, routine blood pressure checks, allergy shots, immunizations and routine injections, employee assistance programs (mental health and other behavior-related counseling), walking clubs, and periodic health education lectures or web-based information exchanges. All three agencies have health units staffed by at least one nurse and a part-time doctor. GSA and Interior have fitness centers, while OPM is developing a fitness room for group classes.

The core difference between the current service level and the new prototype is that we will offer a comprehensive worksite wellness program that will track employee progress in a systematic way. Employees enrolled in the program will complete a health risk appraisal (HRA) in the form of a questionnaire that asks about health history, health-related behaviors (e.g., exercise), and current health status. Additionally, employees will be given certain biometric tests (e.g., cholesterol screening) to establish their baseline health status. Based on the results of the HRA and biometric testing, employees may be referred to individual health coaching and/or specific on-site programs such as smoking cessation, weight management, chronic disease management or stress management. Health coaches will work with employees to achieve individualized goals.

Results from the annual HRA and biometric testing will be reported to employees to measure their individual progress and will be reported on an aggregate, non-identifiable basis to the agencies to measure collective progress.

Participation in the program is voluntary. Employees who participate in the program will be eligible for certain non-monetary incentives such as free or discounted fitness center memberships. The worksite program does not replace the employee's primary care provider or the benefits they receive through the Federal Employees Health Benefits (FEHB) Program. Rather, we expect that the worksite service provider will coordinate with the employee's primary care provider and FEHB plan to optimize use of resources.

We are currently using a competitive procurement process to select a service provider to provide the comprehensive service package. We expect the service provider to begin providing services before the end of May.

We are working with HHS to identify and fund two additional worksite wellness demonstration projects on Federal campuses. These sites will be outside the Washington, DC, area.

Studies in the private sector have yielded promising, though inconclusive results regarding the positive health and fiscal outcomes of these types of programs. For example, in a February 2010 Health Affairs article, researchers from Harvard School of Public Health and Harvard Medical School found that "medical costs fall by about $3.27 for every dollar spent on wellness programs and that absentee-ism costs fall by about $2.73 for every dollar spent." However, most programs have been implemented selectively, so further research is needed to determine the poten-tial effects of large-scale adoption.

This demonstration represents the first study of its kind for the Federal govern-ment with its unique employment landscape. As a result, we recognize the impor-tance of a valid and robust evaluation, and are contracting with an external evaluator to measure our progress according to the metrics described previously. The evalu-ation design will include interim reports that will enable us to receive ongoing feedback.

Savings from worksite health promotion programs generally become apparent within three to five years of the investment. However, for some programs, such as those aimed at better management of diabetes or other chronic diseases, the payoff[1] can occur in less than three years; on the other hand, the results from better nutrition intake for people without serious health problems may take longer to show a benefit.

OPM's Government-Wide Wellness Initiatives

OPM is also getting the message out to Federal agencies and employees about health and wellness activities and programs. OPM's health and wellness promo-tion activities include requiring agencies to establish and implement a comprehen-sive health and wellness program, providing agency guidance, offering training opportunities for agency work–life coordinators, keeping communications lines open with agency coordinators, and coordinating governmentwide health and well-ness activities in conjunction with other Federal partners.

OPM has set a high priority goal of requiring all executive agencies to estab-lish and implement a plan for a comprehensive health and wellness program that will achieve a 75 percent participation rate by the end of FY 2011. OPM will pro-vide agencies guidance on the definition of a comprehensive health and wellness program and other resources to aid with the development of their plans.

OPM provides guidance through one-on-one consultation with agencies on pro-gram development and improvement and through information posted in the Health and Wellness section of our website. OPM works closely with agency work–life coordinators to improve the quality of worksite wellness programs and pro-mote their wider use by employees. OPM offers training opportunities to agency coordinators. They include:

- The Cooper Institute for Aerobics Research Health Promotion Director Training and Certification course for select agency coordinators. Successful completion of this course results in a nationally recognized credential (Cer-tified Health Promotion Director). Twenty-eight Federal agency coordina-tors successfully completed this course.
- The Business Case for Breastfeeding training for workplace staff. This train-ing includes the elements of a good lactation support program at a work-place. Training was completed by 35 Federal agency staff.

- HealthyPeople (HP) 2010/2020 training. This training provided an overview of the Elements of a Comprehensive Worksite Wellness Program. Training was provided to 40 attendees through OPM's fall training for Federal Benefits Officers.
- Wellness as part of the entire workplace work–life portfolio. This is one of four courses toward professional work–life credentialing. Twenty Federal agency staff attended.
- Employee Assistance Program (EAP) administrator training developed in collaboration with HHS. This training provides an overview of effective EAP programs. EAP administrators from 60 Federal agencies have completed this training.
- HP 2010/2020 workshop in partnership with the OPM Benefits Officers Group and HHS. This training explains each of the elements of HP2010/2020 and gives practical implementation strategies for Federal workplaces. This training will be offered in May 2010.

We keep the communication lines open to agency coordinators via:

- E-mails with updates on government-wide initiatives, upcoming conferences and events in health, wellness, and EAP
- Agency "best practices" and unique programs
- A listserv that allows subscribers to share problem and solutions
- Regular meetings to share best practices, ideas, upcoming initiatives
- Expert speakers who present on a wide variety of health promotion topics

OPM also coordinates government-wide health and wellness activities such as physical activity challenges, tobacco cessation (which is currently underway), and Feds Get Fit. OPM launched Feds Get Fit in October 2009 with a walk around the National Mall led by OPM Director John Berry and involving employees from a dozen or more agencies. The Feds Get Fit wellness campaign is intended to raise employee awareness about wellness through fun and interactive events. In March and April, Feds Get Fit sponsored a recipe challenge where more than 500 Federal employees from across the country submitted healthy recipes. A celebrity panel awarded prizes to those recipes that were the most nutritious and best tasting.

The messages communicated through the Feds Get Fit campaign highlight the four pillars of a healthy lifestyle: physical activity, nutrition, healthy choices, and prevention.

Thank you for holding this important hearing. I would be happy to address any questions that you may have.

Note

1. Baicker, K., Cutler, D., and Song, Z. "Workplace Wellness Programs Can Generate Savings." *Health Affairs*, Vol. 29, No. 2 (2010): 304.

Source: Office of Personnel Management. Available online at www.opm.gov/news/testimony/111th-congress/work-life-programs/

PRESIDENT BARACK OBAMA: MEMO ON WORKPLACE FLEXIBILITIES AND WORK-LIFE PROGRAMS (2014)

President Barack Obama executed a memo to the heads of the government's executive departments and agencies on June 23, 2014, to encourage the development and better use of workplace flexibilities and work–life programs. Supervisors must consider all requests for flexible work such as telework, part-time work, and job sharing as well as the availability of WLB perks such as EAPs (employee assistance programs), child care, and health and wellness programs. The President elaborates on the Telework Enhancement Act of 2010 (see Chapter 5), using data from the Federal Employee Viewpoint survey to generate a Workplace Flexibility Index that indicates to what degree federal employees are taking advantage of flexible opportunities.

To attract, empower, and retain a talented and productive workforce in the 21st century, the Federal Government must continue to make progress in enabling employees to balance their responsibilities at work and at home. We should build on our record of leadership through better education and training, expanded availability of workplace flexibilities and work–life programs, as appropriate, and improved tracking of outcomes and accountability. In doing so, we can help ensure that the Federal workforce is engaged and empowered to deliver exceptional and efficient service to the American public while meeting family and other needs at home.

Therefore, it is the policy of the Federal Government to promote a culture in which managers and employees understand the workplace flexibilities and work–life programs available to them and how these measures can improve agency productivity and employee engagement. The Federal Government must also identify and eliminate any arbitrary or unnecessary barriers or limitations to the use of these flexibilities and develop new strategies consistent with statute and agency mission to foster a more balanced workplace.

By the authority vested in me as President by the Constitution and the laws of the United States of America, and in order to support executive departments and agencies (agencies) in their efforts to better utilize existing and develop new workplace flexibilities and work–life programs, I hereby direct as follows:

Section 1. Right to Request Work Schedule Flexibilities

    a. Agencies shall make Federal employees aware, on a periodic basis, that they have the right to request work schedule flexibilities available to them under law, pursuant to an applicable collective bargaining agreement, or under agency policy, without fear of retaliation or adverse employment action as a consequence of making such a request.

b. To facilitate conversations about work schedule flexibilities, each agency shall review, and if necessary amend or establish, procedures within 120 days of the date of this memorandum. Subject to collective bargaining agreements, agency procedures must provide:
  i. employees an ability to request work schedule flexibilities, including telework, part-time employment, or job sharing;
  ii. that, upon receipt of such requests, supervisors (or their designees) should meet or confer directly with the requesting employee as appropriate to understand fully the nature and need for the requested flexibility;
  iii. that supervisors must consider the request and supporting information carefully and respond within 20 business days of the initial request, or sooner if required by agency policy; and
  iv. that the agency should remind employees on a periodic basis of the workplace flexibilities available to them.
c. The Director of the Office of Personnel Management (OPM) shall issue guidance to Chief Human Capital Officers regarding the requirements set forth in this section within 60 days of the date of this memorandum, and shall assist agencies with implementation of this section.
d. Nothing in this section shall be construed to impair or otherwise affect the discretion granted to an employee's supervisor in making a decision on the request for work schedule flexibilities, in accordance with the agency's mission-related requirements.

Sec. 2. Expanding Access to Workplace Flexibilities

Agency heads shall ensure that the following workplace flexibilities are available to the maximum extent practicable, in accordance with the laws and regulations governing these programs and consistent with mission needs:

a. part-time employment and job sharing, including for temporary periods of time where appropriate;
b. alternative work schedules, including assurance that core hours are limited only to those hours that are necessary;
c. break times for nursing mothers and a private space to express milk;
d. telework;
e. annual leave and sick leave, including the advancement of leave for employee and family care situations;
f. sick leave for family care and bereavement;
g. sick leave to care for a family member with a serious health condition;
h. sick leave for adoption;
i. leave pursuant to the Family and Medical Leave Act (FMLA), including allowing employees to take their FMLA leave intermittently as allowed under the Act, including for childbirth, adoption, and foster care;
j. leave transfer programs, including leave banks;

k. bone marrow and organ donor leave; and
l. leave policies related to domestic violence, sexual assault, and stalking situations.

Sec. 3. Expanding Availability and Encouraging Use of Work-Life Programs

Agency heads are encouraged to take steps to increase the availability and use of the following work–life programs to the maximum extent practicable:

a. dependent care programs, including the availability of on-site child care, child care subsidies, emergency child care, and elder care;
b. Employee Assistance Programs, including counseling, resources, and referrals;
c. support for nursing mothers, including worksite lactation support programs and resources; and
d. worksite health and wellness programs, and opportunities to utilize those resources.

Sec. 4. Helping Agencies Encourage the Use of Workplace Flexibilities and Work-Life Programs

The Director of OPM (Director) shall work with agencies to:

a. provide appropriate education and guidance to all agency employees, including managers and supervisors, on the use of workplace flexibilities and work–life programs as strategic tools to assist with the recruitment and retention of employees, with an emphasis on furthering positive outcomes for employees and the agency that result from optimizing their use;
b. support agencies in their efforts to develop training programs that educate employees, managers, and supervisors about the resources that are available to meet work–life needs;
c. support agencies in promoting workplace cultures in which workplace flexibilities and work–life programs are a standard part of operating procedures, and identify any arbitrary, unnecessary, or cultural barriers limiting use;
d. review the Federal Employee Viewpoint Survey data related to supervisor and senior leadership support for work–life, as well as use and satisfaction with alternative work schedules, telework, and work–life programs;
e. implement the President's Management Agenda efforts in a manner that improves Senior Executive Service focus on creating inclusive work environments where workplace flexibilities and work–life programs are used effectively;
f. create, annually update, and electronically publish a Workplace Flexibility Index using data from the Federal Employee Viewpoint Survey, reporting

required by the Telework Enhancement Act of 2010, and other appropriate measures of agencies' effective use of workplace flexibilities;

g. within 120 days from receipt of the agency reports submitted pursuant to section 5 of this memorandum, prepare a report to the President that includes information on agency best practices with regard to the use of workplace flexibilities, any barriers to or limitations that may unnecessarily restrict the use of existing workplace flexibilities and work–life programs, recommendations for addressing or eliminating such barriers or limitations, proposals for future data reporting, and metrics for tracking the use and cost-benefit of work-life programs; and

h. review, for the purpose of identifying relevant trends related to workplace flexibility issues, the annual report that agencies provide to OPM under the No FEAR Act, which includes the agency's analysis of violations of anti-discrimination and whistleblower laws, an examination of trends, causal analysis, practical knowledge gained through experience, and any actions planned or taken to improve programs within the agency.

Sec. 5. Agency Review of Workplace Flexibilities and Work–Life Policies and Programs

Within 120 days of the date of the issuance of guidance pursuant to section 1(c) of this memorandum, each agency shall review its workplace flexibilities and work–life policies and programs to assess whether they are being effectively used to the maximum extent practicable and submit a report to OPM that includes:

a. any best practices the agency has employed to create a culture and work environment that supports the productive and efficient use of workplace flexibilities and work–life programs; and

b. any barriers to or limitations that may unnecessarily restrict the use of existing workplace flexibilities and work–life programs and recommendations for addressing or eliminating such barriers or limitations.

Sec. 6. General Provisions

a. Nothing in this memorandum shall be construed to impair or otherwise affect:
    i.   the authority granted by law or Executive Order to an agency, or the head thereof; or
    ii. the functions of the Director of the Office of Management and Budget relating to budgetary, administrative, or legislative proposals.

b. This memorandum shall be implemented consistent with applicable law and subject to the availability of appropriations.

c. This memorandum is not intended to, and does not, create any right or benefit, substantive or procedural, enforceable at law or in equity by any party against the United States, its departments, agencies, or entities, its officers, employees, or agents, or any other person.

d. The Director is hereby authorized and directed to publish this memorandum in the *Federal Register*.

Source: White House, "Enhancing Workplace Flexibilities and Work–Life Programs." Available online at www.whitehouse.gov/the-press-office/2014/06/23/presidential-memorandum -enhancing-workplace-flexibilities-and-work-life-

OPM Memo: "Enhancing Workplace Flexibilities and Work–Life Programs" (2014)

On Friday, August 22, 2014, Katherine Archuleta, director of the Office of Personnel Management (OPM) issued a memo stating that per President Barack Obama's June 2014 memo, the OPM would be promoting a workplace culture to support WLB and to retain a talented workforce. To enable this, Director Archuleta summarized three documents: an overview of the Right to Request Work Schedule Flexibilities outlining a promise of no retaliation and a program to inform employees on agency policies concerning flexibility requests and denials; an overview of leave and workplace flexibilities, including information on the FMLA (Family and Medical Leave Act), leave transfer programs (donated annual leaves), excused absences, and paid time off; and an overview of work–life programs, including telework, EAPs (employee assistance programs), and dependent care programs. (The previously cited documents follow this memo.)

Friday, August 22, 2014
CPM 2014-11
From:
Katherine Archuleta Director

Since the beginning of his Administration, the President has focused on how we can create real, lasting security for the middle class by strengthening our nation's workplaces to better support working families. On June 23, 2014, President Obama signed a memorandum to further promote a workplace culture for the 21st century that will support the Federal Government's ability to attract, empower, and retain a talented and productive workforce by expanding the use of workplace flexibilities and work–life programs as appropriate and consistent with agency mission.

To achieve this goal, the President directs the U.S. Office of Personnel Management (OPM) to work with agencies to (1) support agencies in their efforts to educate and train the Federal workforce on the various workplace flexibilities and work–life programs available, (2) support agencies in promoting workplace environments that incorporate workplace flexibilities and work–life programs into their organizational cultures, (3) ensure employees are aware of the right to request work schedule flexibilities without fear of retaliation, (4) review the Federal Employee Viewpoint Survey data related to supervisor and senior leadership support for work–life, as well as use and satisfaction with alternative work schedules, telework, and work–life programs; (5) implement the President's Management Agenda efforts in a manner that improves Senior Executive Service focus on creating inclusive work environments where workplace flexibilities and work–life programs are used effectively; (6) establish a Workplace Flexibility Index using data from the Federal Employee Viewpoint Survey, reporting required by the Telework Enhancement Act of 2010, and other appropriate measures of agencies' effective use of workplace flexibilities, (7) report to the White House on agency best practices, potential barriers or limitations, and recommendations for improvements, and (8) review the relevant trends related to workplace flexibility issues in the annual reports that agencies provide to OPM under the No FEAR Act. Agencies are encouraged to begin the process of identifying appropriate contacts who will communicate with OPM on these various deliverables. In doing so, we can help ensure that the Federal workforce is engaged and empowered to deliver exceptional and efficient service to the American public while meeting family and other needs at home.

The following sections and noted attachments provide guidance on the right of an employee to request work schedule flexibilities without fear of retaliation, and an overview of the various workplace flexibilities and work–life programs available to agencies and employees for their use.

Right to Request Work Schedule Flexibilities without Fear of Retaliation

Federal employees have the right to request, without fear of retaliation or adverse employee action as a consequence of making such a request, work schedule flexibilities available to them under law, pursuant to any applicable collective bargaining agreement or under other agency policy. Federal agencies and supervisors should ensure that procedures and policies are in place that will allow Federal employees to make such requests without fear of retaliation. As stated in the President's memorandum, "nothing in this section shall be construed to impair or otherwise affect the discretion granted to an employee's supervisor in making a decision on the request for work schedule flexibilities, in accordance with the agency's mission-related requirements."

Overview of Leave and Workplace Flexibilities

The Federal employee leave program is a dynamic system that has evolved to meet the needs of both employees and Federal agencies. Combined with other workplace flexibilities, the program has progressed to serve the contemporary workforce in a manner that is both generous to employees and responsive to agency mission requirements. Although employees have a wide range of flexibilities available to them, supervisors and employees must understand both the entitlements and flexibilities in order to make decisions that will allow employees to balance their work and family obligations in a manner consistent with agency mission.

Overview Work–Life Programs

Work–life is the business practice of creating a flexible, supportive environment to engage employees and maximize organizational performance. Work–life programs are critical management, recruitment, and retention tools for the Federal community as we strive to maintain an excellent, engaged workforce. Key work–life programs offered to Federal employees include worksite health and wellness, Employee Assistance Programs, workplace flexibilities, telework, and dependent care. When implemented according to today's best practices, work–life programs can demonstrate significant benefits for agencies and employees.

Study of Workplace Flexibilities and Work–Life Programs

In response to the President's memorandum, *OPM will be issuing separate guidance* regarding the agency's review of its workplace flexibilities and work–life policies and programs to assess whether they are being effectively used to the maximum extent practicable. The President's memorandum requires agencies to submit a report to OPM that includes—

a. any best practices the agency has employed to create a culture and work environment that supports the productive and efficient use of workplace flexibilities and work–life programs; and
b. any barriers to or limitations that may unnecessarily restrict the use of existing workplace flexibilities and work–life programs and recommendations for addressing or eliminating such barriers or limitations.

We look forward to working with you on the upcoming report. Agencies should review the information in the attachments to this memorandum and look for a separate information request in the near future.

Additional Information

Employees should contact their agency human resources office for further information on this memo. Agency headquarters-level human resources offices may contact the Pay and Leave office at pay-leave-policy@opm.gov or (202) 606-2858 or the Work–Life Office at worklife@opm.gov.

Source: Chief Human Capital Officers Council. Available online at www.chcoc.gov/content /enhancing-workplace-flexibilities-and-work-life-programs

STEVE SHIH: "CELEBRATING A CULTURE OF WORK–LIFE BALANCE AND WELLNESS" (2015)

Deputy Associate Director Steve Shih of the U.S. Office of Personnel Management gives three important recommendations to achieving WLB in an OPM blog dated October 30, 2015. He suggests acting strategically by creating a personal plan with goals and a practical method of reaching your aims. He also says supervisors should use their communication abilities to be receptive to employees' and colleagues' ideas, needs, and concerns and to create a trusting environment. Furthermore, Shih recognizes how technology must be balanced so it does not monopolize home life or become a requirement rather than a faster, more efficient way to get the job done. Shih also references an online training course for employees and a "Manager's Corner" section of ideas on how to carry out his recommendations.

In the Federal Government, we emphasize the importance of work–life flexibilities for attracting, empowering, and retaining a talented and productive workforce. Earlier this month—in celebration of National Work and Family Month—Acting Director Cobert issued a memo on the progress we've made across government to improve our use of work–life flexibilities. From telework to employee assistance programs to free preventive health programs, there are many resources and tools available to employees to help them succeed in their work and their personal lives.

I'm thrilled to serve as a senior executive where my job includes leading work–life policy for the Federal Government. I am able to model work–life integration with my own team and support the well being of my colleagues. I want to share some of the strategies I have found successful. Below are three ways agencies, leaders, and employees can support and practice work–life success.

1. Act Strategically

Take a strategic approach to achieving excellence in your work and personal lives. Start by figuring out where you want to end up. Then create a personal plan that lays out your goals—from individual to family to professional. Finally, identify the milestones you want to accomplish.

Once you've developed your plan, act purposefully to implement it, regularly measure your progress, and adjust your plan if necessary. Make sure to involve important people in your life to help you along the way and keep you accountable for following your plan. A free, online training course is available for Federal employees through OPM's "Manager's Corner" that teaches these concepts and strategies.

2. Engage Others and Communicate

Your success in balancing work and life priorities will often depend on the support you receive from your supervisor and your colleagues. Supervisors should strive to be open to their employees' needs, goals, ideas, and concerns and provide a safe, trusting environment where employees are comfortable having candid conversations. Leaders should share information on work–life flexibilities and resources available in their agencies. Employees should be mindful of the opportunities that exist and their responsibility to inform their supervisors of their needs and priorities. They should also take ownership by proposing solutions that can achieve both organizational and personal goals. Partnership is the key.

3. Manage Technology

Technology is absolutely vital in our lives; it maximizes our access to information and communication, and it increases our productivity and ability to telework. But technology can also be a distraction.

Be cognizant of how and when you use electronics at work and at home. Use your devices to save time, increase communication, and better manage schedules. At work, consider if a phone call may be more effective than an e-mail or if an instant message could replace an in-person meeting. When you're home, be mindful of how electronics can divert your attention from loved ones, household tasks, or sleep. Achieving a balance in how we use our devices can make a big difference in our quality of life.

For more information about work–life programs and what is available to you, visit OPM.gov and contact your agency's human resources office. These tools are crucial to the continued success of our workforce's ability to succeed at home and on the job.

Source: Office of Personnel Management. Available online at www.opm.gov/blogs/Director/2015/10/30/Celebrating-a-Culture-of-Work-Life-Balance-and-Wellness/

HEATHER BOUSHEY'S TESTIMONY IN FAVOR OF WASHINGTON, DC'S UNIVERSAL PAID LEAVE ACT (2015)

This document amplifies Chapters 5 and 10, which describe government's WLB interventions. In this testimony by Chief Economist Heather Boushey, she describes the good points regarding the District of Columbia's Universal Paid Leave Act of 2015 (Bill 21-415). She stresses four positives: that paid family leave can better fulfill caretaking responsibilities, which unpaid leaves discourage; that family economic security contributes nationally because it keeps talented people employed so they do not require public assistance; that local entities need to support this bill because private employers and federal policymakers are not on board; and that paid family leave heightens consumer buying power, boosts local tax revenues, and lowers governmental expenditures. This bill emphasizes government's potential legislative power to lower family stress and improve WLB.

Thank you, Chairman Mendelson, for calling this hearing. And thank you to the DC Council for extending an invitation to speak to you today. I am honored to be here.

My name is Heather Boushey and I am Executive Director and Chief Economist at the Washington Center for Equitable Growth. We seek to accelerate cutting-edge analysis into whether and how structural changes in the U.S. economy, particularly related to economic inequality, affect economic growth.

I am also the author of a forthcoming book from Harvard University Press, *Finding Time: The Economics of Work–Life Conflict*, where I go into great detail on the need for policies such as the Universal Paid Leave Act of 2015. What I've learned through my research is that the economic evidence points in one direction: Smoothing and securing people's participation in the economy is good for families, good for firms, and good for the economy. Family and medical leave insurance would help all DC workers be less economically vulnerable when balancing work, illness, and family care.

I recognize that there are some added costs for businesses when implementing paid family leave—most importantly, the expenses incurred when coping with an employee's absence. However, the cost of coping with an employee's absence is not new to businesses in the District of Columbia since the District of Columbia Family and Medical Leave Act of 1990 already grants employees 16 weeks of family leave and 16 weeks of medical leave within any 24-month period. The additional step of universal paid leave will enable workers to meet the needs of their families and of the firms they work for in better and more productive ways. This will help make the District of Columbia more—not less—economically competitive and broadly benefit families.

I will make four points in my testimony today:

1. Paid family leave is a necessary policy for modern families.
2. Family economic security is important for our overall economic strength and stability.
3. Localities—like the District of Columbia—should consider action because neither private employers nor federal policymakers have thus far addressed this urgent economic issue.
4. There are models from three states that have led the way that show paid family leave is good for the economy.

Paid Family Leave Is a Necessary Policy for Modern Families

The majority of families do not have a stay-at-home parent to provide care for children or for ailing family members.[1] At the top of the income ladder, families are more often comprised of two earners, while at the bottom, they typically have one earner, often someone playing the dual role of sole earner and sole caretaker/parent. Among children, 71 percent live in a family with either two working parents or a single working parent, and the percentage of adult children providing care for a parent has tripled over the past 15 years.[2] Among workers who were employed at some time while caregiving, one in five reported that they took a leave of absence from work in order to address caregiving responsibilities.[3]

Because of the changes in how families interact with the economy, when a new child comes into the family, when a family member is seriously ill, or when a worker himself is ill, an employee needs a few weeks or more to be at home. Most families no longer can rely on a stay-at-home caregiver to provide this care, and firms cannot assume that families have someone at home. Instead, employees must negotiate time off with their employer. The District of Columbia was at the forefront of addressing the need to better balance family care and work responsibilities when it established the right to 16 weeks of unpaid leave in 1990.

However, for many low-, moderate-, and even high-income families, unpaid leave is nice, but unaffordable. The loss of income—even for just a few months—can cause a serious economic pinch for most families. Most families' savings will cover barely a few months' expenses.[4] Families must have the money to pay the rent or mortgage and put food on the table (and pay the utility bill, the health insurance copayments, and everything else), which is possible only with a regular paycheck, or at least a portion of it. This leads many to refuse unpaid leave, even when it would help them and their families address their care needs. According to a recent survey by the U.S. Department of Labor and Abt Associates, 46 percent of those who need leave but don't take it cited an inability to afford the time off.[5]

Paid family leave addresses a key conflict caused by the lack of a full-time, stay-at-home caregiver and keeps caregivers in the workforce. Over the past 40 years, this added employment of women has been responsible for much of the gains in family income across the income distribution. From 1979 to 2007, low-income women were responsible for all of the growth in their family income. Their earnings as a source of total family income increased by 156 percent, which more than made up for the 33 percent decrease in men's contribution during the time.[6] Families cannot afford to go back to having a stay-at-home caregiver.

Family Economic Security Is Important for Our Overall Economic Strength and Stability

The economy is a system in which both firms and families matter. Each is a key player in our economy. Families buy goods and services from firms and, in turn, supply firms with workers by selling time. Firms buy people's labor, or time, to produce goods and services, which they then sell to families, completing the cycle.

However, where the very purpose of a firm is to engage in the economy, the purpose of families is both economic and non-economic. Families are where we raise children and care for one another. These roles may be subjectively more important to family members than their role in the economy, which raises the importance policies such as paid family leave play in our economy.

In order to see how paid family leave will affect the DC economy, we need to look at all kinds of costs and benefits. Costs include all the hidden costs that may be hard to see. Costs aren't only what firms pay out of pocket, and benefits aren't only about more money. We also need to look at the long-term effects. Upfront costs might be obvious, but benefits may take a while to show up, especially those that affect productivity.

Policies that keep good people in their jobs save firms money. Sociologist Sarah Jane Glynn and I conducted a review of the literature on the cost of job turnover and found that up and down the pay ladder, businesses spend about one-fifth of a worker's salary to replace that worker. Among jobs that pay $30,000 or less, the typical cost of turnover was about 16 percent of the employee's annual pay, only slightly below the 19 percent across all jobs paying less than $75,000 a year.[7]

Paid family leave improves wages and earnings for caregivers. In my research, I found that women who had access to paid leave when they had their first child had wages years later that were 9 percent higher than similar women who had not had access to paid leave.[8] Other researchers have found that women who had access to job-protected maternity leave were more likely to return to their original employer. This reduced the gap in pay that mothers experience relative to nonmothers. The Rutgers University Center for Women and Work found that working mothers who took paid family leave for 30 days or more for the birth of their child are 54 percent more likely to report wage increases in the year following their child's birth, relative to mothers who did not take leave.[9]

Economists find that the lack of paid family leave is one reason that the United States ranks 17th out of 22 OECD countries in female labor force participation. In one recent study, Cornell University economists Francine D. Blau and Lawrence M. Kahn found that the failure to keep up with other nations and adopt family-friendly policies such as parental leave is a reason for this lack of employment.[10]

A lower employment rate for caregivers has dramatic economic consequences. In my work with Eileen Appelbaum and John Schmitt, we estimated that, between 1979 and 2012, the greater hours of work by women accounted for 11 percent of the growth in gross domestic product. In today's dollars, had women not worked more, families would have spent at least $1.7 trillion less on goods and services— roughly equivalent to the combined U.S. spending on Social Security, Medicare, and Medicaid in 2012.[11]

The economic effects of paid leave are also important for families caring for an elder. According to the Bureau of Labor Statistics, about one in six Americans (16 percent) cares for an elder for an average of 3.2 hours a day. Most unpaid family caregivers—63 percent—also hold down a job; most of those with a job are employed full time.[12] The National Alliance for Caregiving's 2015 survey found that among those caring for an aging or ailing loved one, 61 percent reported that this negatively affected their paying job, because they needed leaves of absence, had to reduce their work hours, or received performance warnings. The survey also found that 38 percent of caregivers reported feeling high stress.[13] This means that the "family" part of family and medical leave is important for large swaths of the

U.S. workforce. This is especially true since, unlike in other countries, few elders receive support from government—about 6.4 percent of seniors are in long-term care in the United States compared with 12.7 percent across other developed economies.[14]

Because paid family leave protects families from suffering financial setbacks when working, parents are not forced to take unpaid leave or exit the labor force entirely in order to provide care for their children. This can reduce long-term costs for state and local governments. Researchers from Rutgers University's Center for Women and Work found that paid family and medical leave reduced the number of women who relied on public assistance. In the year after they had their child, women who took paid leave were 39 percent less likely to receive public assistance, like TANF, compared with mothers who did not take leave but returned to work. They were also 40 percent less likely to receive food stamp income in the year following a child's birth.[15]

Paid family leave improves a family's ability to care for the next generation. The economists Raquel Bernal and Anna Fruttero explain that paid parental leave can increase a child's average human capital as parents use their leave to spend time with their new baby, which, as research indicates, increases a child's future skill level. Parental leave also enhances children's health and development and is associated with increases in the duration of breastfeeding and reductions in infant deaths and later behavioral issues. Similarly, returning to work later is associated with reductions in depressive symptoms among mothers.[16]

Localities—like the District of Columbia—should consider action because neither private employers nor federal policymakers have thus far addressed this urgent economic issue.

Private employers do not typically provide paid family leave. A paid family leave program covers only about 13 percent of employees. There are a number of high-profile exceptions, such as Google, which now provides 18 weeks of paid maternity leave and 12 weeks of paid paternity leave for its employees, but they are rare.[17]

When firms do provide leave, they often only give it to their higher-paid employees. Only 5 percent of workers in the bottom quarter of earners have paid family and medical leave through their employer, compared with 21 percent in the top quarter. The trends look similar across educational categories. Unlike pensions and health insurance, uniform leave policies are not mandatory. Low-income families are least likely to be able to afford paid help to care for loved ones, so this lack of leave can quickly lead to an exit from employment or a sharp reduction in family spending.[18]

There is no federal guarantee of paid family leave. In the absence of federal action, there is an opportunity for states and localities to develop programs and policies that provide this increasingly critical piece of help to working families. The United States is the only advanced industrialized nation without a federal law providing workers access to paid maternity leave, and one of only a handful of nations that does not offer broader family and medical leave insurance. In fact, among OECD countries, mothers are, on average, entitled to 17 weeks of paid maternity leave around childbirth alone, so the DC proposal is modest.[19]

Three states—California in 2002, New Jersey in 2008, and Rhode Island in 2013—provide a model for this kind of program. In these states, paid caregiver leave for new parents and workers who need to care for a seriously ill family member was an expansion to their longstanding statewide temporary disability insurance programs. Benefits are for six weeks in California and New Jersey, four weeks in Rhode Island, and typically cover about half or more of an employee's pay, capped at around what the typical, or median, worker earns in a week. Benefits in those states are paid for through an employee payroll deduction for family leave, though the New Jersey temporary disability insurance plan, the most expensive portion of their paid leave program, is two-thirds employer funded.

In the current bill, DC employers pay the insurance premium for paid leave, which makes it different than in these three states. This is due to the unique nature of our city's ability to tax. However, like in the three states, the program spreads the costs of leave through an insurance pool. While the tax is on employers, economic research tells us that they will pass on this additional cost to either consumers, through minimal price increases, or to employees through nominal salary adjustments over time.

Paid Family Leave Is Good for the Economy

Research on the effects of paid leave policies finds that leave periods up to a reasonable length of time is positive for employment outcomes, and those positive employment outcomes are consequently beneficial to the entire economy. In an extensive survey of employers and employees, the sociologist Ruth Milkman and the economist Eileen Appelbaum found that in California, the overwhelming majority of employers—9 out of 10—reported that the paid family leave program has had either no effect or positive effects on profitability or performance. Further, the researchers found that 9 out of 10 employers (87 percent) reported no increase in their costs.[20]

Some might also argue that paid leave is bad for business because it hurts their bottom line. The truth of the matter is that this argument fails to consider the opportunity costs of not providing paid leave, the costs that businesses here in the District and around the United States face currently. Further, a standard that provides workers with paid leave that is funded in a fair, administratively effective way levels the playing field and gives all businesses the ability to compete for talent, not just those that are large and can treat paid leave as a perk rather than a right.

Paid family and medical leave fosters economic security—boosting local demand—by making it possible to sell time in a way that works for families. After California implemented paid family leave, researchers found workers, especially low-wage workers, who took paid family leave through the state program were more likely than those who did not to transition back into their job and remain in the labor force. Among workers in low-paying jobs, 88.7 percent of those who used the leave returned to their jobs, compared with 81.2 percent of those who did not use the leave. The economist Tanya Byker found that the paid family and medical leave programs in California and New Jersey increased the number of mothers in the labor force around the time when they had a child. This was particularly the case for women without a college degree. Similarly, access to family leave to care for an elder can keep people in the workforce.[21]

Paid family leave helps close the gender pay gap because it gives both men and women time to care for their families, boosting family incomes. The percentage of leave taken by men in California has increased since the institution of the state's paid leave program. Men's share of parent-bonding family leave—as a percentage of all parent-bonding family leave claims—increased from 17 percent in the period from 2004 to 2005 to 30.2 percent in the period from 2011 to 2012. In addition, men in California are taking longer leaves than they did before family and medical leave insurance was available.[22]

Conclusion

As a District resident, I am proud that the DC Council is considering legislation that would help not only families across the income spectrum, but our entire economy. Families living in the District and considering moving here are different from those decades ago. They don't often have the luxury of having a parent who doesn't have to work, but they still have to deal with the challenges of welcoming a new baby or caring for an aging spouse or parent. And helping these families stay connected to the workforce helps businesses retain quality employees and keep people who otherwise might drop out connected to the workforce. That means these families can still spend time shopping at DC stores and paying income taxes, rather than cutting their budgets or relying on public assistance. We know from experience in states that have implemented paid leave that these changes are benefiting both workers and businesses. I, again, am honored to be here testifying about the Universal Paid Leave Act of 2015, and I thank you for the opportunity.

Allow me to restate two key points from my testimony. First, with an added cost per employee, it is less important whether the employer or the employee pays the bill. In the end, the cost will in all likelihood be passed onto employees through either changes in nominal pay over time or a marginal addition to consumer prices.

Second, the key economic point is that having families with working caregivers isn't just nice, it's an economic imperative for families and for our economy more generally. This is the kind of policy that keeps people in the workforce and sustains family income. This will, in turn, sustain consumer buying power, boost local tax revenues, and lower government expenditures on programs to support the unemployed and caregivers who have trouble addressing conflicts between work and life.

Notes

1. Sarah Jane Glynn, "Breadwinning Mothers. Then and Now" (Washington, DC: Center for American Progress, June 2014), cdn.americanprogress.org/wp-content/uploads/2014/06/Glynn-Breadwinners-report-FINAL.pdf.

2. Heather Boushey, Ann O'Leary, and Alexandra Mitukiewicz, "The Economic Benefits of Family and Medical Leave Insurance" (Washington, DC: Center for American Progress, December 12, 2013), cdn.americanprogress.org/wp-content/uploads/2013/12/PaidFam Leave-brief.pdf.

3. Ibid.

4. Christian Weller and Jessica Lynch, "Household Wealth in Freefall: Americans' Private Safety Net in Tatters" (Washington, DC: Center for American Progress, 2009).

Source: Testimony before the Committee of the Whole, Council of the District of Columbia on the Universal Paid Leave Act of 2015 (Bill 21-415). Available online at equitablegrowth.org/research-analysis/paid-leave-good-our-families-our-economy/

MAYTE FIGUEROSA: "WORK–LIFE BALANCE DOES NOT MEAN AN EQUAL BALANCE" (2016)

Cardiologist and Washington University School of Medicine Professor Mayte Figueroa opines about WLB in a 2016 editorial in the journal Frontiers in Pediatrics. *Chapter 1 delved into the different definitions of WLB and Figueroa describes how her definition of work–life balance has evolved through the years but has always gravitated to four life areas: career, family, friends, and self. A wife and mother as well as an academic, Figueroa expresses the importance of shared values with a spouse or partner who can support challenging situations. She also emphasizes the need to foster mentoring, networking, and coaching in academic or clinical medicine. Her conclusion: WLB is not always equal, but it can be rewarding and nurture inner happiness.*

As I reflect on the different phases of my life as a physician, wife, mother, and physician leader, I realize that my expectations or definition of work–life balance have varied. I might even dare to say that my expectations vary on a daily basis. The concepts that remain at the crux of what I consider most important are a feeling of daily achievement and joy in each of my four life quadrants. These consist of Career, Family, Friends, and Self. At each stage of my life, I have challenged myself with changes that could potentially have caused an imbalance but instead increased my sense of self achievement and enjoyment. Literature has shown that female leadership in medicine is still disproportionately small which might be due to the barriers of combining work and family (1, 2). Compared with the early 1950s, today the number of women and men who successfully finish medical school is approximately equal. Despite this, a publication by Nonnemaker in the *New England Journal of Medicine* in 2000 showed that women who enter academic medicine have been less likely than men to be promoted or to serve in leadership positions (3). Some of the individual barriers to career development include the sporadic focus on career advancement, time-consuming child care, family responsibilities, and a woman's tendency toward understatement. Despite these barriers, work–family enrichment has been shown to have a positive spillover effect that spreads positive energy and helps to balance the work–life relationship (4). My communication, teamwork, and leadership skills influence my work and home environments in a positive way. Within my marriage, there is a mutual support that we both rely on as well as recognition of the important role each member plays. If asked, what would we say our strategies for success are in a two-career family? First, having a set time for synchronizing schedules; second, frequent verbal support; and third, shared decision making (5). Other strategies that have been reported to play an important role in the medical marriage include defining and recognizing the important roles of each family member (6). For example, determining who does certain chores, pays the bills, or carpools, it is important to have clarity of our own and our partner's responsibilities. Having shared values with a spouse/partner really defines the foundation of a marriage/relationship and serves as a frame of reference when competing commitments arise or when faced with challenges and difficult issues.

Family life in the United States has changed. A recent survey reported that most dual-earning families include a parent working long hours at atypical times (7). Academic medicine can develop so that it supports family life and retains women, but there are several steps that must be taken. First, we must have realistic expectations of what one can accomplish in a day. For me, family time is valuable and my daughter and spouse are not a hindrance or burden to academic or clinical medicine, they are what grounds me in the real world. Second, we need to foster the right kind of mentoring. A mentor should be one who appreciates the things that make our lives work. Third, we need to develop collaborative links between women to support and learn from each other through coaching and networking. Most barriers to career progression are shared. We are not alone in feeling undervalued and overwhelmed.

The Institute of Medicine's landmark publication, "Beyond Bias and Barriers: Fulfilling the Potential of Women in Academic Science and Engineering," explored why women are underrepresented in academic medicine (8). Their conclusion was that women's underrepresentation was due to a steady attrition of women throughout their careers rather than a shortage of women entering these fields. Data from AAMC benchmarking surveys indicate that a number of medical schools already have programs that support the professional development of female faculty, but the nature of such support varies substantially (9). Successful programs should provide an inclusive and supportive climate and unique opportunities for female faculty to network, interact, and collaborate with each other.

Lastly, coming to the realization that work–life balance does not mean an equal balance will make life more realistic and rewarding. We should not have to place our different roles at odds with each other competing for time. Instead of desiring work–life balance perhaps one should seek inner happiness.

This instead should be our measure of success.

References

1. Shambaugh R. *It's Not a Glass Ceiling, It's a Sticky Floor: Free Yourself from the Hidden Behaviors Sabotaging Your Career Success.* New York, NY: McGraw-Hill (2008).
2. Wietsma A. Barriers to success for female physicians in academic medicine. *J Community Hosp Intern Med Perspect* (2014) **4**:246–65.
3. Nonnemaker L. Women physicians in academic medicine: new insights from cohort studies. *N Engl J Med* (2000) **342**:399–405. doi: 10.1056/NEJM20000 2103420606
4. Scheller-Wedekamm C, Kautsky-Willer A. Challenges of work–life balance for women/physicians/mothers working in leadership positions. *Gend Med* (2012) **9**(4):244–50. doi:10.1016/j.genm.2012.04.002
5. Isaac C, Petrashek K, Steiner M, Manwell L, Byars-Winston A, Cranes M. Males spouses of women physicians: communication, compromise and carving out time. *Qual Rep* (2013) **18**:1–12.
6. Perlman R, Ross P, Lypson M. Understanding the medical marriage: physicians and their partners share strategies for success. *Acad Med* (2015) **90**(1):63–8. doi:10.1097/ACM.0000000000000449
7. Murphy EA. *A Vocation to Academic Medicine.* (1987). Available from: http://www.theway.org.uk/back/s060Murphy
8. Institute of Medicine, National Academy of Sciences, National Academy of Engineering. *Beyond Bias and Barriers: Fulfilling the Potential of Women in Academic Science and Engineering.* Washington, DC: National Academies Press (2007).
9. Joliff L, Leadley J, Coakley E, Sloane RA. *Women in U.S. Academic Medicine and Science Statistics and Benchmarking Report 2011–12.* Washington, DC: Association of American Medicine Colleges (2012).

Source: Figueroa, M. "Work–Life Balance Does Not Mean an Equal Balance." *Frontiers in Pediatrics*, March 14, 2016. Available online at journal.frontiersin.org/article/10.3389 /fped.2016.00018/full

25,000 years ago	Prehistoric humans craft stone tools for the work of hunting, fishing, and foraging for food.
15,000 BCE	Storytelling and cave paintings become recreational respites from the work of survival.
12,000–10,000 BCE	Neolithic humans start growing crops and raising livestock, which necessitates the building of permanent cities and delegating specialized workers for tool making, farming, herding, and soldiering. A small select number of people could then devote time to thinking and innovation.
500–400 BCE	Greeks, Romans, and Hebrews work at agriculture or another life-sustaining occupation in this classical period, but a minority of elites pursue intellectual aims.
350 BCE	Aristotle, the Greek philosopher, publishes *Nicomachean Ethics and Politics*, which explores WLB. Life was divided into business and leisure.
400–1400 CE	Christian values develop during the Middle Ages. Work becomes punishment for man's original sin.
1250	Thomas Aquinas compiles an encyclopedia listing in hierarchical arrangement all the professions and trades. Ideal occupation is the monastic life.
1517–1648	During the Reformation period, John Calvin and Martin Luther announce that people should serve God best through a chosen occupation.
1630–1640	Calvinist precepts permeate the American colonies via the Puritans, Quakers, and other Protestant groups. Settling in the New World took hard work and determination.

1759   *Poor Richard's Almanack* is published by Benjamin Franklin, including adages that extol the integrity and commonsense of the Protestant work ethic.

1764   James Hargreaves invents the spinning jenny, a machine that enables textile employees to spin multiple spools of thread simultaneously. This marks the official start of the Industrial Revolution.

1770s   James Watt invents the steam engine, which revolutionizes transportation and industrial machinery.

1820s–1850s   Machines emerge as the stars of industry. Assembly-line division of labor slowly replaces manual labor.

1880s   Output from factories exceeds demand, and salaries plunge, proving the realization that the work ethic could not guarantee riches or even a livelihood.

1904   Max Weber, a sociologist and philosopher, coins the phrase "Protestant work ethic" to underscore the significance and important value of work. *The Protestant Ethic and the Spirit of Capitalism* was published in 1905, marking the shift from a pragmatic ideology of work to a theologically-based philosophy.

1930s   W.K. Kellogg Company creates four six-hour shifts per day to replace the usual three eight-hour shifts, and the new shifts increase employee morale and efficiency.

1938   The Fair Labor Standards Act (FLSA) sets the standard for a 40-hour work week with minimum per-hour wages.

World War II (1939–1945)   Women begin to join the workforce to fill jobs abandoned by men who went off to fight the war in Europe and Japan.

Late 1940s   The psychological theories of labor supersede the traditional model. Experts argue that workers are not lazy but became so if not sufficiently challenged.

1947   By this date, 28 percent of the workforce is composed of women.

1950s   Job enrichment theories emerge, such as the Theory X (authoritarian) and Theory Y (participatory) management styles.

1960s–1970s   Women's Liberation Movement dawns, and women—led by author Betty Friedan and feminist Gloria Steinem, who co-founded *Ms. Magazine*—enter the workforce in droves. Believing they could have it all—work, marriage, and children—they used their college degrees and began to make inroads in professions such as law and medicine.

1963   The Equal Pay Act of 1963 amends the Fair Labor Standards Act, abolishing wage disparity based on sex. It awards equal pay for equal work.

1964   Title VII of the Civil Rights Act is passed. It prohibits employers from discriminating against employees on the basis of sex, race, color, national origin, and religion. It applies to employers with 15 or more employees, including federal, state, and local governments.

1965   Mothers and fathers work an average of eight hours and 42 hours, respectively, per week; housework occupied 32 hours for women and four hours for men. Women also put in 10 hours a week in child care and men two and one-half hours.

1967   The Age Discrimination in Employment Act (ADEA) is passed. It protects applicants and employees 40 years of age and older from discrimination on the basis of age.

1977   Rosabeth Moss Kanter's book *Work and Family in the United States: A Critical Review and Agenda for Research and Policy* brings WLB to the forefront of research.

1978   The Pregnancy Discrimination Act is passed as an amendment to Title VII of the Civil Rights Act of 1964. It makes it illegal to discriminate on the basis of pregnancy, childbirth, or related medical conditions because this would constitute unlawful sex discrimination.

1979   *Working Mother Magazine* debuts, and women read it to gain advice about getting jobs and merging family with work commitments.

1979   The term "work–life balance" is coined by Working Families in London, England.

1980   Approximately 42.5 percent of the workforce in the United States is women.

1980s   Psychologist Hans Selye defines stress and dis-stress and launches a movement to find ways to moderate negative stress to avoid physical and emotional damage.

1985   *Working Mothers 100 Best Companies* debuts and has been re-released every year since.

Late 1980s   Boston College Center for Work & Family is established with support from corporations.

1990   Nearly 50 percent of the U.S. workforce is now made up of women.

1993   The Federal Family and Medical Leave Act (FMLA) entitles eligible employees to take up to 12 weeks of unpaid, job-protected leave in a 12-month period for specific family and medical reasons.

1995   Professor Lotte Bailyn of the Massachusetts Institute of Technology (MIT) writes a nationally recognized paper on women in science.

2002   California becomes the first state to pass a paid family leave act to allow employees to take six weeks leave while guaranteeing up at least 55 percent of their weekly wages.

2008   The National Defense Authorization Act (NDAA) would allow eligible military employees to take up to 12 weeks of job-protected leave in a 12-month period for any "qualifying exigency."

2009   The Lilly Ledbetter Fair Pay Act restores protection against pay discrimination by extending the time period in which women can recover wages lost to discrimination.

2010   The Telework Enhancement Act requires all federal executive agencies to incorporate telework into their functions as a means of accomplishing agency objectives as well as enhancing employee work–life balance.

2014   San Francisco's Retail Workers Bill of Rights provides predictable schedules for hourly workers at the city's retail stores, restaurants, and banks and extends fair treatment to part-time workers.

2015   The California Fair Pay Act ensures that women in that state will receive equal pay for doing "substantially similar work" (not just "equal work") as their male counterparts.

2015   The mayor of New York City signs an executive order that gives 20,000 city employees six weeks of paid leave after the birth or adoption of a child.

2016   In California, the state Fair Pay law takes effect, closing the gap in wages between women and men.

2016   Ellen Kossek presents her 2016 paper "Managing Work Life Boundaries in the Digital Age," dividing workers into categories, such as separators, integrators, and cyclers.

2016   The Department of Defense makes several WLB amendments to policies with the goal of attracting more Millennials.

SOURCES FOR FURTHER INFORMATION

BOOKS

Connerley, Mary, and Jiyun Wu, eds. 2015. *Handbook on Well-Being of Working Women*. New York: Springer.

Friedman, Stewart D. 2014. *Leading the Life You Want*. Boston: Harvard Business Review Press.

Lockett, Katherine. 2008. *Worklife Balance for Dummies*. Milton, AU: Wiley Publishing.

Lu, Luo, and Cary Cooper, eds. 2015. *Handbook of Research on Work-Life Balance in Asia*. Northampton, MA: Edward Elgar Publishing.

Paludi, Michelle A., and Presha E. Nedermeyer, eds. 2007. *Work, Life, and Family Imbalance: How to Level the Playing Field*. Westport, CT: Praeger.

ORGANIZATIONS

American Association of Retired Persons
www.aarp.org
Large national organization that lobbies for people age 50 and over in the areas of health, insurance, and state and national legislation. It is one of the most powerful advocacy groups in Washington, DC.

American Institute of Stress
www.stress.org
A nonprofit organization that furnishes information on stress reduction and stress in the workplace that was founded in 1978 at the request of Dr. Hans Selye. It provides knowledge and leadership on stress-related topics.

American Management Association
www.amanet.org/new-homepage.aspx
Based in New York, the AMA is a corporate training and consulting group that
provides a variety of educational and management development services to businesses, government agencies, and individuals.

American Psychology Association Center for Organizational Excellence
www.apaexcellence.org
An organization that showcases good employers and provides resources on healthy
workplace practices, the latest issues, and the newest resources.

American Staffing Association, Workforce Monitor
americanstaffing.net/asa-workforce-monitor
An organization that promotes legal, ethical, and professional practices for the
staffing industry. It links to the Workforce Monitor, an online survey conducted
by Harris Poll among 1,000 adults that focuses on current workforce trends and
issues.

A Better Balance
www.abetterbalance.org/web
Organization that works for the rights of workers in areas such as fair pay, sick
leave, fairness in the workplace, pregnancy rights, and family leave.

Catalyst
www.catalyst.org
The leading nonprofit organization for working women, Catalyst is dedicated to
creating workplaces where diverse employees can thrive. It provides pioneering
research and programs.

Center for American Progress
www.americanprogress.org
An independent nonpartisan policy institute dedicated to improving the lives of
Americans through progressive ideas, strong leadership, and concerted action.

Engage for Success
engageforsuccess.org
An organization promoting employee engagement as a better way to work and one
that benefits individual employees, teams, and organizations.

Families and Work Institute
www.whenworkworks.org/about-us/our-partners/families-and-work-institute-fwi
A nonprofit research-to-action institute dedicated to providing research for living
in today's changing workplace, family, and community. Founded in 1989, it

addresses issues in three major areas: the workforce/workplace, youth, and early childhood.

Gallup Inc.
www.gallup.com/home.aspx
National survey source led by the American Institute of Public Opinion or its British counterpart that gathers the views of a representative cross section of the population. Results are used especially as a means of forecasting voting.

Glassdoor
www.glassdoor.com/index.htm
A website where employees and former employees anonymously review companies and their management.

Great Place to Work Institute
www.greatplacetowork.com
Company that provides executive coaching and culture consulting services to businesses, nonprofits, and government agencies in over forty countries on six continents.

Human Resource Executive Online
www.hreonline.com/HRE
A premier publication focusing on strategic issues in HR, it is written primarily for vice presidents and directors of human resources departments. The magazine provides news, profiles of HR visionaries, and success stories of human resource innovators.

Institute for Women's Policy Research
www.iwpr.org
An organization that conducts research and disseminates its findings to address the needs of women, promote public dialogue, and strengthen families, communities, and societies.

National Alliance for Caregiving
www.caregiving.org
Established in 1996, it is a nonprofit coalition of national organizations focusing on advancing family caregiving through research, innovation, and advocacy. The Alliance also does policy analysis, develops national best-practice programs, and works to increase public awareness of family caregiving issues.

National Association for the Self-Employed
www.nase.org/home.aspx
Organization providing a broad range of benefits to help entrepreneurs and their small businesses successfully compete in a competitive marketplace.

National Conference of State Legislatures
www.ncsl.org
The champion of state legislatures, this organization gives them the tools, information, and resources to solve difficult problems. It fights against unwarranted actions in Congress and conducts workshops to sharpen the skills of lawmakers and legislative staff.

National Partnership for Women and Families
www.nationalpartnership.org
An organization that fought for every major policy advance that helped women and families. It promotes fairness in the workplace, reproductive health and rights, access to quality, affordable health care, and policies that help women and men meet the double demands of work and family.

New Ways of Working
www.newwaysofworking.org.uk
The United Kingdom's New Ways of Working Network (NewWOW) has ceased operations, but the website still offers a great deal of information on the initiative, flextime, telecommuting, and the use of office space for better cooperation.

Organisation for Economic Co-operation and Development (OECD)
www.oecd.org
An organization that functions to promote policies to improve the economic and social well-being of people around the world.

Pew Research Center
www.pewresearch.org
A nonpartisan American think tank based in Washington, DC that provides information on social issues, public opinion, and demographic trends shaping the United States and the world.

Population Reference Bureau
www.prb.org
An organization that informs people around the world about population, health, and the environment and empowers them to use that information to further the well-being of current and future generations.

React: Respect a Caregiver's Time
respectcaregivers.org
An organization that seeks to create a supportive business environment for caregivers juggling the demands of both work and caregiving for an adult with a chronic age-related disease. The group helps employees better meet their personal and professional responsibilities.

Society for Human Resource Management
www.shrm.org
Based in Alexandria, VA, it is the largest association in the United States to promote the role of HR as a profession. It provides education, certification, and networking to its members while lobbying Congress on issues relating to labor management.

Status of Women in the States
statusofwomendata.org
An organization that provides data on women's progress in all 50 states, the District of Columbia, and the United States overall. The data is used to raise awareness, improve policies, and promote women's equality.

Total Leadership
www.myfourcircles.com
Based on Stuart Friedman's book *Total Leadership,* the purpose of the Total Leadership website is to help improve performance in all four domains of life—work, home, community, and self—by creating mutual value among them.

When Work Works
www.whenworkworks.org
This website is a nationwide initiative that brings research on workplace effectiveness and flexibility into community and business practice. It is a project of Families and Work Institute (FWI) and the Society for Human Resource Management (SHRM).

World at Work, Human Resources Association
www.worldatwork.org/home/html/home.jsp
This is a nonprofit human resources association for professionals and organizations focused on compensation, benefits, work–life effectiveness, and total rewards. It provides comprehensive education, certification, research, and advocacy, enhancing the careers of professionals.

College and Government Affiliated Agencies

Boston College Center for Work and Family
CDC, National Institute for Occupational Safety and Health (NIOSH)
Center for Families at Purdue University
Center for WorkLife Law—UC Hastings College of Law
Corporate Voices for Working Families
Substance Abuse and Mental Health Services Administration
United States Breastfeeding Committee
U.S. Department of Labor, Bureau of Labor Statistics
U.S. Equal Employment Opportunity Commission

U.S. Office of Personnel Management
Work and Family Researchers Network, University of Pennsylvania
Work, Family & Life Network, Kaiser Permanente Center for Health Research
Work-Life Fit, Drexel University
Work/Life Integration, Wharton, University of Pennsylvania

MAGAZINES

Business Management Daily
Employee Benefits News
Fast Company
Harvard Business Review
HR Professionals Magazine
Inc.
MIT Sloan Management Review
Sage Business Researcher
Working Mother Magazine

ARTICLES

AARP. 2016. "More Americans are Postponing Retirement." *AARP Bulletin.*
Adkins, Amy. 2015. "Only One in 10 People Possess the Talent to Manage."
    Gallup.
American Academy of Neurology. 2015. "Can Work Stress Be Linked to Stroke?"
American Association of University Women. 2016. "The Simple Truth about the
    Gender Pay Gap." www.aauw.org/research/the-simple-truth-about-the-gender
    -pay-gap
American Psychological Association. 2012. "Work-Life Balance Education."
Anxiety and Depression Association of America. "Highlights: Workplace Stress
    & Anxiety Disorders Survey" and "Tips to Manage Anxiety and Stress." www
    .adaa.org.
Bedoya, Jaclyn, et al. 2015. "How to Hack It as a Working Parent." *Code {4} lib
    Journal.*
Ben-Ishai, Liz. 2014. "The Schedules That Work Act." www.clasp.org
Billings-Harris, Lenora. 2015. "On the Evolution of Corporate Diversity." *Atlanta
    Tribune.* www.atlantatribune.com/2015/09/02/lenora-billings-harris-on-the
    -evolution-of-corporate-diversity
Bird, Jim. 2004. "Work-Life Balance Defined." *The Officer.*
Blackett, Karen. 2016. "Why Diversity Matters." *Campaign.* www.haymarket.com
    /home.aspx
Boushey, Heather. 2014. "A New Agenda for American Families and the Econ-
    omy." www.dissentmagazine.org/article/a-new-agenda-for-american-families
    -and-the-economy

Bresman, Henrik. 2015. "What Millennials Want from Work, Charted across the World." *Harvard Business Review.*

Brown, Courtney, et al. 2016. "Trusting Telework in the Federal Government." *The Qualitative Report.*

Campos, Belinda, et al. 2013. "Positive and Negative Emotion in the Daily Life of Dual-Earner Couples with Children." *Journal of Family Psychology.*

Cappelli, Peter, et al. 2010. "Leadership Lessons from India." *Harvard Business Review.*

Compson, Jane. 2015. "The CARE Heuristic for Addressing Burnout in Nurses." *Journal of Nursing Education and Practice.*

Davidson, Paul. 2016. "New Rule Would Mean More OT for Workers." *USA Today.*

Davies, Andrea Rees, and Brenda D. Frink. 2014. "The Origins of the Ideal Worker: The Separation of Work and Home in the United States from the Market Revolution to 1950." *Work and Occupations.*

DePasquale, Nicole, et al. 2015. "The Psychosocial Implications of Managing Work and Family Caregiving Roles: Gender Differences among Information Technology Professionals." *Journal of Family Issues.*

Dionisi, Angela M., and Julian Barling. 2014. "Spillover and Crossover of Sex-Based Harassment from Work to Home: Supervisor Gender Harassment Affects Romantic Relationship Functioning Via Targets' Anger." *Journal of Organizational Behavior.*

Dishman, Lydia. 2015. "Why Managing Work-Life Balance Is Harder Than Ever." *Fast Company.* www.content-loop.com/managing-work-life-balance-harder-ever

Earnest, David J., et al. 2016. "Sex Differences in the Impact of Shift Work Schedules on Pathological Outcomes in an Animal Model of Ischemic Stroke." *Endocrinology.*

Eichler, Leah. 2015. "Let's Kill the Myth of the Ideal Worker." *Globe and Mail.*

Eisen, David. 2015. "Genuine Diversity Has Nothing to Do with Black or White." *Hotel Management.*

Elmer, Vickie. 2015. "Minority Women Face Double Bind." *Sage Business Researcher.*

Fairchild, Caroline. 2015. "Is There a Legal Case for Work–Life Balance?" *Fortune.*

Feminist Newswire. 2016. "U.S. Women's Soccer Team Players File Wage Discrimination Complaint." feminist.org/blog/index.php/2016/03/31/u-s-womens -soccer-team-players-file-wage-discrimination-complaint

Ferguson, Merideth, et al. 2015. "The Supportive Spouse at Work: Does Being Work-Linked Help?" *Journal of Occupational Health Psychology.*

Friedman, Stewart. 2015. "Keep Your Home Life Sane When Work Gets Crazy." *Harvard Business Review.* hbr.org/2015/02/keep-your-home-life-sane-when -work-gets-crazy.html

Frizzell, Rebecca E. 2015. "Manufacturing Satisfaction with Work–Family Balance." Kansas State Dissertation.

Gagliordi, Natalie. 2016. "IBM Watson Teams with Welltok, AHA to Develop Workplace Health Program." *Between the Lines.*

Gastfriend, Jody. 2014. "No One Should Have to Choose between Caregiving and Work." *Harvard Business Review*.

Gille, Ann, et al. 2015. "Manager Behavior, Generation, and Influence on Work–Life Balance: An Empirical Investigation." *Journal of Applied Management and Entrepreneurship*.

Gino, Francesca, et al. "Compared to Men, Women View Professional Advancement as Equally Attainable, But Less Desirable." *PNAS*.

Grawitch, Matthew J. 2015. "Check Your Baggage—Assumptions about Work–Life Balance." American Psychological Association Center for Organizational Excellence.

Grossman, Jonathan. "United States Department of Labor, Fair Labor Standards Act of 1938: Maximum Struggle for a Minimum Wage." www.dol.gov/oasam /programs/history/flsa1938.htm

Groysberg, Boris, and Robin Abrahams. 2014. "Work–Life Balance: Manage Your Work, Manage Your Life." *Harvard Business Review*. hbr.org/2014/03/manage -your-work-manage-your-life

Hackbarth, Natalie. 2016. "Why Employee Recognition Is Important for Business Performance." www.quantumworkplace.com/future-of-work/infographic -employee-recognition-important-business-performance

Hadley, Joelle. 2015. "Clarify Your Values in Order to Live by Them." *Arizona Republic*.

Harrington, Brad. 2007. "The Work–Life Evolution Study." Boston College Center for Work and Family. www2.bc.edu/~harrinb/Docs/Publications/Work%20 Life%20Evolution%20Study%20final.pdf

Hill, Roger B. 1996. "Historical Context of the Work Ethic." workethic.coe.uga .edu/historypdf.pdf

Holder, Aisha M. B. 2015. "Racial Microaggression Experiences and Coping Strategies of Black Women in Corporate Leadership." *Qualitative Psychology*. www.apa.org/pubs/journals/features/qua-0000024.pdf

Houghton, Trinnie. 2015. "Coping with the 'Myth' of Work–Life Balance." *New Hampshire Business Review*.

Hunt, Vivian, et al. 2015. "Why Diversity Matters." McKinsey & Company.

Ibarra, Herminia, et al. 2010. "Why Men Still Get More Promotions Than Women." *Harvard Business Review*.

Jamieson, Dave. 2015. "Democrats Want to Guarantee Your Right to Seek a Flexible Work Schedule." *Huffington Post*.

Jenkin, Matthew. 2015. "Millennials Want to Work for Employers Committed to Values and Ethics." *The Guardian*.

Jhunjhunwala, Soniya. 2012. "Review of Indian Work Culture and Challenges Faced by Indians in the Era of Globalisation." *Interscience Management Review*.

Jimenez, Paul, et al. 2015. "Workplace Incivility and Its Effects on Value Congruence, Recovery-Stress-State and the Intention to Quit." *Psychology*.

Jones, Trina. 2014. "Single and Childfree! Reassessing Parental and Marital Status Discrimination." scholarship.law.duke.edu/cgi/viewcontent.cgi?article =6188&context=faculty_scholarship

Keiko, Yamada, et al. 2016. "Influence of Work-Related Psychosocial Factors on the Prevalence of Chronic Pain and Quality of Life in Patients with Chronic Pain." *BMJ.*

Kelly, Erin L., et al. "Changing Work and Work–Family Conflict: Evidence from the Work, Family, and Health Network." *American Sociological Review.*

Kossek, Ellen Ernst, et al. 2015. "Balanced Workplace Flexibility: Avoiding the Traps." *California Management Review.*

Kossek, Ellen Ernst, et al. 2015. "Line Managers' Rationales for Professionals' Reduced-Load Work in Embracing and Ambivalent Organizations." *Human Resource Management.*

Kratz, Greg. 2014. "Survey Shows Executives' Views of Work–Life Balance." *Deseret News.*

Laubenthal, Christina. 2016. "6 Ways Employees Can Reduce Stress in the Workplace." www.quantumworkplace.com/future-of-work/6-ways-employees-can -reduce-stress-in-the-workplace

Lavee, Yoav, et al. 2007. "Relationship of Dyadic Closeness with Work-Related Stress." *Journal of Marriage and Family.*

Ledbetter, Bernice. 2014. "Despite Regional Differences, Women across the Globe Face Same Career Advancement Challenges." *Huffington Post.*

Lee, David. 1997. "Employee Stress: The True Cost." *The John Liner Review.*

Lee, Kyu. "World Happiness Report 2016 Update Ranks Happiest Countries." worldhappiness.report

Lies, Mark. 2015. "Workplace Violence—Putting Employers on the Horns of a Dilemma." *Mondaq Business Briefing.*

Lipman, Victor. 2014. "Study: Stress Sources Differ for Managers and Employees— and Why It Matters." *Forbes.*

Lobosco, Katie. 2016. "New York Will Pay Your Student Loan Bills for Two Years." money.cnn.com/2016/01/04/pf/college/new-york-student-loan-forgiveness

Locklear, Mallory. 2016. "Social Anxiety Isn't Helping Women Close the Pay Gap." *Women's eNews.*

Lynch, Shana. 2015. "Why Your Workplace Might Be Killing You." *Stanford Business Insights.*

Malcolm, Hadley. 2015. "Paid Leave Benefits are on the Rise." *USA Today.*

Malos, Stan. 2015. "Overt Stereotype Biases and Discrimination in the Workplace: Why Haven't We Fixed This By Now?" *Employee Responsibilities and Rights Journal.*

Martin, Michel. 2014. "On Balancing Career and Family as a Woman of Color." *National Journal.*

Martin, William, and Helen LaVan. 2009. "Workplace Bullying: A Review of Litigated Cases." *Employee Responsibilities and Rights Journal.*

Mazerolle, Stephanie M., et al. 2015. "Perceptions of NCAA Division." *Journal of Athletic Training.*

McDonald, Glenda, et al. 2015. "Surviving Workplace Adversity: A Qualitative Study of Nurses and Midwives and Their Strategies to Increase Personal Resilience." *Journal of Nursing Management.*

Medved, Caryn E., et al. 2006. "Family and Work Socializing Communication: Messages, Gender, and Ideological Implications." *Journal of Family Communication*.

Miller, Claire Cain. 2015. "More Than Their Mothers, Young Women Plan Career Pauses." *New York Times*.

Miller, Claire Cain. 2016. "Paid Family Leave Gets More Attention, But Workers Still Struggle." *New York Times*.

Moen, P., et al. 2015. "Is Work-Family Conflict a Multilevel Stressor Linking Job Conditions to Mental Health? Evidence from the Work, Family and Health Network." *Research in the Sociology of Work*.

Mohrman, Susan Albers, and Kay Quam. 2000. "Consulting to Team-Based Organization: An Organizational Design and Learning Approach." *Consulting Psychology Journal: Practice and Research*.

Mosdale, Mike. 2015. "Study: Poor Lawyers Less Miserable Than Rich Ones." *New Orleans CityBusiness*.

Murphy, Tom. 2015. "Netflix's Benefit Prompts Review of Leave Policies." *Arizona Republic*.

Nagel, Marilyn. 2015. "Women Network Differently than Men and It Hinders Our Advancement." www.huffingtonpost.com/marilyn-nagel/women-network-differently_b_8259538.html

Nappo-Dattoma, Luisa. 2015. "Striving for a Healthy Work–Life Balance in a 24/7 World." *Access*.

New York University. 2014. "Fighting Parents Hurt Children's Ability to Recognize and Regulate Emotions." www.nyu.edu/about/news-publications/news/2014/09/17/fighting-parents-hurt-childrens-ability-to-recognize-and-regulate-emotions.html

News Staff. 2015. "Why Your Workplace Might Be Killing You." *Obesity, Fitness & Wellness Week*.

Nink, Marco. 2015. "German Managers Not Strengths-Focused." Gallup.

North, Scott. "Boston College Center for Work & Family, Work–Life in Japan: The Past Is Prologue." www.bc.edu/content/dam/files/centers/cwf/research/publications/pdf/BCCWF%20EBS%20Work%20Life%20in%20Japan.pdf

O'Neil, Deborah A., and Margaret M. Hopkins. 2015. "The Impact of Gendered Organizations Systems on Women's Career Advancement." *Frontiers in Psychology*.

Parker, Kim, and Wendy Wang. 2013. "Modern Parenthood: Roles of Moms and Dads Converge as They Balance Work and Family." Pew Research Center.

Pascoe, Robin. "Mobility Is a Work–Life Challenge." www.expatexpert.com

Paugh, Amy L. 2005. "Learning about Work at Dinnertime: Language Socialization in Dual-Earner American Families." *Discourse & Society*.

Pedersen, Daphne E. 2014. "Spillover and Crossover of Work-to-Family Conflict and the Health Behaviors of Dual-Earner Parents with Young Children." *Sociological Focus*.

Perlow, Leslie A., and Erin L. Kelly. 2014. "Toward of Model of Work Redesign for Better Work and Better Life." *Work and Occupations*.

Preidt, Robert. 2016. "Financial Incentives Don't Spur Employee Weight Loss, Study Finds Workplace Wellness Programs Must Get More Creative, Researchers say." www.nlm.nih.gtov/medlineplus/news/fullstory_156560.html

Preidt, Robert. 2016. "Paid Family Leave Tied to Decline in Child Abuse." www .nlm.nih.gov/medlineplus/news/fullstory_157492.html

Pyrillis, Rita. 2012. "Specialty Drug Costs: Hard Pills to Swallow." *Workforce Management.*

Quantum Workplace and Limeade. 2015. "Workplace Well-Being."

Ramos, Romualdo, et al. 2015. "Busy Yet Socially Engaged: Volunteering, Work–Life Balance, and Health in the Working Population." *Journal of Occupational and Environmental Medicine.*

Rehel, Erin, and Emily Baxter. 2015. "Men, Fathers, and Work–Family Balance." www.americanprogress.org/issues/women/report/2015/02/04/105983/men -fathers-and-work-family-balance

Ruggless, Ron. 2016. "NY Paid Family Leave Approved in Minimum Wage Deal." *Nation's Restaurant News.*

Sabattini, Laura, and Faye J. Crosby. 2015. "Work–Life Policies, Programs, and Practices: Helping Women, Men, and Workplaces" in *Handbook on Well-Being of Working Women,* edited by Mary L. Connerley and Jiyun Wu. New York: Springer.

Sadia, R. 2016. "The Relationship between Employee Health, Quality Culture and Organizational Effectiveness: Findings from the Literature." *Journal of Design & Nature and Ecodynamics.*

Sahdat, Madiha, et al. 2011. "Emotional Intelligence and Organizational Productivity: A Conceptual Study." *World Applied Sciences Journal.* www.idosi.org /wasj/wasj15(6)11/9.pdf

Schulte, Brigid. 2014. "Aging Population Prompts More Employers to Offer Eldercare Benefits to Workers." www.washingtonpost.com/local/aging-population -prompts-more-employers-to-offer-elder-care-benefits-to-workers/2014/11 /16/25f9c8e6-6847-11e4-a31c-77759fc1eacc_story.html

Scommegna, Paola. 2014. "Family, Friends Help Shape Childbearing Choices." Population Reference Bureau. www.prb.org/Publications/Articles/2014/child bearing-choices.aspx

Secord, Richard. 2015. "Managing Cultural Diversity." *Leadership Excellence Essentials.*

Senden, Marie Gustafsson, et al. 2014. " 'She' and 'He' in New Media Messages: Pronoun Use Reflects Gender Biases in Semantic Contexts." *Sex Roles.*

Shellenbarger, Sue. 2015. "Go from Grumpy to Happy: Rethink the After-Work Routine." *Wall Street Journal.*

Sorkin, Andrew Ross. 2015. "Heavy Toll of Working on Wall St." *International New York Times.*

Spanjol, J., et al. 2015. "Employer–Employee Congruence in Environmental Values: An Exploration of Effects on Job Satisfaction and Creativity." *Journal of Business Ethics.*

Steier, Gabriela. 2013. "Womenomics for Nursing Growth: Making the Case for Work Time Flexibility and Mother-Friendlier Workplaces." *Buffalo Journal of Gender, Law and Social Policy*.

Streit, Jessica, et al. 2015. "Work, Stress, and Health: Help Us Plan the Next 25 Years." NIOSH. blogs.cdc.gov/niosh-science-blog/2015/07/01/workplace-stress

Sugg, Wendy. 2015. "My Boss Drives Me Nuts! But Is That a Disability?" *Mondaq Business Briefing*.

Tanner, Lindsay. 2015. "Women Dominate Nursing Field, Yet Men Make More." USA Today Network. www.usatoday.com/story/news/nation-now/2015/03/25/male-nurse-gender-pay-gap-women-nursing/70419356

Taylor, Nicole Fallon. 2016. "Overcoming the Top 5 Business Challenges of 2016." *Business News Daily*.

U.S. Equal Employment Opportunity Commission. 2015. "EEOC Releases Report on the American Workplace." www.eeoc.gov/eeoc/statistics/reports

Valade, Jodie. 2016. "Working Like a Dog." *All Animals*.

Vidon, Maya. 2016. "Bill Would Let French Shun Work Emails at Home." *USA Today*.

Weber, Lauren, and Sue Shellenbarger. 2013. "Office Stress: His vs. Hers—Chronic Tension Hurts Mental Clarity." *Wall Street Journal*.

Weintraub, Karen. 2015. "Work–Life Balance Keeping You Awake?" *The Boston Globe*.

Weisberg, Anne. 2015. "The Workplace Culture that Flying Nannies Won't Fix." *New York Times*.

Weiss, Yoram. 2008. "Work and Leisure: A History of Ideas." *Journal of Labor Economics*.

Williams, Dwight C., and Dorcey L. Applyrs. December 2015. "Making the Case: Why Diversity Matters in the Health Care Workforce." *Diverse Issues in Higher Education*.

Williams, Joan C., et al. 2016. "Beyond Work–Life 'Integration.' "*Annual Review of Psychology*.

Williams, Ray. 2014. "How the Millennial Generation Will Change the Workplace." *Psychology Today*. www.psychologytoday.com/blog/wired-success/201403/how-the-millennial-generation-will-change-the-workplace

Wolever, Ruth. 2016. "Views Mindfulness Training Improves Focus, Employee Performance." *Employee Benefit News*.

Women's Sports Foundation. 2011. "Pay Inequity in Athletics." www.womenssportsfoundation.org/home/research/articles-and-reports/equity-issues/pay-inequity

"Workforce Stress: Employer/Employee Disconnect." www.slideshare.net/TowersWatson/workforce-stressinfographic2014

Yost, Cali Williams. 2015. "Design a Work–Life Improvement Pilot Project." *Harvard Business Review*.

Zoratti, Jen. 2015. "Women Still Haven't Come Far Enough." *Winnipeg Free Press*.

WEBSITES

blog.hubspot.com/marketing/work-life-balance
A website for a company that develops and markets a software product for inbound marketing. The company advocates for the inbound marketing concept in its own marketing through viral videos, Twitter, webinars, and an annual inbound marketing report. Includes essay on WLB.

www.careerarc.com
Company that helps HR leaders worldwide succeed in their recruitment and outplacement efforts. Has resources, including a blog.

www.careerbuilder.com
Company that helps job seekers and employers around the world connect. Operates in the United States, Europe, Canada, Asia, and South America.

www.Deloitte.com
Company that provides audit, consulting, financial advisory, risk management, tax, and related services. Has more than 220,000 professionals at member firms delivering services in more than 150 countries and territories.

www.dol.gov/oasam/programs/history/flsa1938.htm
U.S. Department of Labor's history page, including a timeline and e-history sources.

www.ebri.org
The Employee Benefit Research Institute is an independent, nonprofit, and nonpartisan organization that analyzes and reports research data. Its objectivity and reliability is the reason EBRI information is the gold standard for private analysts and decision makers, government policymakers, the media, and the public.

www.fierceinc.com
A global leadership development and training company that changes the way people communicate and transforms organizational cultures by building conversational skills.

www.flexjobs.com
An innovative, professional job service to help people find available flexible jobs.

www.intuit.com
Company with well-used products—QuickBooks TurboTax, and Mint—that help people manage their personal finances, run small businesses, and pay employees. Serves customers in Canada, the United Kingdom, Australia, Singapore, and India.

www.opm.gov/retirement-services
Information from the Office of Personnel Management on the U.S. phased retirement program with links to blogs and news releases and other sources.

www.outandequal.org
Organization that educates and empowers companies, HR professionals, and individual employees through programs and services resulting in equal policies, opportunities, practices and benefits in the workplace regardless of sexual orientation and gender identity.

www.randstadusa.com
One of the largest staffing organizations in the United States, Randstad provides temporary, temporary-to-hire, and permanent placement services to people through its network of more than 900 branches and client-dedicated locations.

www.vitalworklife.com
A national behavioral health consulting company that provides support to people facing life challenges while also assisting organizations to improve workplace productivity. Offers Employee Assistance Programs, specialized support, training, and consulting for a wide variety of industries.

www.worklifebalance.com
Company that provides work–life and time management programs to boost productivity. The programs teach people how to attain a higher level of achievement and enjoyment both on and off the job.

www.workplacetrends.com
A research and advisory membership service for HR professionals. Provides a database of research covering all aspects of HR—from recruiting to employee benefits to training and development.

www.wmmsurveys.com
Website for *Working Mother Magazine's* Best Company surveys, including the 100 best companies for women, multicultural companies, and law firms.

NOTES

CHAPTER 2

1. Mercer.com, "Bridging the Gap between Employers' and Employees' Needs Is Key to 'Future-Proofing' HR," April 11, 2016, www.uk.mercer.com/newsroom /2016-global-talent-trends-study.html

2. Society for Human Resource Management, ondemand.shrm.org/conference /shrm-2013-annual-conference-and-exposition/session/managing-workplace -conflicts

3. Aldo Svaldi, "Stress Leave a Rising Source of Contention for Employers," *Denver Post*, May 27, 2013, www.denverpost.com/2013/05/027/stress-leave-a -rising-source-of-contention-for-employers

CHAPTER 3

1. The Muse, blog.avelist.com

2. GAO Report, "Employee Arrangements: Improved Outreach Could Help Ensure Proper Worker Classification," July 2006, www.gao.gov/new.items/d06 656.pdf

3. Great Leadership, www.greatleadershipbydan.com

4. Maria Burke, "A Third of Australian Women in Science and Engineering Ready to Quit," *Chemistry World*, January 4, 2016, https://www.chemistryworld. com/news/a-third-of-australian-women-in-science-and-engineering-ready-to-quit /9299.article

5. Christina Porvath, "No Time to Be Nice at Work," *New York Times*, June 19, 2015, www.nytimes.com/2015/06/21/opinion/sunday/is-your-boss-mean.html?_r=0

6. Mila Lazarova, "Work Family Issues on International Assignments," books .google.com/books?id=nbVO4tjFULQC&pg=PA109&lpg=PA109&dq=relocation +Mila+Lazarova,+a+business+professor+at+Simon+Fraser+University+in+Vanc ouver,+Canada.&source=bl&ots=fie1x1pwn6&sig=7pZqk3Fp508Bw0dDIXS

Bs1X-Cds&hl=en&sa=X&ved=0ahUKEwjJnpem75vPAhUGFz4KHRBMBQkQ
6AEIMTAD://

7. Laurier website, legacy.wlu.ca/homepage.php?grp_id=13140

8. International Federation for Family Development, iffd.org

9. Kelsey D. Howard, "Occupational Burnout and the Causes, Predisposing
Factors, Consequences, and Prevention Strategies," Spring 2015, spark.parkland
.edu/ah/140/

10. Canadian Policy Research Networks, www.cprn.org/doc.cfm?l=en

11. "A 21st-Century Benefits Challenge: Striking the Right Balance," Inc.com, inc
.com/principal/a-21st-century-benefits-challenge-striking-the-right-balance.html

12. Lonnie Golden, "The Effects of Working Time on Productivity and Firm
Performance: A Research Synthesis Paper," www.ilo.org/wcmsp5/groups/public
/@ed_protect/@protrav/@travail/documents/publication/wcms_187307.pdf

13. Teressa Moore Griffin, *Working Mother*, www.workingmother.com/teressa
?page=6

14. Spirituality Mind Body Institute, Columbia University, Teachers College,
Clinical Psychology Program, spiritualitymindbody.tc.columbia.edu

15. Kansas State University, "Study Finds That Employees Who Are Open about
Religion Are Happier," December 17, 2014, www.k-state.edu/media/newsreleases
/dec14/religion121714.html

16. Chuck Lucier, "Herb Kelleher: The Thought Leader Interview," June 1,
2004, www.strategy-business.com/article/04212?gko=8cb4f

CHAPTER 4

1. Laura Shin, "Work from Home: The Top 100 Companies Offering Telecommuting Jobs In 2015," January 21, 2015, www.forbes.com/sites/laurashin/2015
/01/21/work-from-home-the-top-100-companies-offering-telecommuting-jobs-in
-2015/#aa602b476c00

2. Shane Ferro, "Netflix Just Made Another Huge Stride on Parental Leave,"
December 9, 2015, www.huffingtonpost.com/entry/netflix-paid-parental-leave
-hourly-workers_us_56685ae1e4b009377b233a79

3. Joanna Allhands, "Will Arizona Lead the Maternity Leave Revolution?,"
September 30, 2016, www.azcentral.com/story/opinion/op-ed/joannaallhands/2016
/04/12/arizona-maternity-leave-bank-america/82757530

4. "The Unexpected Secret Behind Bigger Profits," March 11, 2014, www.jlnick
.com/j-l-nick-blog

5. Luke Geiver, "Oil Execs Give Insight on Oil Impact to Unconventional Operations," *The Bakken*, February 18, 2015, http://thebakken.com/articles/1018/oil
-execs-give-insight-on-oilimpact-to-unconventional-operations

6. "eLogic Learning Partner, SWBC, Takes Fifth Place in 'Learning! 100
Awards' for Outstanding Employee Mentoring Program," August 15, 2015, www
.swbc.com/about/about-swbc/press-releases/articletype/articleview/articleid/96

/elogic-learning-partner-swbc-takes-fifth-place-in-learning-100-awards-for-out
standing-employee-mentoring-program

7. Center for Workplace Leadership, www.workplaceleadership.com.au/press
/page/7

8. "Roth 401(k) Contributions: Employers and Employees Are Missing Out
on a Golden Financial Well-Being Opportunity," May 4, 2016, www.willistowers
watson.com/en/press/2016/05/roth-401k-contributions-employers-and-employees
-missing-out

9. Rebecca Veseley, "Tapping into Workplace Wellness Technology Trends,"
Association of Health Care Journalists, July 12, 2016, healthjournalism.org/blog
/2016/07/tapping-into-workplace-wellness-technology-trends

10. Chestnut Global Partners, chestnutglobalpartners.org/Portals/cgp/Publica
tions/Effectiveness-of-an-employment-based-smoking-cessation-assistance-pro
gram-in-China-March20

11. "All Work and No Pay: The Impact of Forfeited Time Off," Project Time Off,
www.projecttimeoff.com/research/all-work-and-no-pay-impact-forfeited-time

12. Sharlyn Lauby, "You Can't Have Self-Managed Teams without Self-Managed
People," HR Bartender, May 3, 2015, www.hrbartender.com/2015/recruiting/you
-cant-have-self-managed-teams-without-self-managed-people

13. PromoCorner, www.promocorner.com/identity_marketing

14. Sodexo, "Population Health Management: A New Business Model for a
Healthier Workforce," 2016, sodexoinsights.com/wp-content/uploads/2016/02/
Population-Health-Managed-Trend.pdf

15. "President and CEO of IncentOne to Address Midwest Business Group on
Health," April 10, 2006, www.prnewswire.com/news-releases/president-and-ceo
-of-incentone-to-address-midwest-business-group-on-health-56170522.html

16. Julie Kantor, "High Turnover Costs Way More Than You Think," February 22, 2016, www.huffingtonpost.com/julie-kantor/high-turnover-costs-way-more
-than-you-think_b_9197238.html

CHAPTER 5

1. Phillip Reese, "California Paid Family Leave Program Growing—Thanks to
Men," July 7, 2014, www.sacbee.com/news/local/article2603053.html

2. Cole Miller, Kohr Harlan, et al., "Oregon Now Has Highest Minimum Wage
in the Country," KOIN6 News, March 2, 2016, http://koin.com/2016/03/02/oregon
-now-has-highest-minimum-wage-in-country/

3. Family Values at Work, familyvaluesatwork.org/about-us

CHAPTER 6

1. Energy.gov, energy.gov/sites/prod/files/NSF_Stemming%20the%20Tide%
20Why%20Women%20Leave%20Engineering.pdf

2. Shan Li, "Self-Doubt Hinders Career Advancement for Women, Survey Says," May 31, 2013, articles.latimes.com/2013/may/31/business/la-fi-mo-women -career-20130530

3. Dr. Bernice Ledbetter, "Despite Regional Differences, Women Across the Globe Face Same Career Advancement Challenges," May 30, 2014, www.huffing tonpost.com/dr-bernice-ledbetter/despite-regional-differences_b_5397444.html

4. Mercer.com, *2016 Global When Women Thrive Report*, www.mercer.com /our-thinking/when-women-thrive-2016-report.html

5. Anne-Marie Slaughter, "Why Women Still Can't Have It All," July/August 2012, www.theatlantic.com/magazine/archive/2012/07/why-women-still-cant-have -it-all/309020

6. Julie Coffman and Bill Neuenfeldt, "Everyday Moments of Truth: Frontline Managers Are Key to Women's Career Aspirations," June 17, 2014, www.bain.com /publications/articles/everyday-moments-of-truth.aspx

7. Kimberly Fitch and Sangeeta Agrawal, "Female Bosses Are More Engaging Than Male Bosses," May 7, 2014, www.gallup.com/businessjournal/183026/female -bosses-engaging-male-bosses.aspx

8. Urban Land Institute, "Women in Leadership in the Real Estate and Land Use Industry," womenincre.uli.org

9. Anne-Marie Slaughter, "Why Women Still Can't Have It All," July/August 2012, www.theatlantic.com/magazine/archive/2012/07/why-women-still-cant-have -it-all/309020

10. Jill Abramson, "Is 'Having It All' as Simple as Getting Men to Demand That, Too?," *Washington Post*, September 25, 2015, http://wpo.st/5Wv92

11. Connie Gersick, Social Science Research Network, *Having It All, Having Too Much, Having Too Little: How Women Manage Trade-Offs Through Adulthood*, January 14, 2013, papers.ssrn.com/sol3/papers.cfm?abstract_id=2200581

12. Public Services People Managers' Association, "Shared Parent Leave Gaining Traction or Hard to Sell?," www.ppma.org.uk/assets/_files/documents/may_16 /FENT__1462873848_SHARED_PARENTAL_LEAVE-_GAINING.pdf

13. "Co-Workers Take Dim View of Women Who Seek Flex Time: Study," August 18, 2014, consumer.healthday.com/mental-health-information-25/beha vior-health-news-56/co-workers-take-dim-view-of-women-who-seek-flex-time -study-690746.html

14. Lauren Weber and Joann S. Lublin, "The Daddy Juggle: Work, Life, Family and Chaos," *Wall Street Journal*, June 12, 2014, www.wsj.com/articles/the-daddy -juggle-work-life-family-and-chaos-1402616356

15. "What Is the Global Cost of Talent?," theundercoverrecruiter.com/global -cost-of-talent

16. "Catalyst Study Highlights the Unique Challenges Asian Women Face in the Workplace," www.catalyst.org/media/catalyst-study-highlights-unique-chall enges-asian-women-face-workplace

17. Katty Klay and Claire Shipman, "The Confidence Gap," *The Atlantic*, May 2014, www.theatlantic.com/magazine/archive/2014/05/the-confidence-gap/359815/

18. Marilyn Nagel, "Women Network Differently Then Men and It Hinders Our Advancement," October 7, 2015, www.huffingtonpost.com/marilyn-nagel/women -network-differently_b_8259538.html

19. *Women in the Workplace*, McKinsey & Co., September 2015, www.mcki nsey.com/business-functions/organization/our-insights/women-in-the-workplace

20. Herminia Ibarra, Nancy M. Carter and Christine Silva, "Why Men Still Get More Promotions Than Women," *Harvard Business Review*, September 2010, hbr .org/2010/09/why-men-still-get-more-promotions-than-women

21. "Women Need to Move Outside Comfort Zones, Financial Women's Association Poll Finds," Financial Women's Association, February 17, 2015, fwa.org/women -need-to-move-outside-comfort-zones-financial-womens-association-poll-finds

22. Kenneth Matos, "STUDY: Paternity Leave Is Not a Luxury, It Is a Responsibility," Life Meets Work, www.lifemeetswork.com/2016/04/27/paternity-leave -not-luxury-responsibility

CHAPTER 7

1. "A Business Case for Older Workers," AARP, states.aarp.org/wp-content /uploads/2015/08/A-Business-Case-for-Older-Workers-Age-50-A-Look-at-the -Value-of-Experience.pdf

2. "New MassMutual Study Finds Employee Benefits' Preferences Vary by Generation and Gender," December 2, 2015, www.massmutual.com/about-us/news -and-press-releases/press-releases/2015/12/02/09/43/new-massmutual-study-finds -employee-benefits-preferences-vary

3. *The Retirement Readiness of Three Unique Generations: Baby Boomers, Generation X, and Millennials*, April 2014, www.transamericacenter.org/docs /default-source/resources/center-research/tcrs2014_sr_three_unique_genera tions.pdf

4. Chris Hogan, "Millennials and Retirement: The Future Is Better Than You Think," August 13, 2016, www.postbulletin.com/business/millennials-and-retire ment-the-future-is-better-than-you-think/article_3abc7795-b274-5139-b1cf -6e9b2cc4f402.html

5. "Inside the Gender Pay Gap," Payscale.com, www.payscale.com/data-pack ages/gender-pay-gap

6. Bella DePaulo, "Do You, Married Person, Take These Unearned Privileges, For Better or for Better?," April 4, 2015, www.huffingtonpost.com/bella-depaulo /do-you-married-person-tak_b_6514796.html

7. Viktor Arvidsson, "Strategy Blindness as Disciplined IT-use Practice: Looking Past the 'Unintended and Unexpected' through the Practice Lens," January 2016, https://www.researchgate.net/publication/281776518_Strategy_Blindness_as _Disciplined_IT-use_Practice_Looking_Past_the_'Unintended_and_Unexpec ted'_through_the_Pr

8. Cort Olsen, "Enticing Young Recruits with Unique Benefits," September 19, 2016, www.benefitnews.com/news/enticing-young-recruits-with-unique-benefits

9. Lawrence S. Krieger, "What We're Not Telling Law Students—and Laywers—That They Really Need to Know," *Journal of Law and Health* 13, no. 1 (1998–1999), www.lwionline.org/uploads/FileUpload/Krieger.pdf

10. Douglas Quenqua, "Lawyers with Lowest Pay Report More Happiness," May 12, 2015, well.blogs.nytimes.com/2015/05/12/lawyers-with-lowest-pay-report-more-happiness/?_r=0

11. "The Status of Women and Girls," Institute for Women's Policy Research, www.iwpr.org/initiatives/the-status-of-women-and-girls

12. "Balancing the Scale: NSF's Career-Life Balance Initiative," National Science Foundation, www.nsf.gov/career-life-balance/

13. Vickie Elmer, "Work–Life Balance," January 12, 2015, businessresearcher.sagepub.com/sbr-1645-94863-2645119/20150112/worklife-balance

14. Kenji Yoshino and Christie Smith, "Uncovering Talent: A New Model of Inclusion," December 6, 2013, deloitte.com/content/dam/Deloitte/us/Documents/about-deloitte/us-inclusion-uncovering-talent-paper.pdf

15. Molly Petrilla, "How Analytics Helped Kimberly-Clark Solve Its Diversity Problem," December 10, 2014, fortune.com/2014/12/10/kimberly-clark-dods-worth-diversity

16. "Lesbian, Gay, Bisexual, Transgender Workplace Issues," May 26, 2015, www.catalyst.org/knowledge/lesbian-gay-bisexual-transgender-workplace-issues

CHAPTER 8

1. "Want to Retain Me? U.S. Workers Say . . . ," Randstad.com, www.randstadusa.com/about/news/want-to-retain-me-us-workers-say-show-me-the-money

2. Steve Crabtree, "Winning Combo: A Dedication to Talent and a Focus on Results," November 4, 2014, www.gallup.com/businessjournal/179132/winning-combo-dedication-talent-focus-results.aspx

3. Anne Weisberg, August 24, 2015, "The Workplace Culture That Flying Nannies Won't Fix," www.nytimes.com/2015/08/24/opinion/the-workplace-culture-that-flying-nannies-wont-fix.html?_r=0

4. *The Values Revolution*, Global Tolerance, www.globaltolerance.com/wp-content/uploads/2015/01/GT-Values-Revolution-Report.pdf

5. Matthew Jenkin, "Millennials want to work for employers committed to values and ethics," May 5, 2015, www.theguardian.com/sustainable-business/2015/may/05/millennials-employment-employers-values-ethics-jobs

CHAPTER 9

1. Tawni Jaakola, *Breastfeeding Support Across Different Socio-Demographic Groups of Society: A Study from Minnesota*, Master's thesis, Institute of Public Health and Clinical, Nutrition Faculty of Health Sciences, University of Eastern Finland, July 2015, epublications.uef.fi/pub/urn_nbn_fi_uef-20150904/urn_nbn_fi_uef-20150904.pdf

2. "About Liz Davidson," Financial Finesse, www.financialfinesse.com/liz

3. "Global Wellness Institute Releases Report and Survey on 'The Future of Wellness at Work,'" Global Wellness Institute, February 17, 2016, www.global wellnessinstitute.org/global-wellness-institute-releases-report-and-survey-on-the -future-of-wellness-at-work

4. Michael Atkin and Joel Keep, "Hepatitis C Sufferer Imports Life-Saving Drugs from India, Takes on Global Pharmaceutical Company," HCMSG, August 20, 2015, www.hepatitiscmsg.org/blog/category/all/5

5. New Benefits Blog, blog.newbenefits.com/category/bloggers/

6. Paul Foery, "Health Care Reform: How a PEO Can Put Your Mind at Ease," www.insperity.com/blog/health-care-reform-how-a-peo-can-put-your-mind-at-ease

CHAPTER 10

1. Bryan Kramer, "How Successful Companies Create Emotional Intelligence," October 19, 2015, www.bryankramer.com/how-successful-companies -create-emotional-intelligence

2. "Current Projects," The Hong Kong Politechnic University, www.polyu.edu .hk/mm/cli/en/research/current_projects.html

3. Gus Gordon et al., "Employee Perceptions of the Manager Behaviors That Create Follower-Leader Trust," *Management and Organizational Studies* 1, no. 2 (2014), www.sciedupress.com/journal/index.php/mos/article/download/4719/2734

4. Nick Otto, "Thriving Workplace Culture Hinges on Trust," April 8, 2016, web.dentalmanagers.com/news/newsarticledisplay.aspx?ArticleID=961

5. National Partnership for Women & Families, "State Paid Family Leave Insurance Laws," April 2016, www.nationalpartnership.org/research-library/work-family /paid-leave/state-paid-family-leave-laws.pdf

6. "What Clinton and Trump Would Do for Gig Economy Workers—Forbes," August 11, 2016, ptla.org/category/states/bak/all?page=65

Glossary

Absenteeism: Habitual pattern of absence from a duty such as employment

Americans with Disabilities Act (ADA): A wide-ranging civil rights law intended to protect against discrimination based on disability. It affords similar protections to Americans with disabilities as the Civil Rights Act of 1964.

Assembly line: A manufacturing process in which parts are added as the semi-finished product moves from workstation to workstation until the final assembly is finished.

Autoimmune diseases: Conditions caused by immune responses to normal healthy tissue.

Autonomous: Responding, reacting, or existing independently, especially regarding moral independence.

Baby Boomers: People born during the post-World War II baby boom approximately between 1946 and 1964.

Better Life Index (OECD): A way to bring together internationally comparable measures of well-being such as WLB (work–life balance) and education with recommendations from the Organization for Economic Cooperation and Development (OECD) (see OECD).

Bipolar disorder: A mental illness characterized by periods of depression and periods of elevated mood.

Bullying: Use of superior strength or influence to intimidate someone, typically to force him or her to do what one wants.

Burnout: To wear out or become exhausted from overwork.

Cadillac Tax: As part of the ACA or Obamacare, an excise tax of 40 percent on high-end health plans above $10,200 for individuals and $27,500 for family coverage starting in 2020. This tax is not deductible.

Captive: An insurance company wholly owned and controlled by its insureds; its primary purpose is to insure the risks of its owners, and its insureds benefit from the captive insurer's underwriting profits.

Civil Rights Acts of 1964: Landmark civil rights legislation that outlawed discrimination based on race, color, religion, sex, or national origin. It also ended unequal application of voter registration requirements.

Cognitive behavioral therapy (CBT): A type of psychotherapy in which negative patterns of thought about the self and the world are challenged in order to alter unwanted behavior patterns or treat mood disorders such as depression.

Cognitive dissonance: Discomfort experienced by someone who holds two or more contradictory beliefs, ideas, or values at the same time and needs to perform an action contradictory to one or more of these beliefs, ideas, or values.

Colitis: Inflammation of the colon.

Company (organizational) culture: Those values and behaviors that contribute to the unique social and psychological environment of an organization.

Concierge programs: Assistance on personal tasks provided to employees so they can focus on work. Especially valuable for companies that bill by the hour, such as lawyers, accountants, architects, and other consultants—where time actually is money.

Consortium: A group of organizations formed to undertake an enterprise and is beyond the resources of any one member.

Contingent workers: A provisional group of workers who work for an organization on a non-permanent basis; also known as freelancers, independent professionals, temporary contract workers, independent contractors, or consultants.

Cortisol: A metabolite of the primary stress hormone cortisone, cortisol is an essential factor in the proper metabolism of starches, and is the major natural glucocorticoid (GC) in humans.

Cro-magnons: The first early human beings.

Division of labor: Separation of tasks so that participants in any industry may specialize.

Egg freezing: Eggs harvested from a woman's ovaries, frozen unfertilized, and stored for later use.

Emotional intelligence (EI): The capacity to be aware of, control, and express one's emotions and to handle interpersonal relationships judiciously and empathetically.

Employee assistance programs (EAPs): Programs that help employees work through various life challenges adversely affecting job performance, such as health and personal well-being, finances, and legal problems.

Employment discrimination: A form of worker discrimination possibly involving litigation against an employer based on race, gender, religion, national origin, physical or mental disability, or age.

Engagement: People who are fully absorbed by and enthusiastic about their work and take positive action to further the organization's reputation and interests.

Equal Employment Opportunity Commission (EEOC): Federal agency that administers and enforces civil rights laws against workplace discrimination.

Extrinsic motivation: The performance of an activity driven by influences outside the individual such as grades or money.

Face time: Time spent in face-to-face contact with someone.

Fair Labors Standards Act (FLSA): Federal law that sets out various employment regulations including minimum wages, requirements for overtime pay, and limitations on child labor.

Federal Family and Medical Leave Act (FMLA): Provides certain employees with up to 12 weeks of unpaid, job-protected leave per year.

Fight or flight response: Physiological reaction occurring in response to a perceived harmful event, attack, or threat to survival.

Flexibility stigma: Flextime options employers offer but also consciously or unconsciously punish employees for using.

Flextime: A system of working a set number of hours with the starting and finishing times chosen within agreed limits by the employee.

Gen (Generation) X: People born after the World War II baby boom whose birth dates range from the early 1960s to the early 1980s.

Globalism: Policy of treating the whole world as a proper sphere for political influence based on the electronic connectedness of media.

Greenwashing: Deceptively promoting the perception that an organization's products, aims, and policies are environmentally friendly.

Healthy Workplace Bill: A bill proposed in 30 states and two territories to outlaw abusive behavior in the workplace by supervisors and others.

Homo-Sapiens: Modern human species.

Hub space: Open space in a building that houses entrepreneurs, solopreneurs, contractors, and freelancers.

Human resource departments (HR): Personnel departments within organizations.

Ideal worker: The committed employee who works full-time and full force for the employer with no discernible family responsibilities.

In vitro fertilization (IVF): A process by which an egg is fertilized by sperm outside the body; commonly called a "test-tube baby."

Intrinsic motivation: Desire driven by an interest or enjoyment in the task itself and existing within the individual rather than relying on external pressures or a desire for reward.

Involuntary part-time workers: Employees who would like full-time work but cannot find it due to economic or other reasons.

Irritable bowel disorder (IBD): Unusual activity in the bowel that causes irritation and discomfort.

Ischemic stroke: Vascular event in which the blood supply to part of the brain is decreased leading to dysfunction of the brain tissue in that area.

Latchkey children: Children at home without adult supervision for some part of the day, especially after school, when parents are still at work.

LGBT: Stands for Lesbian, Gay, Bisexual, and Transgender.

Lilly Ledbetter Fair Pay Act: Restores the protection against pay discrimination that was negated by the Supreme Court decision in *Ledbetter v. Goodyear Tire & Rubber Co.*

Metabolic syndrome: A clustering of at least three of five medical conditions: abdominal obesity, elevated blood pressure, elevated glucose, high serum triglycerides, and low levels of high-density lipoprotein (HDL).

Millennials: People born following Generation X whose birth years range approximately from the early 1980s to early 2000s.

Mindfulness: Awareness of the present moment without judgment.

Mirroring or **matching:** Getting into rhythm with the person on as many levels as possible, such as emotionally and physically, even matching the tone, tempo, inflection, and volume of a person's voice.

National Recovery Act (NRA): An act to encourage national industrial recovery, to foster fair competition, and to provide for the construction of certain useful public work and for other purposes.

Neanderthals: Species or subspecies of human beings.

Neolithic: A period in the development of human technology beginning about 10,200 B.C.E.

NIOSH: National Institute for Occupational Safety and Health. The only federal institute responsible for conducting research and making recommendations for the prevention of work-related illnesses and injuries.

Obsessive compulsive disorder (OCD): A mental disorder in which people feel the need to check things repeatedly, perform certain routines or rituals, or have certain repeated thoughts.

Organization for Economic Cooperation and Development (OECD): An international economic organization of 34 countries founded in 1961 to stimulate economic progress and world trade.

Participatory management: Empowering members of a group, such as employees of a company, to participate in organization decision making.

Patient and Affordable Care Act (Obamacare): Legislation enacted to increase the quality and affordability of health insurance, lower the uninsured rate by expanding public and private insurance coverage, and reduce the costs of health care for individuals and the government.

Phased retirement: Plan that enables an employee who is approaching retirement age to continue working with a reduced workload, eventually transitioning from full-time work to full-time retirement.

Plebeians: Common people in Roman times.

Positive psychology: A branch of psychology focusing on improving mental functioning through, for example, mindfulness and compassion to achieve happiness.

Post-traumatic stress disorder (PTSD): A mental disorder that can develop after a person is exposed to a traumatic event such as a sexual assault, warfare, traffic accidents, or other threats to a person's life.

Predestination: The doctrine that God in his infallibility guides chosen people to their salvation.

Presenteeism: The act of attending work while sick.

Professional employer firm (PEO): Firm that provides a service under which an employer can outsource employee management tasks, such as employee benefits, payroll and workers' compensation, recruiting, risk/safety management, and training and development.

Protestant work ethic: Concept that hard work, discipline, and frugality will result in a person's salvation.

Reduction in force (RIF): The act of suspending or dismissing an employee as for lack of work or because of corporate reorganization.

Resilience: The capacity to recover quickly from difficulties; toughness.

Results only work environment (ROWE): A human resource management strategy wherein employees are paid for result (output) rather than for the number of hours worked.

Retention: Management measures that lead to employees remaining on staff, including activities that influence the bonding, performance, and degree of loyalty of staff.

Return on investment (ROI): Benefit to an investor (such as a company) resulting from an investment of some resources in an employee.

Sandwich generation: A generation of people who care for their aging parents while supporting their own children.

Schizophrenia: A group of psychotic mental illnesses characterized by disorganization of personality.

Second shift: A term used to describe people who work to earn money but are also responsible for significant amounts of unpaid domestic labor.

Self (funded health care): A concept involving an employer providing certain benefits—generally health benefits or disability benefits—to its employees and funding claims from a specified pool of assets rather than through an insurance company.

Sign-on bonus: A sum of money paid to a new employee by a company as an incentive to join that company.

Small Necessities laws: Laws that give employees the right to take leave for family obligations for a limited number of hours annually, covering specific activities that are not included under the Federal Family and Medical Leave Act (FMLA), such as for parents to attend school-related events and activities for their children.

Snowbirds: Northerners who move to a warmer southern state in the winter.

STEM: Career fields in the areas of science, technology, engineering, and math.

Stress: Physical or psychological distress that causes tension and may be implicated in disease formation.

Surrogacy: A process of artificial insemination of sperm into a woman who carries the fetus to term for another woman.

SWOC: Single without children; singlism.

Theory X and Theory Y: Theories of management and motivation in which Theory X stresses the importance of strict supervision, external rewards, and penalties and Theory Y emphasizes the motivating role of job satisfaction and creative approaches to tasks.

Time management: Planning and exercising control of time and tasks to maximize efficiency and productivity.

Title VII to the Civil Rights Act of 1964: Prohibits employment discrimination based on race, color, religion, sex, and national origin.

Turnover: The number of people hired within a time frame to replace those left or dropped from an organization.

Values clarification: The determination of one's moral, religious, ethical beliefs to pursue goals that will not conflict.

Women's Liberation Movement: Feminist campaigns begun in the 1960s for reforms on issues such as reproductive rights.

Work–life balance (WLB): The individual prioritization of career with lifestyle so that individuals feel they are fulfilling their goals, needs, and commitments.

World Health Organization (WHO): A specialized agency of the United Nations that is concerned with international public health and is headquartered in Geneva, Switzerland.

Zero-drag worker: Employee who would have neither family, possessions, commitments or social life to pull him or her away from the job at hand.

Zero-hour contract: A type of contract between an employer and worker in which the employer is not obliged to provide any minimum working hours and the worker is not obliged to accept any work offered.

INDEX

AARP (American Association of
Retired Persons), 187
AARP Bulletin, 106
AAUW (American Association of
University Women), 93
Abramson, Jill, 98
Absenteeism, 24, 69–70
ADA Amendments Act of 2008, 33
ADA (Americans with Disabilities
Act), 33
ADEA (Age Discrimination in
Employment Act of 1967), 76
Adkins, Amy, 125
Administrative Science Quarterly,
107
Adoption, 79
Affordable Care Act (ACA), 78–79,
133, 136
African-Americans, 113–114
Age: communication preferences,
120–121; freelancers versus
entrepreneurs, 41; having it all,
98; impact on view of work–life
balance, 105–107; Latinos, 112;
pay inequity, 94; preventive
health program resistance, 62;
priorities and, 50–51; retention,

70; retirement delays, 13–14;
values and differences in, 128;
wellness programs, 69
Age Discrimination in Employment
Act of 1967 (ADEA), 76
Aggressive behavior, 31–35
Allen, Catherine, 64
Alternating locations, 57
Amaez, Karina, 111
American Association for Women in
Science (AWIS) survey, 110
American Association of Retired
Persons (AARP), 187
American Association of University
Women (AAUW), 93
American Institute of Physics report,
40
American Institute of Stress, 187
American Management Association,
45, 188
American Psychological Association
(APA), 5, 42, 125
American Psychology Association
Center for Organizational
Excellence, 188
American Staffing Association,
Workforce Monitor, 188

ABOUT THE AUTHOR

Janice Arenofsky is a writer specializing in health, environmental, and human interest topics. She is author of *Beyoncé Knowles: A Biography* (Greenwood, 2009) and *The Healing Sounds of Music* (American Media, 2002).